Educational Transformation

Educational Transformation

Akamai University

Copyright © 2019 by Akamai University.

ISBN: Softcover   978-1-7960-4895-7
        eBook   978-1-7960-4896-4

All rights reserved. No part of this book may be reproduced or transmitted in any form or by any means, electronic or mechanical, including photocopying, recording, or by any information storage and retrieval system, without permission in writing from the copyright owner.

The views expressed in this work are solely those of the author and do not necessarily reflect the views of the publisher, and the publisher hereby disclaims any responsibility for them.

Any people depicted in stock imagery provided by Getty Images are models, and such images are being used for illustrative purposes only.
Certain stock imagery © Getty Images.

Print information available on the last page.

Rev. date: 08/01/2019

To order additional copies of this book, contact:
Xlibris
1-888-795-4274
www.Xlibris.com
Orders@Xlibris.com
626029

CONTENTS

Preface vii

Chapter 1   The Responsibilities Facing the
University in the New Millennium
by Douglass Capogrossi, PhD 1

Chapter 2   Where Science Meets Policy: The Nexus
of Decision-making in Modern Society
by Anthony R. Maranto 10

Chapter 3   With Justice For All: A Remedy for the
Key Omission in Higher Education
by Michael J. Cohen 29

Chapter 4   How to Communicate Effectively
to be a Successful Professional
by Dr. Niranjan Ray 85

Chapter 5   Neo-Platonism, its influences in the
Italian Renaissance and Connection to the
Advancement of the Human Condition
by Sandra L.M. Kolbl (Koelbl) Holman Ph.D. 98

Chapter 6   The Foundations of eCampus Excellence
by Khoo Voon Ching 107

Chapter 7   Teaching And Learning For Working
Adult Students (WASs)
by Prof. Dr. Lee Karling, PhD 121

Chapter 8   Power of Service Healing Hearts and
Following Dreams: Complementary and
Alternative Medicine as a Positive Force for
Love, Renewing, and Revitalizing Health
by Dr. Mary Jo Bulbrook, RN, CEMP/S/I 149

Chapter 9   Video as a Medium for Online and
            Social Media-centric Education
            by Dr Seamus Phan 164
Chapter 10 Neoliberal Transformation of Education in
            Turkey: Political and Ideological Analysis of
            Educational Reforms in the Last Decade
            by Dr Kemal Yildirim 174
Chapter 11 E-Learning System Evaluation towards
            Improving Entrepreneurial Competencies
            Supported by Modern Automated Systems:
            Case Study of Balkan Countries
Chapter 12 The Debates between Quantitative and
            Qualitative Method: An Ontology and
            Epistemology of Qualitative Method-
            The Pedagogical Development
            by Medani P. Bhandari 232

Biographies of Authors 293
Endnotes 307

PREFACE

Akamai University is an advanced institution of higher learning with headquarters in Hilo, Hawaii. Established as a non-profit tax-exempt corporation, Akamai is governed by a voluntary Board of Directors, the majority being residents of the United States of America and others from 42 other nations. Akamai is operating in good standing and is functioning in accordance with all applicable laws and regulations, its corporate charter, Hawaii Regulation HRS446E and the IRS 501(c)(3) tax-exempt codes.

    The mission of Akamai University is founded upon the premise that amelioration of major world problems and the creation of sustainable lifestyles and global practices are the hallmarks of responsible individual and corporate world citizenship. As generators of new knowledge and developers of new systems, our sole mission as an institution is the advancement of the human condition and sustainability of the planet.

    The Introductory Chapter written by Dr. Douglass Capogrossi examines major challenges facing the human community, its advancement, and the sustainability of the planet. The chapter discusses how higher education is responsible for moving human culture forward in areas such as mental health, human services, economic development, environmental and ecological issues, education and literacy, health and wellness, sustainability, and peace, diplomacy and international relations. It discusses the current status of these challenges requiring amelioration.

Chapter 2 presented by Dr. Anthony Maranto discusses how society relies on a fragile and often tense relationship between policy and science to make informed decisions about everything from how much water can be drawn from an aquifer to where to site radioactive waste repositories. While accurate projections and a deep understanding of the second and third order effects of the decisions we collectively make as a society should be based on scientifically-sound data, evidence, and observations, often the connection between these two foundational elements is not well understood. Policy makers have little understanding of the scientific process, the meaning of the data they use, or the ramifications of scientific uncertainty. Similarly, scientists often have little insight into how the data and hypotheses they generate will ultimately be used to form or modify governing principles. In order to strengthen the vital connection between science and policy, universities need to explore the inter-connectivity of those realms in their hard science as well as their political science students.

Chapter 3 written by Dr. Michael Cohen examines education and holistic aliveness. Dr. Cohen asserts that we suffer most of our human disorders because we treat Planet Earth as a dead resource that has no purpose or direction when, in reality, it is a living organism in the process of supporting all life. Dr. Cohen presents that as an antidote for this error, the art of Educating, Counseling and Healing with Nature (ECHN) enables scientific inquiry to give our mind, body and spirit rare, whole life, self-evident information that includes sensory and material facts beyond reasonable doubt. He further explains how ECHN increases efficacy and reduces budgets for when conflicts or fractures appear it heals them with natural attraction energies that remedy stress and disorders without producing adverse side effects.

Chapter 4, presented by Dr. Niranjan Ray, discusses in some detail how to communicate effectively in becoming a successful professional. He further explains that the key to success in life, in relationships, and in work depends on good communication skills. Effective communication sends or receives an unambiguous message that brings success in life. Following higher education, it is communication that makes the difference between success and failure. Addressing these issues better assures that higher education institutions better serve the needs of their students.

Chapter 5, written by Dr. Sandra L.M. Kolbl (Koelbl) Holman, explores Neo-Platonism and its influences in the Italian Renaissance Period and how it may impact the advancement of the human condition.

Chapter 6, is a highly beneficial presentation by Dr. Khoo Voon Ching concerning the foundations of eCampus excellence. Dr. Khoo advances how technology management is important in distance learning education because it can improve the efficiency of the conventional distance learning approach. He states that, the study material and the distance learning support staff should be student centric to ensure successful completion of their program. The innovative virtual campus approach fostered by Dr. Khoo was implemented to incorporate technology management into the distance learning environment to improve the operational efficiency of virtual study.

Chapter 7, prepared by Dr. Lee Karling discusses rationale behind working adult returning to university studies and provides an understanding on how their learning differs from traditional counterparts. Dr Karling provides insight into classroom management, teaching strategies and learning methodologies to help working adult students learn more effectively. The design of an Assessment Rubric for Working Adult Students is also provided to help higher education institutions more effectively address learning.

Chapter 8, is an application by Dr. Mary Jo Bulbrook of the theories and healing arts of Dr. Virginia Satir. The chapter reviews the historical roots, describes the theory, and discusses the force for change in individuals' lives, via a transformed educational model in partnerships with traditional health and healing, honoring cultural perspectives.

Chapter 9, presented by Dr. Seamus Phan explored the ways video provides for excellent as a medium for online and social media-centric education. Dr Phan examines options of equipment, software, and techniques that are now more easily available to educators, and how best to think as a filmmaker and storyteller when approaching an educational topic.

Chapter 10, written by Dr. Kemal Yildirim concentrates on a well-theorized, and biting evaluation of the neoliberal-cum-Islamo-conservative reformation & reformulation of schooling and education in Turkey over the last 15 years. The primary part of the chapter examines political and ideological analysis of educational reforms in the Age of the Justice and Development Party (AKP).

Chapter11, written by Dr. Mirjana Radović-Marković discusses e-learning systems evaluation and how this is able to improve entrepreneurial competencies, when supported by modern automated systems. Dr. Radovic presents a case study of Balkan Countries.

Chapter 12, presented by Dr. Medani P. Bhandari, describes the pedagogical development and the debates between quantitative and qualitative methods and the ontology and epistemology of the qualitative method.

CHAPTER 1

The Responsibilities Facing the University in the New Millennium

Douglass Capogrossi, PhD
Akamai University

> Education is the most powerful weapon which you can use to change the world.
> -Nelson Mandela, 2007

There are many diverse challenges facing the human community in the new millennium which can be addressed internationally by university systems worldwide. Let us take a look at some of the more damaging challenges facing humanity over the past couple decades.

Just prior to the turn of the millennium, The World Conference on Higher Education assembled at UNESCO Headquarters in Paris to conceive of the vital actions necessary to transform higher education in support of human sustainability across the twenty-first century and beyond. Those in attendance from the global community of higher education fashioned a valuable foundational document important to policy-making. This paper is the *World Declaration on Higher Education for the Twenty-First Century: Vision and Action*. An excerpt from that valuable document states:

Higher education has given ample proof of its viability over the centuries and of its ability to change and to induce change and progress in society. Owing to the scope and pace of change, society has become increasingly *knowledge-based* so that higher learning and research now act as essential components of cultural, socio-economic and environmentally sustainable development of individuals, communities and nations. Higher education itself is confronted therefore with formidable challenges and must proceed to the most radical *change and renewal it has ever been required* to undertake, so that our society, which is currently undergoing a profound crisis of values, can transcend mere economic considerations and incorporate deeper dimensions of morality and spirituality.

(UNESCO, Transformation Towards a World-Class University, 1998)

The future holds many vital challenges for the human community, and the planet humans call home. A number of prominent international organizations have made available to the University the scope of real challenges with which it might be confronted, presenting an alarming picture of what the University now must address.

Roughly 1.3 billion people live in absolute poverty with nearly 25 million being added to their numbers each year. Hundreds of millions of people have no running water to drink or bathe themselves. One hundred million people do not have homes to live in and must spend their lives on the streets and pavements, their children never knowing the security of a suitable shelter.

(World Bank and United Nations, Press Release, 2016)

Already, more than ten percent of the earth's vegetated surface has been degraded, an area larger than India and China combined. This desertification, caused by overgrazing domestic animals, over-cultivation, salinization, and deforestation, has already begun to impact over 35percent of the land surface of the Earth and the situation is worsening

        (The State of Planet Earth, Project NatureConnect, 2012)

The children of many nations suffer appalling abuses at the hands of their own countrymen and represent a huge and voiceless population seldom represented in the international human rights arena. Street children are frequently abused by police, or imprisoned in inhumane conditions. Because of their vulnerable condition, young people are often used as soldiers, and bonded laborers. Governments are also known to perpetrate or acquiesce in systematic human rights violations against women, citing customs and rigid concepts of privacy as justifications for the subordination of women.

        (Human Rights Watch, **Children's Rights,** https://www.hrw.org/topic/childrens-rights 2019)

Human culture now has the potential to inflict irreversible damage on the environment and on its life sustaining systems and resources. Already, critical stress suffered by our environment is clearly manifest in the air, water, and soil, our climate, and plant and animal species. Should this deterioration be allowed to continue, we can expect to alter the living world to the extent that it will be unable to sustain life, as we know it

        (Union of Concerned Scientists, World Scientists' Warning to Humanity 1992).

More than half the world population lacks access to the badly needed essential drugs. More than 150 million children are born every year worldwide and approximately 10% of these will never see their fifth birthday. One child dies every other second, due to malnutrition, hunger and poverty. It is estimated that one quarter of the world population is subject to chronic intestinal parasitic infections, which have insidious effects on growth, malnutrition, and cognitive functions

        (World Health Organization, *World Health Report,* 1992).

It is no small aspiration to strive for a world filled with greater peace, balance, cooperation, and the promise of an evolved human fellowship. These seem to be noble foundation stones upon which to establish the fundamentals of sustainable human culture. As we look to the future, as a higher education community, the transformations in our thinking must be sound-minded, if we are to be a power and catalyst for change in the betterment and sustainability of the human community.

According to Anthony Cortese in his *The Critical Role of Higher Education in Creating a Sustainable Future*, Planning for Higher Education, v31 n3 p15-22 Mar-May 2003 presents strong evidence for the need to transform education is the current condition of humanity as can be understood from the incredible endeavors of the nongovernmental organizations across our global community.

Additionally, The Millennium Project, the world's most profound assembly of futurists, operating as an independent non-profit global participatory futures research think tank, was originally founded as a project of the United Nations University. The most meaningful contribution of this organization has been the identification and discussion of fifteen global challenges that must be overcome if we are to sustain the livability of our home planet into the future and maintain the health and vigor of our human community worldwide.

(The Millennium Project, 2014, http://www.millennium-project.org/projects/challenges/)

The ninth global challenge, focusing upon education, has been stated as follows:

> How can education make humanity more intelligent, knowledgeable, and wise enough to address its global challenges?

According to The *Millennium Project Papers; The Future of Higher Education in the Knowledge-Driven, Global Economy of the 21st Century,* it is essential for institutional transformation in higher education that educational leaders diligently reassess the vital roles and missions of the university to assure effective change. The paper states that universities must look to the challenges they face in the future and develop strategies. In that light, it would be fair to state that if higher education is to make an impact upon the future and serve as a catalyst for our survival, it must fundamentally modify its vision and mission.

(The Millennium Project Papers, National Governors Association, 2001)

In that light, the best future vision and mission for higher education must be to establish the wherewithal to recognize the challenges facing human culture and the critical challenges impacting sustainability of the planet. Thereafter, higher education must advance future-oriented academic programs most conducive to achieving the mission of human survival. According to the Akamai University community, the foremost areas of focus might be viewed as these seven: psychology and human services, business and economic development, environmental and ecological studies, education and literacy, health and wellness, engineering and technology, and sustainability and security.

These areas of focus seem to have the most potential to prepare future participants to combat major world problems and contribute toward achievement for the human community. There also seem to be instructional models with inherent potential for future success, including mentorship, therein linking students to the best of the best among the knowledge holders, individualization of study to match outcomes for isolated populations, project-oriented learning environments, which provide for integration with real world challenges.

In conclusion, it must become apparent to higher education worldwide that a transformation must rapidly take place with regard to the mission, vision, goals and objectives of all wise and well-intentioned institutions of higher learning. The status quo is no longer sustainable, and we must see a major transformation, so that the great minds and institutions are able to take a leadership role in bringing the human community forward in its thinking, its values, and approach to life on our planet, assuring its sustainability into the future for the benefit of our children and our grandchildren.

As an example, let us now examine a uniquely designed university, which has struggled to implement a mission that addresses amelioration of major world problems and sustainability of the planet.

In early 2002, a group of likeminded academics and futurists from across the global community undertook to envision a new style higher education institution, one designed to exclusively pursue human advancement and sustainability for our planet. These dedicated professionals were somewhat dissatisfied with the lack of leadership and direction across traditional higher education and sought a new vision; one of sincerity and effectiveness, establishing a new foundation for the future of higher education, a transformation, whereby the university of the future shall serve as the catalyst for human advancement. Thereby, Akamai University was founded as a unique non-governmental organization with a vision that higher learning should serve as a catalyst for human betterment and in that manner successfully serve the needs of its students.

The mission and vision of Akamai University as an institution of higher learning was the advancement of the human condition and sustainability of the planet. From its start, Akamai University believed it is no small aspiration to strive for a world filled with greater peace, balance, cooperation, and the promise of an evolved human fellowship. The founders believed these goals to be noble foundation stones upon which to establish the fundamentals of sustainable human culture. They are spiritual principles that demand a worthy mission, and although the tasks and goals before the University seemed immense, they believed them attainable with adequate understanding of the problems and solutions, and the full commitment and participation of the global community.

As educators, since its founding, Akamai has been most comfortable with instructional methods that empower its students to think beyond the confines of the classroom, building achievement and new learning while fully engaged with their personal and professional lives. Akamai respects each student as a unique individual, academically and professionally. Freed from traditional residency requirements, the students are able to pursue advanced study in a personalized and self-paced manner while maintaining full time employment and family responsibilities. Akamai honors the life pursuits of our students by providing opportunities for them to integrate professional activities within their programs. As a non-profit organization, Akamai has established the fairest tuition rates possible to provide access for students from across the global community.

Since its founding on the Island of Hawaii in the Central Pacific, Akamai's primary academic quest has been the delivery of meaningful educational programs, individualized to the academic and professional goals of its students. Under the direction of quality faculty, all students are encouraged to create and evaluate, do independent and original thinking, make judgments, communicate unique ideas, feelings, and experiences; and design effective solutions within "real life" situations. This type of outcome contributes in a powerful manner to the development of effectiveness for these professional-minded individuals.

Further, Akamai encourages and expects its adult students to seek a path that permits them to contribute to the amelioration of major problems worldwide, within nations, and in their profession. To help engage them in addressing these human needs, the University leadership continues to research and plan ways to achieve its vision, mission, goals and objectives.

To assure the highest level of guidance in deriving its operations, Akamai entered an affiliation in our infancy with the top level futures research think tank, The Millennium Project, comprised of futurists, scholars, business planners, and policy makers who work for international organizations, governments, corporations, NGOs, and universities. As Akamai developed, it strived to build a robust faculty of like-minded professionals. Akamai also was able to affiliate with nationally recognized universities, and training agencies from seventeen nations. As it progressed, Akamai has enrolled and instructed more than 5,000 students from across 47 nations. The University's faculty led its students to create and evaluate, do independent and original thinking, make judgments, communicate unique ideas, feelings, and experiences; and design effective solutions within "real life" situations and firmly sought to influence its students to become colleagues for human betterment. Many of Akamai's alumni have pursued areas that contribute powerfully toward the advancement of the human condition and sustainability of the planet. The University remains proud to have its graduates collaborate in the field of research and international programs, following similar life missions, as did the founders of Akamai University.

References

Cortese, A. D. (2003). *The critical role of higher education in creating a sustainable future.* Retrieved from http://www.aashe.org/resources/pdf/Cortese_PHE.pdf

Human Rights Watch. *Youth for human rights: Human rights abuses.* Retrieved from http://www.youthforhumanrights.org/voices-for-human-rights/human-rights-abuses.html

The Millennium Project. (2005). *Investing in development: A practical plan to achieve the millennium development goals.* [Report to the UN Secretary General]. Retrieved from http://www.unmillenniumproject.org/documents/MainReportComplete-lowres.pdf

Union of Concerned Scientists. (1992). *World scientists' warning to humanity.* Retrieved from http://www.ucsusa.org/about/1992-world-scientists.html#.VWO36Ebg_oc

United Nations Environmental Program. (2015). *Environment for development.* Retrieved from http://www.unep.org/

The World Bank and United Nations. (2008-2015). *Poverty around the world.* Retrieved from http://www.globalissues.org/article/4/poverty-around-the-world#Introduction

The World Conference on Higher Education, UNESCO. (1998). *World declaration on higher education for the twenty-first century: Vision and action.* Retrieved from http://www.unesco.org/education/educprog/wche/declaration_eng.htm

World Health Organization. *World Health Report.* Retrieved from http://www.globalissues.org/article/588/global-health-overview

CHAPTER 2

Where Science Meets Policy: The Nexus of Decision-making in Modern Society

Anthony R. Maranto
Akamai University

Abstract

Society relies on a fragile and often tense relationship between policy and science to make informed decisions about everything from how much of a food additive should be allowed to where to site radioactive waste repositories. While accurate projections and a deep understanding of the second and third order effects of the decisions we collectively make as a society should be based on scientifically sound data, evidence, and observations, often the connection between these two foundational elements is not well understood. Policy makers often have little understanding of the scientific process, the meaning of the data they use, or the ramifications of scientific uncertainty. Similarly, scientists often have little insight into how the data and hypotheses they generate will ultimately be used to form or modify governing principles. In order to strengthen the vital connection between science and policy, universities need to explore the interconnectivity of those realms in their hard science as well as their political and social science curricula.

Overview

Throughout most of human history there has been an uneasy relationship between the fundamental disciplines of the hard sciences and the sphere of public policy, politics, and governance. Public policy drives the development of our societal framework, lays out the purpose and objectives for our collective efforts, and coalesces into the guidelines for how we operate in society. In order to develop sound policy based on observed conditions and relationships, politicians require unbiased, accurate, and high-quality science to support their decision-making processes. At the same time, scientists and policy makers often have very different goals, standards for information, time schedules, and professional language, resulting in significant barriers to information sharing, knowledge transfer, and even fundamental trust between the two groups (Choi et al., 2005).

An additional complication to the relationship between scientists and policy makers rests in the fact that political decision makers have a level of control over a substantial amount of the support required for scientific research and technological development, thereby influencing the course of science itself. Additionally, while most politicians and policy makers will publicly state a strong desire to have sound science as the basis for their policy frameworks, they are by no means, bound to use scientific data properly, or even at all. Indeed, policy makers are free to eschew or completely disregard objective data and observations when it does not support their objectives, with little or no real consequence for their political careers. These conditions are the chief source of the ever-present tensions between the scientific and political communities (Silver, 2005).

While the term "sound science" is part of the ubiquitous political dialogue at all levels of government, the term tends to have an un-fixed meaning in policy circles which shifts in relation to the intent and motivation of the speaker. The term often is used as a descriptor for science which supports the views and actions of the policy maker, rather than an accurate characterization of the rigor and standards observed in the collection of the data or development of the analysis. Policy makers often look for evidence to support their positions, thus creating a systematic bias in the way they look at data (Choi et al., 2005). This, to many scientists, is the opposite of what "sound science" should be.

Alternately, the term is often used by bureaucrats to signify a scientific theory for which there are no controversial (or at least difficult to dismiss) counterpoints. The unvarnished truth of the matter is that there are rarely issues in science that are resolved to the point of absolute certainty. There are, after all, only a few hundred scientific principles which rise to the level of scientific laws. These deal primarily with mathematically provable relationships in gravitation, relativity, thermodynamics, electromagnetism, fluid dynamics, chemistry, geophysics, and the like. The number of scientific theories, however, that have been and currently are postulated to explain what we observe in nature and we have experimentally derived in the laboratory are, quite literally, beyond measure. These theories are all subject to scrutiny and debate.

Sound science (i.e., research that follows the scientific method, has appropriate methodologies, institutes appropriate controls, has proper statistical applications, has survived the peer review process, etc.) can go a long way towards eliminating weak theories and establishing a body of evidence to support stronger ones, but it usually doesn't provide absolute confirmation of anything. The concepts of uncertainty and probability functions are absolutely vital for understanding the significance of any piece of research. These factors, however, are generally not well understood by either the general public nor by non-scientist policy makers.

While the differences between scientists and policy makers are very real, each community must have an understanding of each other's strengths, weaknesses, and purposes. Building a broader understanding of the use and meaning of scientific data is a concept that should be integrated into the political and social science curricula of tertiary institutions in order to facilitate the better use of scientific research as a support for public policy decisions.

What Science Can and Cannot Do

Decisions which balance the public good with the competing interests of individual and civil liberties, social order, national security, resource usage, resource conservation, economic drivers, future needs, strategic initiatives, ethics, and a host of other important factors, cannot and probably should not be based solely on a scientific valuation or quantification of the observable factors underlying the position. Scientific research and observations can only provide a piece of the puzzle when solving social problems. This is a difficult fact for many scientists to digest.

In traditional science education, students are taught that science is the unbiased search for truth. The reality of it, however, is that science is better characterized as the search for facts. Facts are measurable, observable, and stand against logical argument (e.g., the melting point of camphor is 175°C). Truth, by way of comparison, is a human construct that weaves together the disparate values of belief, desire, culture, perception, and history and may or may not be supported by fact (Price, 1989).

Facts, when scientifically derived, can be strongly supportive of public policy decisions. As a result, we can rely on properly structured and executed scientific research to:

- describe the characteristics and conditions of whatever is being observed;
- explain how a system works;
- assess the linkages and connections between different systems;
- identify where our understanding of a system is incomplete;
- identify potential problems which need to be addressed by policy;
- set a standard set of conditions upon which to evaluate policy decisions;
- set limits and thresholds for policy actions;
- provide a neutral evaluation of alternatives to some course of action;

- provide evidence as to the effects of implemented policies; and
- predict, to some statistical level, what may happen under different policy scenarios.

Science cannot, however, provide all perspectives that often factor into human decision processes like governmental policy. No matter how sound the research methodology, experimental controls, or statistical analysis, we cannot expect the scientific community to:

- identify the full range of values and variables that must be considered;
- determine which values should be prioritized and which should be minimized;
- determine what levels of risk or uncertainty are acceptable to a particular policy decision;
- make legal, moral, or ethical judgments;
- make aesthetic or cultural valuations;
- develop quality science on accelerated timelines;
- provide answers to complex questions with absolute certainty;
- guarantee that scientific results will not be misused to bolster a political interest;
- guarantee that any sector of the public will garner interest/passion in the debate of ideas; and
- be the sole determinant in a policy decision.

In an examination of the integration of forestry science with policy, the USDA noted that "the turn to science often reflects a failure of other processes (political management, legal, regulatory, negation)" (Clark et al., 1998). It is important that all scientists and science students learn the limits of what we can ask of scientific research and to avoid drawing their analysis into the areas of value judgments, ethical equivalencies, and prioritization of societal goals. That is the job of the policy maker who will integrate scientific facts, with economic analysis, and the values, mores, and cultural preferences of their constituent groups. While scientists need to be careful when faced with situations that can put their credentials as unbiased observers into question, they also must understand that once released into the public domain, their observations can and will be used in ways they did not intend.

Politics is more Difficult than Physics

When asked by a Princeton conference attendee in 1946, "Dr. Einstein, why is it that while the mind of man has stretched so far as to discover the structure of the atom, we have been unable to devise the political means to keep the atom from destroying us?," the legendary Nobel scientist replied, "That is simple, my friend. It is because politics is more difficult than physics" (Clark, 1955).

There is no question that science is an integral part of the political process. National and even regional/state governments require significant scientific capacity to perform and disseminate their own scientific research; monitor and evaluate outside scientific research; and assess the impact of policy decisions on issues with complex scientific content (Homer-Dixon et al., 2014).

Scientists are, from the beginning of their training, taught to be objective and as unbiased as possible in their work. If that means that a scientist spends that better part of his or her career trying to advance a theory that is ultimately disproven by their own work, then so be it. All of us who have undergone classical training as scientists, understand that we have an ethical responsibility to report our findings as we record them, even when they show results contrary to our interests or personal agendas.

While the standards for sound science are well established, the current state of scientific theory has never been in stasis, unless it was artificially arrested at a given level of inquiry (as in the Roman Catholic Church's treatment of the research of Galileo Galilee). The body of human knowledge is in constant flux. What the scientific community took as gospel yesterday, may prove to be misguided fiction tomorrow. That is why science must strive to remain an open and self-correcting process. To be of value, a theory or experimental protocol need not be agreed upon by all experts. Indeed, if we required unanimity among the opinions of all scientists, very little would ever be accomplished. What is required of scientific research, however, is that it be consistently logical in its reasoning, it be testable, and ultimately, that it be reproducible (Maranto, 1998).

The realm of political decision-making, however, is bound by a different set of guidelines and many competing interests. In the body of governance, if the outcome of a scientific study does not support the stated objectives and goals of a policy, then it is often discarded. This is not a cynical statement, but rather a realization that there may be societal values or goals that influence the ultimate decision process that are not borne out by a purely scientific examination of the data at hand.

Early in my career, I was given a small dose of reality in terms of how policy decisions were shaped by perception as much as they were by the actual underlying science. When working as a consultant for the US Army Environmental Command, I was fortunate enough to be part of a ground-breaking initiative which focused on leveraging small amounts of federal funding as a partially matching incentive program for private organizations to spend their resources in natural resource conservation efforts near to and adjoining military training lands. These projects had the effect of conserving thousands of acres of critical habitat, reducing urbanization pressures near military installations, and protecting a number of threatened and endangered species which had concentrated on military lands because of habitat destruction outside of the installation fence-lines, all while helping to ensure that the military could continue to use its training lands in support of national defense. The projects were a win for the conservation groups, a win for the natural environment, and a win for national security. Nonetheless, one of our larger projects was politically attacked and even made it into the "Congressional Pig Book" of wasteful government pork-barrel projects, largely for the sin of being based in Hawaii. Obviously, anything the government funds on a beautiful Pacific island has to be wasteful. No logical statement of the underlying conservation science or the economic return on investment for those projects could persuade their detractors otherwise.

The Goal of Evidence-Based Policy

While it is possible for bad policy to be developed based on good science, and conversely, for good policy to be developed with bad or no scientific basis at all, there has been a general consensus among governing bodies, that sound science before and after a policy decision helps to frame the problem and to assess the effectiveness of the policy itself (Choi, et al., 2005; Haskins & Baron, 2011). Over the last several decades, the importance of using science as a supporting platform for public policy has been recognized, yet there remains a debate over how to best achieve this goal. The framework of "evidence-based policy" has led to greater integration of science and scientists into the policy making process (Homer-Dixon, et al., 2014). This has also been furthered through the steady growth of centers of scientific expertise within government bodies (in the United States, prime examples would include the many federal agencies with a science-based mission focus like NASA, NOAA, USDA, CDC, etc.).

Despite efforts to better encapsulate scientific data into the public policy process, full integration has not yet been broadly achieved. One factor that has limited the broad implementation of an evidence-based policy approach relates to the timeliness of available data and analysis. While public policy makers like to talk about being proactive and progressive in their approach to planning and policy development; in reality, most governmental policy is based on a reactive timeline. Often, decisions and policies are developed in response to a rapidly developing situation or under emergency conditions, and as such, cannot fully afford the long timelines required for the development, review, and verification of sound science (Clark et al., 1998).

Policy makers can often be frustrated because the body of science cannot provide a quick, clear, and understandable answer to a problem as it occurs. Likewise, scientists are similarly befuddled by demands from politicians for expedient and absolute responses to problems where data may not exist or where detailed answers may be years or decades away (Choi et al., 2005).

Science and policy have at their core different decision drivers. Scientists have long (often generational) attention spans, allowing answers to be probed based on successive rounds of improving observations and experimentation. The scientific process is designed to be slow, ponderous, and deliberate. Policy makers, however, do not enjoy the luxury of time. They look for concise nuggets of information that are readily available and can be pressed into service when needed. The data need not always be rigorous and often encompasses unscientific polls, anecdotes, and limited case studies (Choi et al., 2005).

How Scientific Uncertainty Affects Public Policy

The concept of uncertainty is one of the key tenants of science and is also one of the most misunderstood by non-scientists. Starting from the most basic formulation that very little in life happens with 100% certainty; then by extension, anything less than that has a degree of uncertainty associated with it. Science is based on inquiry and observation. Sometimes our observations are imperfect, and those imperfections carry over in predictions we make based on observed patterns (SAS, 2013).

Uncertainties can generally be placed in three categories: statistical, model, and fundamental. These categories correspond to the nature of observational inexactness, unreliability, and insufficient knowledge (Funtowicz & Ravetz, 1992). Both the kind and the degree of scientific uncertainty have significant implications for the how policy makers can and should use scientific data.

When looking at new or evolving research, there is a heightened risk of uncertainty when compared with fundamental scientific principles or settled science that is supported by large bodies of evidence from the peer reviewed literature. While there are often changes to our understanding of systems based on improved experimentation, instrumentation, or research design, these discoveries rarely change our understanding of scientific principles (i.e., settled science) (SAS, 2013).

Uncertainty, while often misunderstood by the general public and by non-scientific policy makers, is not completely absent from every aspect of governance. It is, for example, a common feature of all evidence-based regulatory decision-making. As an example, the basis for human, occupational and environmental health regulatory standards is to develop uncertainty- and risk-based judgments about protective thresholds (NRC, 2002).

The public tends to construct their understanding of scientific uncertainty based on the conflicting accounts of risk presented in the media. This adds an additional layer of filter to the already complex interactions between science and public policy, in that journalists can bring their own perceptions to the coverage of controversial issues in emerging research. Uncertainty is therefore, often viewed by the public as battling interpretations between politicians, scientists, and journalists, where all three start from a common set of facts, but then construct their accounts of uncertainty related to those facts in progressive layers upon each other (Friedman et al., 1999). This has led to much confusion in the general public, and sometimes outright panic, as observations and policy decisions are reported without proper context for their scientific uncertainty.

An additional issue that compounds the misunderstanding of uncertainty is the near universal trend for scientists to "hedge their bets" in publications. Indeed, it is a long running joke in the scientific community that no journal manuscript can end without a clear statement that "additional research is required." While a clear statement of the assumptions, conditions, and uncertainties associated with any research is absolutely required, many scientists go beyond an assessment of the limitations of their data and attempt to provide proof "beyond a reasonable doubt," which in turn requires complex caveats to their work.

Policy makers who have to exercise rapid judgments, rely on a standard that is better defined as "on balance, reasonable" (Choi et al., 2005). This creates a condition where policy makers are looking for a "bottom line," while scientists seek to provide "fine print," creating another disconnect between how science is produced and how it is consumed.

The Precautionary Principle

A common framework in public policy (especially as it relates to health, safety, and environmental protection) where there is insufficient science or elevated uncertainty is to incorporate what has become known as the "precautionary principle." This term, derived from the German "Vorsorgeprinzip" (which translates to fore-caring principle), takes its roots from the 1970's German clean air policies that called for forward planning to prevent harmful effects of pollution (Boehmer-Christiansen, 1994). The concept has since been incorporated in numerous regional, national, and international policies and regulations as a standard of protection for a variety of health and environmental standards (Schettler, Barrett, & Raffensperger, 2002).

A policy decision based on the precautionary approach incorporates the ethical aspects of proactively preventing harm. It is structured on the recognition that scientific uncertainty and gaps in the body of scientific data can lead to real and serious risks to human health and the environment (Schettler, Barrett, & Raffensperger, 2002). When boiled down to its simplest form, the precautionary principle is an extension of the ages old adage that "it is better to be safe than sorry."

One would be very challenged to find either a scientist or a policy maker anywhere who would not agree with the statement that human health and the environment need to be protected. Where differences rapidly emerge, however, is in the level of precaution that should be incorporated into public policy to reasonably protect human health and the environment. Again, scientific uncertainty plays a role in the different views on this matter, however, there are also cost issues and ramifications from second- and third-order effects from precautionary regulations.

While from a political standpoint, the precautionary principle has a great deal of appeal, in and of itself it offers little guidance for practical public governance. Additionally, many scientists and policy makers alike have noted that precautionary decisions can themselves have their own risk and uncertainty (Sunstein, 2005). While from a policy standpoint, it may seem prudent to ban the use of an industrial chemical until it is deemed safe (assuming for a moment that it is even possible to prove such a thing); a precautionary regulation along those lines may have dramatic and unexpected impacts for society as a whole which could include unemployment in those industries which used the compound, dependence on other compounds which may pose even higher health risks, loss of key goods to the economy, etc. Herein lays another of the conflicts that exist between scientifically derived data and the policy imperatives of proactive protection.

The Vectors of Money, Bureaucracy, and Power

While it is clear that science can have a direct impact on the course of public policy, the realm of politics can have an even greater impact on the course of science. It is not uncommon for federal agencies to create rules that direct government scientists (and to a lesser extent those funded through government grants), to seek bureaucratic approval before presenting their findings at conferences or publishing their research. Within government research agencies, travel for the purposes of attending symposia and conferences is tightly controlled. Gag-orders preventing researchers from communicating with journalists are also not uncommon in government-developed research (Homer-Dixon et al., 2014).

Additionally, within bureaucracies, there is often a reluctance to examine the overall effectiveness of policies and publicly funded programs. Agencies can be resistant to such examination because there is an acknowledged understanding that many government programs, when subjected to rigorous scientific evaluation, show null results, and since no agency wants to be identified with programs that are ineffective, it becomes easier to simply not measure program effectiveness (or not accurately measure it) rather than to face potential losses in budgets and organizational power (Haskins & Baron, 2011).

While scientists are accountable to their research institutions and to the editors and peer reviewers who are involved in the publication and validation process, policy makers are accountable to a wide range of stakeholders including their constituents, the tax-paying public, political parties, other government agencies, other politicians, and the bureaucratic hierarchy of their respective agencies (Choi, et al., 2005). In this complex matrix of accountability, budget considerations and organizational weight play significant roles in the balance of power and the direction of public policy.

Government as a singular entity, can and does use its control over the public coffers to not only drive research in a direction that supports current public policy, but it likewise can use those funding powers to shut down or dissuade research in areas which are perceived to be counter to the political direction of a given governmental agency or regime. Be that as it may, in the US, the diversity of funding sources available to the broad scientific community does allow for research that isn't strictly assessed to be in the policy-based public interest but can still compete for non-federal resources to support their research. In the US, federal research funding accounts for just over 30% of the totality of available funding pool, with private industry funding approximately 60%, and all other funding sources (i.e., non-profits, universities, non-federal governments, etc.) accounting for just under 10% (AAAS, 2014).

While current government objectives and focus can, from time to time, impair the development of competing scientific inquiry, there are intervals when the push for scientific discovery matches lock-step with the stated policy directives and goals of the time. One of the best examples of this was when President Kennedy announced that America would place a man on the moon by the end of the 1960s. The geopolitical environment of the Cold War helped spur significant scientific developments and advanced much of the technology which would later drive the computer revolution (Silver, 2005).

When national interests line up with the trends in research and development, the scientific community can be the beneficiary of massive levels of resources and funding made available from the public treasury. This results in the relatively high percentages of federal research dollars focused on basic research, applied research, and development related to key governmental interests of Defense (51%), Health and Human Services (26%), and Energy (7%) (Kennedy, 2012). Scientists whose research aligns with government interests tend to have a larger pool of funding available for competition, and thus, development in those areas is supported to the detriment of others.

Education Challenges for the Next Generation

Introducing public policy concepts and perspectives into science courses has been a concept that has been resisted by many traditional hard science faculties, especially at the undergraduate level. This fact may stem from the reality that few tertiary science professors have been explicitly educated to teach science from such a perspective (Labov & Huddleston, 2008). In light of the ever tighter integration of complex scientific issues in the realm of public policy, however, many now believe it to be a critical component of a balanced and multi-disciplinary science education.

It has also been observed that many non-science majors are becoming more interested in aspects of the hard sciences when they can see the relevance of the subject to other topics of interest (i.e., environmental protection, food scarcity, energy independence, crime and civil liberties, etc.) (Labov & Huddleston, 2008). This interest may in turn, be utilized to help ingrain basic scientific concepts in social science or political science students.

The National Science Foundation has acknowledged the need for integrated science and public policy education and since 2001 has supported the Scientific Education for New Civic Engagements and Responsibilities (SENCER) program. SENCER seeks to apply current Science, Technology, Engineering, and Mathematics (STEM) content to critical local, national, and global challenges in an effort to make science more useful and civically important. SNECER has supported the development of over 50 educational models including such topics as climate change, nanotechnology, urbanization, pregnancy outcomes, and evolutionary medicine (NCSCE, 2015).

Initiatives like these will be paramount to the inclusion of cross-discipline and multi-discipline concepts in both science and social science curricula. When perused at the tertiary educational level, these programs may have the effect of focusing academic and post-academic research into a form that is more accommodating and inclusive of broader societal factors. Likewise, these efforts may help engender a higher degree of scientific literacy in the next generation of policy makers, government workers, lawyers, and social policy advocates.

Conclusions

There are several prerequisites that must be considered to successfully integrate science and public policy. These include having clear objectives and processes; having clear roles and responsibilities which include participation from the science community, policy makers, and the general public; quality control processes including peer, technical, and public review; and open communication with all stakeholders (incorporating translational scientists if necessary) (Clark et al., 1998).

Educators and institutions of higher education can facilitate the movement of social policy towards a more evidence-based approach which recognizes the value of sound science along with the other social, ethical, and economic drivers that support reliable decision-making by integrating the following concepts into curriculum development and delivery.

- **Establish well-reasoned benchmarks for scientific and technological literacy at all levels of education.** Raising the understanding of the population-at-large in the areas of scientific process and current developments will support the public's understanding of developing scientific research and will provide flexibility for policy makers to move towards a more solid scientific basis for their policy decisions.
- **Provide ethical and regulatory guidance to young scientists.** Integration of both scientific ethics and regulatory standards into classical science education will engender deeper consideration for these issues among research institutions, scientific publications, and in the development of research protocols.

- **Develop a shared scientific and political language**. The situational meaning of such basic terms as uncertainty, risk, significance, etc., has led to heightened tensions and misunderstandings between scientists and policy makers. Development of common usages for these terms (or the development of alternate terms) should be integrated into both science and political science curricula, so that communications and information sharing can transpire in a more precise fashion.
- **Integrate professional organizations into the development of well-reasoned policy which properly uses science as a decision support tool**. Support the development of networking, outreach, and educational programs with key professional and academic organizations like the American Association for the Advancement of Science, the American Chemistry Society, the American Medical Association, the International Association for Political Science Students, and the like, focused on better integration of science and policy.

References

http://blog.apastyle.org/apastyle/2009/08/formatting-apa-references-with-more-than-seven-authors.html

http://blog.apastyle.org/apastyle/2011/01/writing-in-text-citations-in-apa-style.html

http://blog.apastyle.org/apastyle/2011/02/et-al-when-and-how.html

http://blog.apastyle.org/apastyle/2013/04/when-to-include-the-year-in-citations-appearing-more-than-once-in-a-paragraph.html

http://blog.apastyle.org/apastyle/2011/01/writing-in-text- citations-in-apa-style.html

http://blog.apastyle.org/apastyle/2013/04/when-to-include-the-year-in-citations-appearing-more-than-once-in-a-paragraph.html

http://blog.apastyle.org/apastyle/2011/02/et-al-when-and-how.html

http://blog.apastyle.org/apastyle/2016/11/writing-website-in-text-citations-and-references.html

http://blog.apastyle.org/apastyle/2009/08/formatting-apa-references-with-more-than-seven-authors.html

References

American Association for the Advancement of Science. (2014). *Historical trends in federal &d.-*Washington, DC: Author. Retrieved from http://www.aaas.org/page/historical-trends-federal-rd

Boehmer-Christiansen, S. (1994). The precautionary principle in Germany: Enabling government. In O'Riordan, T. & Cameron, J. (Eds.). *Interpreting the Precautionary Principle.* London, UK: Earthscan Publications.

Choi, B. C. K., Pang, T., Lin, V., Puska, P., Sherman, G., Goddard, M.,... Clottey, C. (2005). Can scientists and policy makers work together? *Journal of Epidemiology and Community Health, 59,* 632-637.

Clark, G. (1955, April 22). Letters to the Times. *New York Times. 24.*

Clark, R. N., Meidinger, E. O., Miller, G., Rayner, J., Layseca, M., Monreal, S. ... Shannon, M. A. (1998). *Integrating science and policy in natural resource management: Lessons and opportunities from North America.* [PNW-GTR-441]. US Department of Agriculture, Forest Service, Pacific Northwest Research Station. Portland, OR: Author.

Friedman, S. M., Dunwoody, S., & Rogers, C. L. (1999). *Communicating uncertainty: Media coverage of new and controversial science*. New York, NY: Routledge, Taylor & Francis Group.

Funtowicz, S. O., & Ravetz, J. R. (1992). Three types of risk assessment and the emergence of post-normal science. In Krimsky, S., & Golding, D. (Eds.). *Social Theories of Risk*, 251–274. Westport, CT: Praeger.

Guston, D. H. (2007). *Between politics and science: Assuring the integrity and productivity of research*. New York, NY: Cambridge University Press.

Haskins, R., & Baron, J. (2011). Building the connection between policy and evidence. London, UK: NESTA.

Homer-Dixon, T., Douglas, H., & Edwards, L. (2014, June 23). Fix the link where science and policy meet. *The Globe and Mail* Retrieved from: https://www.theglobeandmail.com/opinion/fix-the-link-where-science-and-policy-meet/article19286655/

Kennedy, J. V. (2012, Summer). The sources and uses of U.S. science funding. *The New Atlantis: A Journal of Technology & Society. 36*, 3-22.

Labov, J. B., & Huddleston, N.F. (2008). Integrating policy and decision-making into undergraduate science education. *CBE Life Science Education, 7*(4), 347-352.

Maranto, A. R. (1998). Classic barriers to novel science. *Exotic Research Report, 2*(4), 61-64.

National Center for Science and Civil Engagement. (2015). The SENCER model series. Washington, DC: Author. Retrieved from http://www.sencer.net/Resources/models.cfm

National Research Council. (2002). *Animal biotechnology: Science-based concerns.* Committee on Defining Science-Based Concerns Associated with Products of Animal Biotechnology. Washington, DC: Author.

Price, H. (1989). *Facts and the function of truth.* New York, NY: Basil Blackwell.

Sense About Science. (2013). *Making sense of uncertainty: Why uncertainty is part of science.* London, UK: Author.

Schettler, T., Barrett, K., & Raffensperger, C. (2002). The precautionary principle: Protecting public health and the environment. *The Collaborative on Health and the Environment.* Retrieved from http://www.healthandenvironment.org/articles/doc/540#2002Schettler

Silver, H. J. (2005). Science and politics: The uneasy relationship. *Open Spaces Quarterly, 8*(1).

Sunstein, C. R. (2005). *The laws of fear: Beyond the precautionary principle.* Cambridge, UK: Cambridge University Press.

CHAPTER 3

With Justice For All: A Remedy for the Key Omission in Higher Education

Michael J. Cohen
Akamai University

In order to change an existing paradigm you do not struggle to try and change the problematic model. You create a new model and make the old one obsolete.
--Robert Buckminster Fuller, Operating Manual for Spaceship Earth, 2006

Abstract

This Chapter is a metaphor for the United States Department of Justice convening a Grand Jury to indict Higher Education Accrediting Associations and the U.S. Department of Education for violating the civil and human rights of the public by denying and withholding the value of Einstein-54 education, counseling, and healing with Nature. Because it consists of and only uses sensory self-evidence, beyond reasonable doubt this tool helps us remedy the dangerous natural resource deficiency people produce that increasingly injures the life of

Planet Earth and its seamless continuum as our body, mind, and spirit (Project Nature Connect, PNC, 2012a).

Overview

This metaphor starts with the opening statement of Robert Goldwater. He is the Prosecutor from the U.S. Department of Justice for a Grand Jury in a class action complaint (Plaintiffs) against both the U.S. Department of Education and Higher Education Accrediting Associations (Defendants). Both federal and state governments depend upon the Defendants to fulfill their responsibilities to all parties concerned.

Opening Statement by Prosecutor

Good Day, Jury members. Thank you for fulfilling your duties as American citizens to help justice for all prevail through trial by jury. The Plaintiffs have filed with the U.S. Department of Justice, a class action complaint against the Defendants, individually and in collusion, for violating a wide range of human and civil rights held in common by the Plaintiffs.

This complaint results from the Defendants' denial and negligence in meeting their responsibility to incorporate and implement legitimate facts, methods, and materials that make education in the United States meet minimum standards to ensure many freedoms and rights guaranteed to all citizens by the Constitution of the United States. To this end, and in good faith I, as the Prosecutor for the Department of Justice, have investigated and selected essential topics that Witnesses will present for you to weigh as evidence.

Along with some of the Plaintiffs, I have questioned the Witnesses so that here this morning they may each make a short statement that presents an overview of their observations and findings. This will allow Jurors to better understand the further testimony of the Witnesses this afternoon and question them with regard to the Plaintiffs' complaint. I will advise you on the relevance of the evidence and on the law as will Judge Marilyn Wilson when necessary.

I have drafted the charges fairly and they will show that you must indict the Defendants so a judge and jury may properly settle this injustice by rule of law later and hear the Defendants. Please note that an additional Plaintiff here, one that all the class action Plaintiffs hold in common, will not be present now and in the possible forthcoming trial. This is because that Plaintiff has no rights or legal standing in the eyes of the law.

I have asked the Witnesses to express their views using information that can also be found on the Internet so that the Jurors can see it is common knowledge, not private or restricted, and that the Defendants had full access to it and they had the responsibility and authority to require its use as well as its distribution. This information is available as well for any Juror. You can locate it in a search engine through its topics.

For greater completeness, I have asked each Witness to cite individuals not present whose statements support their testimony. For example, if the real, alive Albert Einstein were on the witness stand rather than just someone who could convey some of his knowledge, the impact and outcome of the testimony would be different even though the information was the same. Many references to the citations are available by entering them in internet search engines.

You 23 Jurors must decide whether the evidence presented by the Witnesses shows due cause for this case to proceed to court so appropriate liabilities, fines, punishments, and a Judge may take necessary steps in this regard. To this end, and with respect to its responsibility to the American people, the Justice Department last month convened a committee of recognized experts in appropriate fields. They vetted all the Witnesses listed by the Plaintiffs and myself. With due diligence, they selected to present facts to this Grand Jury only from witnesses (a) with the strongest qualifications in their area of expertise, (b) who had the greatest preponderance of evidence beyond reasonable doubt for their testimony, (c) had the most unblemished records for abiding by the law, and (d) swore or guaranteed to tell the truth, the whole truth, and nothing but the truth in this hearing. Kept in separation, the Witnesses are unaware of each other's testimony.

The 23 of you have been selected as a fair cross section of society because with respect to the claims of the Plaintiffs, your charge is for you to be reasonable, to evaluate, and to blend from the wide range of your own personal education and life experiences the fairness, appropriateness, well-being, and truth that you find in the testimony of each Witness. This will challenge you since you have been educated and put in denial by the Defendants. This morning you are to pay attention to what makes the most sense to you in this complaint. Then this hearing will examine further details this afternoon and tomorrow when we will bring the Witnesses back for full information and questioning.

Jurors must know that they are considering for the Justice Department at this time, only a limited number of rights allegedly violated. If you decide to send this case to trial, the Department will hold additional inquests into other rights ~~that have also~~ allegedly ~~to be~~ violated. In these future hearings the prosecution will subpoena the most influential members of society to appear. This will assure that their power is brought to protect the people through these Witnesses' areas of influence as well as through the Justice system.

The central issue of this hearing is that the civil and human rights of the Plaintiffs ~~have been breached~~ were through undue prejudice and negligence. This is because the Defendants ~~have~~ had the opportunity to provide, but irresponsibly neglected to provide, federal government and private non-profit research, information, and educational services that they are established to make available for the public good. Because we undeniably live in the time and space of our living planet, Earth, when negligence by some parts of our society damages its health, they damage the health of others and they can be held legally responsible for their acts by those whose rights have been violated. In real life 2016, several suits against corporations for damages incurred from unabated climate change are presently in the process of trial by jury. The Defendants here are alleged to have fraudulently reduced public health and welfare through their omission of the scientifically valid *Albert Einstein Unified Field 54-Sense Equation* (Einstein-54 or GreenWave-54), and the process of *Educating, Counseling, and Healing With Nature* (ECHN). They include the *Natural Attraction Ecology Model* (PNC, 2007B) also known in some circles as *Organic Psychology* and the *Natural Systems Thinking Process* ("Natural Attraction Ecology," 2003). Hereinafter they all will collectively be referred to as *Einstein-54, GreenWave-54* or *ECHN*.

Einstein-54 does the seemingly impossible. It validates that we have 54 natural senses that are part of Albert Einstein's Unified Field of the Big Bang Universe, that we call Nature, so they register it as themselves and it guides them in natural areas (Cohen, 2013). This enables people to come out of denial and unify their personal lives with others, society, and the environment. It helps folks apply the high tech ways of objective science to 54 often conquered, subjective sensory facts (Cohen, 2014). This connection produces the value and beauty of whole life relationships in balance, locally and globally (Albert Einstein, 2014). It increases personal, social, and environmental well-being at every level of endeavor while decreasing the costs of coping with the disorders caused by the deterioration of personal and global wellness due to our excessive disconnection from Nature (Cohen, 2015).

While this inquest is convened, during breaks Jurors are welcome to examine any detail of Einstein-54 at its website (http://www.mjcnow.info). I will officially introduce you to it later.

Society paid and trusted the Defendants to make the unique contribution of Einstein-54 to them. Because they failed to do this, the Plaintiffs demand reparations for health, life, and livelihood losses they have suffered, penalties for corrupt and unreasonable practices by the Defendants, and enactment of new acts and laws that reverse as well as restore the damages that have been and are still being inflicted daily on them. These include the Defendants' effects on the US Department of Health and Human Services that make it liable for its violation of human rights and environmental justice.

The Witnesses will explain to you the Plaintiffs' case mostly using self-evidence or empirical evidence from Einstein-54. It consists of the benefits of unified scientific facts, reasonable thinking, and rational passion. Illegally, these have not taken place—disregarded by the Defendants in their contracted duties to promote excellence in Education.

Opening Statements by Witnesses

Witness 1 Harold Dorn
Einstein-54 Testimony: *Measurement of Earth's Carrying Capacity*

Earth Overshoot Day has increased each year since 1975. This day marks the annual date when humanity exhausts Nature's resources on Planet Earth. It signifies that all year long, since 1975, we, personally and planet-wise, have produced, registered, and sensed a natural resource deficiency, an emptiness, an unexplainable, discomforting void in the whole life integrity of body, mind, spirit, and environmental quality (*The State of Planet Earth and Us*, 2001). Its destructive source along with its remedy, although known for decades, has yet to be offered and integrated by educators because they are not required to acknowledge or include Einstein-54 in their curriculums. Meanwhile, in 2015 we are operating at 150% greater resource use than our planet can provide yearly and this along with the misery factors it produces is increasing every year. Now, to come into balance with Earth we need an additional planet half the size of Earth to connect with and restore the capacity of Earth's integrity to stop, rather than continue to diminish, the quality of life and health of its biosphere and populations. Based on the environmental impact of the United States, we would need four additional planets to make up this alarming deficit. As Henry David Thoreau said, "The price of anything is the amount of life you exchange for it," (Searls, 2009). We are each part of the deficit problem as well as its solution for we are part of Nature. In 1653, Blaise Pascal recognized, "*The least movement is of importance to all nature. The entire ocean is affected by a pebble*" (Blaise Pascal, Thoughts, 1995).

Witness 2 Jennifer Long
Einstein-54 Testimony: *Integrity and Connectedness of the Global Life Community*

As an edited letter by Chief Seattle states, "All things are connected like the blood that unites us all. Man did not weave the web of life; he is merely a strand in it. Whatever he does to the web, he does to himself" (Chief Seattle, We May be Brothers After All, 1854).

The form and process of any single individual or environmental system is connects to everything else on Earth. As demonstrated by the complete recycling every few years of all the atoms in the human body, all life is connected to being a contributing and cooperating part to how the life of Earth works and vice versa. Every living thing survives by relationships with every other living thing and their environmental intimacy. All things intertwine in a complex web of hidden and subtle relationships. Any one form of life depends on the rest of a life community to provide the conditions needed for its existence. For example, as our fingers are connected to our toes, insecticides applied on Canadian crops end up in Antarctic penguins.

Like Einstein-54 stopping an approaching meteor, humanity not using Einstein-54 is causing the sixth great mass extinction happening now. Over 50% of species may disappear because local and global extinction is now up to 1000 times the natural background rate (Kluger, 2014). As present symptoms show, this loss threatens ecosystem services of food and water, flood and disease control and our spiritual, aesthetic, recreational, and emotional demands along with nutrient recycling and carbon storage. Our morals, ethics, and values must direct us to intensely care about the fact that, on average, we spend over 95% of our time indoors and 99% of our felt-sense thinking and relationships out of tune with the natural world and its balanced ways around and within us. The loss and wanting, conscious or subconscious that this separation produces *deteriorates our normal ability to give and receive love*. It makes us demand excessive fulfillments from Earth's resources. We are brainwashed to uncomfortably sense that we need more of everything. For example, no matter how rich or poor we are, we believe we need 15% more money. As if we are insane, we are bankrupting our natural economy along with our body, mind, and spirit. We must use existing rescue packages that work before it is too late.

Today, the Educating, Counseling and Healing with Nature process (ECHN) based on Albert Einstein's Unified Field Equation (Cohen, 2013) may be the only scientific program available that works to make the unchangeable change. It successfully addresses our extreme 54 natural sense estrangement from our Planet as being a habit or psychological/psychiatric denial or addiction problem, or an emotional attachment disease that we can remedy (Cohen, 2014). Our 54 senses are the tools we use to register, love, believe, and relate to the world. When they are lost or distorted nothing can be trusted.

Einstein-54 works simply because our excessive disconnections from Einstein's Unified Field allows us to eviscerate our planet and produce our disorders. This is why our genuine reconnections with the Unified Field remedy them.

> *We are like islands in the sea, separate on the surface but connected in the deep.*
> —William James, The Collected Works of William James, 2011

Witness # 3 Stanley Farrel
Einstein-54 Testimony: *Personal Field Journal Report*

I was thinking about my right to equality and my love of it as many of my colleagues returned from their walk on campus discontented at the school's lack of nature and the limitation of space to walk around as others have elsewhere. My reasoning mind could have agreed with them but my new, whole-life, sensory way of knowing could not. I experienced united Einstein-54 non-verbal awareness and nature's intelligence found me. I felt more at peace, connected, and open. Without addressing the questions for this Einstein-54 assignment, I would not have understood the entire connection as deeply as I do now. I have repeated it many times and it opens and softens me further when I do. I look forward to retrieving more of these experiences from where I have learned to store them, my mind, where they will remain intact and strong for my use at will. This makes me feel very connected, happy, and real. Our lives cannot afford to be without it.

> *Equality is the soul of liberty; there is, in fact, no liberty without it.*
> —Frances Wright, Reason, Religion, and Morals, 2004

Witness 4 Arnold Raquette
Einstein-54 Testimony: *Education and Citizenship*
The Defendants have harmfully omitted that, as John Dewey said, "The purpose of education has always been to everyone, in essence, the same—to give the young the things they need in order to develop in an orderly, sequential way to become contributing and wholesome members of society. To develop into a member of society in what was needed in ancient times has almost nothing in common with developing into a member of society with what is needed in the advanced science and technology of today and its effects. To maintain and support well being any education and its methods and materials, is an outgrowth of the needs of the society and the environment in which it exists" (Dewey, 1934). Einstein-54 is an important contribution in this regard and the Defendants are negligent in their legal duties to make it available in all areas by including it as a required part of Higher Education.

> *Democracy cannot succeed unless those who express their choice are prepared to choose wisely. The real safeguard of democracy, therefore, is education.*
> —Franklin D. Roosevelt, Quotations of Franklin D. Roosevelt, 2010

Witness 5 James Darnell
Einstein-54 Testimony: *The U.S. Department of Education*
Amongst many things the purpose of the U.S. Department of Education includes getting information on what works in education to teachers and education policymakers for the improvement of

science, mathematics, and environmental instruction in elementary and secondary schools, graduate fellowships, and vocational-technical training. The Department is required to raise national and community awareness of the education challenges confronting the Nation, to disseminate the latest discoveries on what works in teaching and learning, and to help communities work out solutions to difficult educational issues by increasing student achievement and preparation for global cooperation and competitiveness, fostering educational excellence and ensuring equal access. Einstein-54 makes an important contribution in this regard because it enables education to include scientific truths concerning relating through natural attraction/love and its benefits. The Department of Education is irresponsible in not insisting that universities receiving federal dollars and offering federal financial assistance be required to teach it.

> *We have repressed far more than our sexuality : our very organic nature is now unconscious to most of us, most of the time, and we have become shrunken into two dimensional social or cultural beings, aware of only five of the hundreds of senses that link us to the rich biological nature that underlies and nourishes these more symbolic and recent aspects of ourselves.*
> —Norman Brown, Love's Body, 1966

Witness 6 Samantha Roswell
Einstein-54 Testimony: *Legality of Regional Accrediting Associations*

Regional accrediting helps evaluate and ensure Higher Education's contribution to the common good and addresses the needs of society and students because it is a fundamental human right to which freedom of inquiry and expression are integral. Accreditation serves as the common unifying denominator of shared values and practices among diverse institutions. At its core are such questions as: What are students learning? Is it the right kind of learning? What difference is the institution making in their lives? What evidence does an institution have that ensures it is worth the student's investment? Considering the already experienced effects of our increasing overuse of Earth's resources, it is hypocritical for accrediting associations to decide such questions and set the standards for federal financial assistance for students while omitting the unifying value of Einstein-54 from their decisions as well as ~~for to~~ the common good. Before the U.S. Department of Education established, federal assistance was accepted if four other accredited schools recognized them. Today that option is gone and in addition, U.S. financial aid to students is paying their tuitions to Wall Street sponsored universities. The latter are making profits from payments by taxpayer-backed student loans. This is just another form of the underlying corrupt relationships that separate us from Nature, in and around us. They result from the missing love and support from Nature that we suffer and that Einstein-54 helps us recover. An analysis of current accreditation would conclude that institutional purposes, rather than public purposes, predominate.

> *Throughout our lives we long to love ourselves more deeply and to feel connected with others. Instead, we often contract, fear intimacy, and suffer a bewildering sense of separation. We crave love, and yet we are lonely. Our delusion of being separate from one another, of being apart from all that is around us, gives rise to all of this pain.*
> —Sharon Salzberg, Loving Kindness, 2014

WITNESS 7 Ben Chapwald
Einstein-54 Testimony: *Personal Field Journal Report*

My studies of the Einstein-54 sensory attraction activities helped me to gain greater self-awareness and health. I feel better and relate more intelligently in general now and I am so much more grounded than I was before I found these rare courses. They fulfill my right to education that my 19 previous years of education denied because they did not and still do not, offer, or validate Einstein-54. Today, I know myself to be a combination of natural sensory awareness and socially conditioned reasoning in regards to what and how I have learned to know and love the world. I have identified illegitimate stories that I attach to certain situations. I understand how these stories hinder my ability to logically connect with the web and people and how to strengthen my ability to correct these stories, become more whole and help others do the same. My greater self-appreciation, adaptability, and happiness are a measure of my growth. I have placed an entire world of continual natural attractions within my psyche to, in any moment, safely unify in balance with my human, environmental, and cosmic communities. I can't teach it to my students because, unreasonably, the Department of Education does not demand it in curriculums.

> *All our knowledge begins with the senses, proceeds then to the understanding, and ends with reason. There is nothing higher than reason.*
> —Immanuel Kant, <u>Critique of Pure Reason</u>, 1781

Probable Cause Summary Prosecutor Goldwater

Here is my Probable Cause summary of the testimony of the witnesses to this point. From them we have learned that to maintain and to support well-being, any education is, in its methods and materials, an outgrowth of the needs of the society and the environment in which it exists.

Today, due to Earth Overshoot all year long we, personally and planet-wise, produce, register, and sense a natural resource deficiency and its effects (*The State of Planet Earth and Us*, 2001). We experience emptiness or an unexplainable, discomforting void in whole life integrity, in our body, mind, spirit, and the natural world. We feel out of balance and dissatisfied; things do not make sense, and this reduces our resilience along with the vitality of our immune system. This results from our society measurably producing an increasing deficit in Earth's environmental quality and resource capacity. It deteriorates the well-being of the environment and of humanity for we are dependent on the health of its purifying and balancing powers. This dilemma is a catastrophe in the making, the root of most of our miseries.

The destructive source and remedy for this problem is known and addressed by Einstein- 54. However, at this late date it is yet to be required, utilized, and offered by Higher Education, by the U.S. Department of Education, or by regional accrediting associations. This is contrary to and a breach of their published contract and responsibility to

- get information on what works in education to teachers and education policymakers for the improvement of science, mathematics, and environmental instruction;
- raise national and community awareness of the education challenges confronting the nation;
- disseminate the latest discoveries on what works in teaching and learning;
- evaluate and ensure higher education's contribution to the common good and address the needs of society and students since this is a fundamental human right to which freedom of inquiry and expression are integral; and
- help communities work out solutions to difficult educational issues by increasing student achievement and preparation for global cooperation and competitiveness, fostering educational excellence, and ensuring equal access.

In consideration of the testimony of Witness #1 with regard to Earth Overshoot and its destructive effects on human and other life forms, the Defendants have violated our constitutional rights to life, love, education, health, and freedom of speech. It may not even be legal for them to use taxpayer money to pass judgment on what is acceptable or non-acceptable education. Who are they to decide this? Their expertise and judgment to date has educated us to be unstoppably excessive and continue to create our still-increasing Earth Overshoot debt and its misery factors.

What Earth Overshoot demonstrates is that due to our excessiveness, for every 25-45 seconds of every minute that each of us live, some other person, place or thing of the Planet is suffering while losing their life. This reduces the quality or possibility of life for any person, no less any other thing or place. By omitting Einstein-54, Higher Education allows this practice to increase each year. It lets us be socialized to reject reasonable material and emotional support from the life of our planet. This defies our right to love and be loved as individuals on legal, moral, and ethical grounds. By not being educated to protect the vitality of natural systems in and around us, we are secretly infringing upon our freedom from torture and degrading treatment, along with the unspoken right to life of all of life. Where are these stalwarts of Education with the right to teach us to continue on this track by not letting Einstein-54 help us remedy this dilemma, no less, help them correct their own warped thinking so they may help the public do the same? Other than the Plaintiffs, the Justice Department, and this jury, who is the investigator who investigates the investigator who investigates the Defendants?

The testimony I will now present shows that Einstein-54 (a) is privately subsidized and scientifically substantiated, (b) has been readily available for any interested party for the past 25 years, and (c) because it has a 50-year history of perfecting its function, the claims by the Plaintiffs of their civil and human rights being unnecessarily violated by the omission of Einstein-54 by the Defendants deserve to be heard in a trial that the best thinking of this Grand Jury must sanction.

Carefully weigh the additional experienced Witnesses and testimony that will provide you with evidence beyond reasonable doubt about the vital contribution of Einstein-54 and that the Defendants are guilty as charged for withholding it without cause. This is not science fiction. If you are clear thinking and not in denial, you will recognize this as a true disaster.

Witnesses' Opening Statements
(continued)

WITNESS 8 Charles Bradbury
Einstein-54 Testimony: *Philosophical Empiricism and Scientific Evidence*

For Justice to prevail the facts must be known and, as demonstrated by the amazing success of our human-built society and advanced technologies, the facts obtained from scientific methodology are trustable. It is self-evident that they work when applied. From a century of research about how the Universe operates and especially from the work of Albert Einstein, scientific methodology has produced the Big Bang model finalized in 2012. Its origin includes a "Higgs boson" attraction net as Einstein's Grand Unified Field predicted. ~~It is the~~ This core ~~that~~ makes up matter, including humanity, the origin of fundamental particles and mass. Its attraction energy unifies and binds all things and relationships together, from subatomic particles to molecules to galaxies including how we think, feel, and act since attraction is the essence of love. The model shows the Universe emerged from a state of extremely high temperature and density—the so-called Big Bang that occurred 13.8 billion years ago. It says that the Universe has no edge; its origin occurred not at a particular point in space but rather throughout whatever existed then at the same time so it is possible to calculate its sequential history of creating its attraction to creating time and space, moment-by-moment since its origin. We are each the life of the Universe continuing to create itself in this very moment as us. The attraction/love essence of each moment and everything in it is identical. This means that our whole Planet is an intelligent living and loving singularity (*Our Living Universe*, 2014).

The self-evidence used in the science of Einstein-54 is undeniable, true, and trustable in word and deed because it registers directly on our 54 natural senses in the moment. Similarly, our science and technology world does not need to be proven because it is obvious. Self-evidence can be gathered in the immediate moment of the Universe that some call the "now." For example, it is self-evident that right now your sense of hearing can register my voice or your eyes read these words of my testimony. Your attraction to do this brought you to this final word.

Empirical evidence based on logic is equally reasonable. For example, the logic of the number sequence from 0-9 is reasonable, and it is reasonable to accept that other members of the jury can hear my voice. Scientific methodology uses both these forms of evidence. Einstein-54 validates that we have 54 natural senses, not just 5, as well as incorporates our key missing truth of the sequential Big Bang time-space universe that Einstein predicted and the discovery of the Higgs boson "God particle" unified attraction field validated in 2012.

Most, if not all of the evidence used in Einstein-54 is organic and either self-evidence or empirical evidence; nothing is subjective. Its power is that it enables us to transform the duality that troubles us into a unified field singularity that our 54 felt-sense reasoning in the moment can tap into (Cohen, 2008). This is because these 54 senses, in concert, are the aliveness, love, and wisdom in us of the Universe's time-space continuum.

Observations of Einstein-54 in action show that learning to think and speak while 54-sense connected to the GreenWave Dance of the Unified Field helps us communicate with the whole of life and its history as part of the attraction/love essence of our personal life in any moment. The Dance attaches us to all past and present leaders, deities, stories, senses, facts, prophecies, and relationships in the history and life of Planet Earth. While we lovingly dance as 54-sense equals with them in the present, we update them about our advanced science and technology progress. In congress together, this enables our natural attraction dance, moment-by-moment, to unify, transform, produce, and support responsible tomorrows in peaceful balance with the whole of life.

> *For more than three decades, the Higgs Boson has been physicists' version of King Arthur's Holy Grail, Ponce de Leon's Fountain of Youth, Captain Ahab's Moby Dick. It's been an obsession, a fixation, an addiction to an idea that almost every expert believed just had to be true.*
> —Stefan Soldner-Rembold, Guardian News and Media Limited, 20189

Witness 9 Anne Barkley

Einstein-54 Testimony: *Applied Psychology*

Jurors, please do the following now. Close your eyes and imagine you are seeing the bright yellow color of a lemon wedge as you hold it.

Notice how its thick skin feels rubbery. Now bring the imaginary lemon towards your nose and with a deep breath, smell it. Place the wedge in your lips, mouth, feel your teeth against the fruit and skin. Bite into the lemon and feel your teeth as they move through the skin and the pulp. What consistency is the juice as it begins to run into your mouth? Feel it on your tongue, and on your teeth and gums. Is it cold? Warm? How does it taste? Is it sour? Is it sweet? Bitter?

Are you salivating now? You probably are; most people do. Our sensory 54 senses do not know the difference between what is real and what is imaginary until our senses of consciousness and reason assess the experience in concert.

Other than humanity, no animal, plant, mineral, or energy is literate. They do not understand stories we write or tell. Everything we have ever sensed with our bodies is stored in our mentality and simply by having one of our senses remember some sensory reality, your mind, body, and spirit will react as if the sensory stimulus were really there. In the Big Bang Universe, the ramifications of this phenomenon are far reaching when a story is inaccurate for it becomes a habitual or fixed, addictive way of thinking that is difficult to unravel or correct its effects (Cohen, 1993).

> *In the beginning was the word and the word was "distortion" or "corrupt" because the beginning was not a word.*
>
> —God <grin>

> *If you wish to make an apple pie from scratch, you must first invent the universe.*
> —Carl Sagan, Cosmos #9, 2009

A thriller movie, or threatening statement, or description of a sad event can make you feel and respond as though it was real yet each of them is imaginary. Any information that that you think is true makes this happen. In addition, our body protectively hides the discomfort of being wrong, stressed, or hurt by storing these feelings in our subconscious mind. There they subconsciously stress us as our daily lives threaten to hook them into feeling their discomfort. This fear influences and often warps how we think, feel, and act. It is a source of corruption (Cohen, 2007a).

A person that never knew what a lemon was or never experienced one would not salivate when I read the lemon instructions. They would be unprepared to know what to expect from a lemon, good or bad. That is the value of the second amendment, the right to free speech. It enables our stories to acquaint us with all the known or imagined so that our reasoning can be more reasonable and our lives more sensible.

I am giving each of you a list that Einstein-54 uses. It names the scientifically validated 54 senses that most normal people are born with to help them register the world correctly and rationally felt—sense, think, and relate in balance with Nature (PNC, 1997). You can use it as a checklist in considering the testimony of the witnesses. Notice that in addition to our five senses it includes our sense groups of temperature, color, reason, pressure, gravity, consciousness, excretion, space, motion, literacy, chemicals, pain, love, humor, place, thirst, humility, fear, time, aliveness, distress, and trust. In the moments when you experienced them, they were undeniable, self-evident facts of your life.

The major difference between the rest of nature and us on Planet Earth is that we alone create and relate through stories that can be accurate for our life in balance or that can mislead and hurt us. Until we can tell the difference and, in addition, reasonably know how to select accurate stories for Nature and ourselves, we are fooled into, habitually or addictively, living in ways that hurt Earth's and our web-of-life as shown by Earth Overshoot (PNC, 2001). Einstein-54 only uses the most accurate stories produced by scientific methodology to provide us with an important safeguard and remedy for this destructive phenomenon (Cohen, 2009). The Einstein-54 story is to develop stories that create moments in natural areas that let Earth teach us what we need to know in its non-story way. Then know and speak true stories from what your 54 senses register in those moments (Cohen, 2007b).

The kind of education science offers teaches us to be neglectful of nothing—not to despise the small beginnings,

for they precede of necessity all great things in the knowledge of science, either pure or applied.
—Michael Faraday, *1857*

Witness 10 William Barlow
Einstein-54 Testimony: *Personal Field Journal Report*

When I was doing this activity in the natural area on campus, I started to shuffle my feet through the dried leaves. I suddenly realized that my pain had stopped and I concentrated on the very pleasant sound of the dried leaves under my feet. I stopped walking through the leaves and slowly the pain returned, so I started walking again and sure enough, the pain resolved again. I thought, "This natural love is Nature's pain reliever. My rights to be free of pain, torture, and degrading treatment are being infringed upon by the absence of Einstein-54 in this school."

Love is the only sane and satisfactory answer to the problem of human existence.
—Erich Fromm, Art of Loving, 1956

Witness 11 Roger Young
Einstein-54 Testimony: *Unified Field Attraction and Applied Logic*

Natural attraction or attractiveness is defined as the act, process, or power of attracting or loving to bring about a unifying response. Natural attraction is unifying force acting mutually between particles of matter, energy, or life relationships that tends to draw them together and resists their separation. When you sense that you want to survive, that feeling is the universal attraction or love to live expressing itself in and as you.

To date no provable deviation has been found to the core principle of Einstein-54, that moment-by-moment all things in the Universe are simultaneously in a self-promoting and self-organizing natural attraction-based relationship with each other as well as with the dance of the whole Big Bang Universe as it creates its own time and space.

This is because Einstein-54 includes John Muir's fundamental ecology principle of connectedness:

> *When we try to pick out anything by itself we find that it is bound fast by a thousand invisible cords that cannot be broken (are attracted/attached) to everything in the universe.*
> —John Muir, My First Summer in the Sierra, 1911

Albert Einstein observed that the Universe is attracted to expanding as a vibrating, immediate moment, unified field of time and space attraction that Einstein-54 calls the Dance of the Universe and its aliveness. Every part of it is an attractive dancer that is connected, attracted, or attached to other dancers as attraction/loves of the Grand Unified Field. Repulsion is non-existent. It is instead a misinterpretation of lesser attraction moving to a greater attraction. It is, running for life not repulsed by danger. It is the singular rhythm and sway of the Dance, not a duality.

The Higgs boson "God particle" is an original Big Bang attraction energy that produces the unified attraction field of the Universe, as Einstein predicted (Green, 2013).

The Universe and its unified field, life, love, and grace are synonymous names for natural attraction and are found everywhere, including "God" when God is unconditional love that includes the web-of-life.

> *For what else is Nature but God and the Divine Reason that pervades the whole universe and all its parts*
> (Seneca the Younger, circa 25 A.D.).

This is also observed in scripture:

> *God is love. Whoever lives in love lives in God, and God in them.*
> (John 4:16 Revised Standard Version).

> (Jesus said) *"I am the light that is above them all. I am the all; the all came forth from me, and the all attained to me. Cleave a piece of wood; I am there. Raise up a stone, and you will find me there"*
>
> (Gospel of Thomas. [77])

Be it God or not, humans possess an innate attraction to seek connections with nature and other forms of life, a passionate love of life/survival and of all that is alive that some scientists call *biophilia*.

Repulsion between dancers in the Dance of the Universe does not exist. It is a misinterpretation of it because the Dance of Nature is solely a vibrant and resonating sway of attractions to more attractive dances and dancers. For example, magnets only repulse each other when our stories or some other force manipulate their poles to do so. In their natural state, their attraction dance attracts them to each other.

Since the essence of the Universe its attraction to produce and sustain the life of its fundamental unifying attraction field in each moment, it can't have repulsions. Rather it has greater or weaker attractions. This means fear, pain, and depression are natural attraction signals to beneficially find and fulfill new or greater attractions. This explains why the life of Nature produces no garbage or negatives. In any moment, all things are attracted to each other. It is our nature-disconnected or conquering stories that produce and are Nature negatives. Since Nature only works with attractions, it is vulnerable to these negatives.

Science works because consistently, like the 0-9 logical sequence of numerals, or like a plant growing from its seed, everything is seamlessly attracted/attached to all that has gone before it and remains attached to all that follows it into the next moment. This reflects the sequential time/space process and continuum of the Big Bang Universe and makes it accessible in any given moment.

The dancers that we call Humanity inherently have 54 natural attraction senses whose sensations are natural attraction facts and intelligence. For example, thirst is our attraction for water; trust is our attraction for safe support. Each different sense and sensation is a form of love, a motivation for fulfillment and the happiness it produces as it supports life. Their unifying powers, in concert and with enthusiasm, reasonably register, guide, balance, and heal relationships. For example, thirst is intelligent and self-fulfilling enough to know when to bring the global water cycle in and through us, while excretion knows when to remove soiled water from us and feed the Planet with it, thus purifying the water. Note that thirst, excretion, and trust are not included in the 5 senses we are taught that we have. However, they are included in Einstein-54 as are our love of consciousness, reason, and literacy. It also includes the means for us to think and feel with our 54 senses habitually.

> *For small creatures such as we, the vastness is bearable only through love.*
> —Carl Sagan, Pale Blue Dot, 1994

Witness 12 Gene Bellvue

Einstein-54 Testimony: *Personal Field Journal Report*

The Einstein-54 courses gave me a previously missing respect for my actions and a feeling of dignity, that I had the Right to Love and Be Loved: I aligned myself with my natural surroundings, letting their energy fill me, while remaining flexible enough to allow it to pass through me without conflict. Aligning and drawing in the attraction energy from various elements of the natural environment increases balance and harmony. When I have feelings of anxiety, I can reasonably connect to the web of life and it is attracted to embrace me with comfort, guidance, and wisdom that I have been missing. I get the feeling of being "one" with its power and beauty and Einstein-54 gave this ability to most folks in the courses I took.

> *There is no remedy for love but to love more.*
> —Henry David Thoreau, Journal, J1839

> *The natural world is the larger sacred community to which we belong. To be alienated from this community is*

to become destitute in all that makes us human. To damage this community is to diminish our own existence.
—Thomas Berry, *The Great Work: Our Way into the Future*, 1999

Witness 13 Sandy Boyle
Einstein-54 Testimony: *Cosmology and Behavioral Physics*

Because it has built itself since its beginning, at any given moment of the Big Bang Universe, the essence of all things in it is a singular identical unified attraction/love energy dance that creates the "now" immediate time and space of the Universe and of the next moment of itself that it builds. We learn to overlook that this means if our essence is alive at any given moment of the Universe, the whole Universe and all parts of it are this aliveness because they are identical. The aliveness consists of attraction/love in the form of energy, atoms, our senses, our Planet, the stars, and galaxies. It explains why rocks, stars, and galaxies are observed to have slow but measureable life cycles.

At this late date, the reason the scientific process still cannot distinguish between life and death is that the essence of everything is alive, all things are attracted to live and love, to stay alive in our living Planet and Universe.

The Big Bang, called "the birth of our Universe" because birth is a life process, is correct. Space telescope scientists who report that the Universe may now be "attracted to" dying, (International Astronomical Union, 2015), confirm its life. Natural attraction is alive and produces different forms of its aliveness, moment by moment. The aliveness part of us today was there in the Big Bang then and is a seamless continuum of it. Our 54 natural senses along with the Unified Field are aliveness in action in any given moment (Michael J Cohen, The Magic of Something from Nothing, 2012).

The purpose of life is to support life because life/survival is attractive. Death is an attraction to transform into another form of attractive aliveness. For this reason, Nature produces no garbage. Everything, including humanity, is attractive, alive, belongs, and cooperatively contributes to the welfare of the whole of life, moment after moment from the beginning of time and space.

Humanity lives in, not on, our Living Planet Earth/Gaia, deep in its atmosphere and biosphere. We are each a uniquely evolved personification of Earth's aliveness, metabolism, and spirit, and we can talk and think in abstracts, too. Experience shows us that the resources and ways of Mother Earth are our placenta to the Universe. A placenta is alive.

> *The whole universe in its different spans and wavelengths, exclusions and developments, is everywhere alive and conscious. There is one fundamental stuff.*
> —William James, A Pluralistic Universe, 1908

Witness 14 Janet Whelm
Einstein-54 Testimony: *Personal Field Journal Report*

I just walked outside, and started walking along the waterfront, connecting with various beings of nature--a person-size bush with yellow blooming flowers, a tree with bulbs that looked like they are getting ready to open; weeds, thorns, grass, sun, air, and water. The bush was the first one I connected with, repeating "unity" in my mind. The reaction was almost immediate, and I had a sense/vision--much like the ending of *The Matrix,* (The Matrix. Dir. Andy Wachowski and Larry Wachowski. Warner Bros. Pictures, 1999.) when Neo sees everything like flowing energy, himself included. I was in a different country, one that protected me from being injured by the hostile lack of unity that I endure when I'm at home or school. I felt very similar, in a deep and visceral way--being one with the bush. There was simply difference in our physical form, yet we were built out of the same "thing"--pure energy or love. It continued with all other beings I encountered along the way back home. I had to slow down, walk slowly and mindfully, and maintain the focus on this experience.

I could feel that we are truly are all one, that I was fulfilling my right to seek asylum if a country treats me badly. In this protective Einstein-54 country, the underlying energy in all being is very much the same, and can be tapped into-almost immediately-once the intention is present I recognize that Einstein-54 helps me get good feelings from being near water, from feeling the sun on my being, and from allowing my senses to wander around, without any specific and particular focus.

> *If you watch how nature deals with adversity, continually renewing itself, you can't help but learn.*
> —Bernie Seigel, MD, Peace, Love and Healing,1989

Witness 15 Robert Brown
Einstein-54 Testimony: *Universal and Living Planet Consciousness*

In Planet and Universe, everything contains an intelligent consciousness. To create and sustain the astounding dance of life, its natural attraction essence must be intelligent enough to achieve this.

Nature's life-dance within and around us consists of conscious, wild, attraction-based, optimums that become stronger and more attractive through cooperating diversity. The dance accomplishes this by being aware of and following its attractions rather than disregarding or omitting their signals.

Natural attraction is both motivation and intelligent awareness in action. The attraction to self-correcting life, love, diversity, balance, fairness, cooperation, sanity, and purity is a conscious attraction. Nature does not create excessiveness, greed, garbage, stress, corruption, depression, madness, abusiveness, dependencies, or conflicting stories because they are not attractive. Any person or thing that can make this happen this would have to be considered intelligent (Michael J Cohen, The Magic of Something From Nothing, 2012).

Any moment in human consciousness consists of Nature-disconnected stories or 54 attraction-connected thoughts, sensations, feelings, and stories.

The fittest survive in Organism Earth because they are the most intelligent builders of attractive, cooperative, mutually beneficial relationships that support the Planet's life dance. They also help other species help their fitness by strengthening their cooperative relationships with them. This makes the wisdom of the ages be that natural attraction love is the only truth.

> *I regard consciousness as fundamental. I regard matter as derivative from consciousness. We cannot get behind consciousness.*
>
> —Max Planck, The Observer, 1931

Witness 16 Susan Aaron
Einstein-54 Testimony: *Personal Field Journal Report*

I am a person who feels great when I take the time to shut off the inner chatter and explore nature with many senses. When I do so, I feel that I am part of a huge organism called earth, and that I share in the collective wisdom and strength of Earth. These activities that I have been doing are deceptively simple: they are powerful and healing. (I spend time in nature, I immerse myself in it, what difference could a few simple words or particular approach make.................all the difference in the world.........yes, deceptively simple....amazingly effective!)

Einstein-54 helps me to gain greater self-awareness and health. I feel better and relate more intelligently in general now, I have strengthened my right to life, liberty, and personal security. I know myself to be a combination of natural sensory awareness and socially conditioned reasoning in regards to what and how I have learned to know the world. I have identified stories that I attach to certain situations, how these stories limit my freedom to use my ability to logically connect with the web and people, and how to strengthen my ability to correct these stories and become ~~more~~ whole. The measure of my greater self-appreciation, adaptability, and happiness is a measure of my growth. By using Einstein-54 I have placed an entire world of continual natural attractions within my psyche to, in any moment, safely unify in balance with my human, environmental, and cosmic communities.

For the things we have to learn before we can do, we learn by doing.
—Aristotle, The Nicomachean Ethics, 340BC

Witness 17 Elijah Colt
Einstein-54 Testimony: *The Lie of Omission*

Here are a few quotes from the past 2500 years that show that the information presented by witnesses today has long been available and known. The negligence of the Defendants denies people's right to it by avoiding or omitting it by not including Einstein-54 in Higher Education. As noted by Baruch Spinoza in 1661: *Nature offers nothing that can be called this man's rather than another's; but under nature everything belongs to all—that is, they have authority to claim it for themselves.*

> *The Universe is a single living creature that encompasses all living creatures within it.*
> —Plato, Father of Philosophical Idealism, 420 BC

> *The Tao is the sustaining Life-force and the mother of all things; from it, all things rise and fall without cease.*
> —Lao Tzu, Tao Te Ching, 600 BC

> *We followers of Spinoza see our God in the wonderful order and lawfulness of all that exists and in its soul as it reveals itself in man and animal. Time and space and gravitation have no separate existence from matter.*
> —Albert Einstein, 1935

> *And because we are alive, the universe must be said to be alive. We are its consciousness as well as our own. We rise out of the cosmos and we see its mesh of patterns, and it strikes us as beautiful. And that feeling is the most*

important thing in the entire universe—its culmination, like the color of the flower at first bloom on a wet morning.
—Kim Stanley Robinson, 1985

We are more likely to destroy ourselves with our persistent and worldwide conflict with nature than in any war with weapons ever devised.
—Fairfield Osborne, Our Plundered Planet, 1948

We are facing an imminent catastrophic ecological collapse and our only hope is to transform humanity into a global interdependent sustainable society, based on respect and reverence for the Earth.
—The Green Agenda, *http://green-agenda.com/globalrevolution.html*, 2014

Witness 18 Elise Whitney

Einstein-54 Testimony: *Hard Science Social Relationships*

The scientific discovery of Nature's Higgs Boson attraction-based birth of the life of our Universe is the essence of our social relationships as well as all other natural relationships. Converging scientific evidence shows that we only exist in the attraction-based sequence of time and space "now" moments of the Universe that we call its Unified Field. The past and future only exist as their influence on the Unified Field of the present moment.

We humans live in immediate attraction relationships either via our 54 natural attraction senses or in our stories, whether they are scientifically accurate or not. Building relationships based on our inaccurate stories produces problems. The attachments or addictions of our senses render our unreasonable stories incapable of solving them; they govern our behavior.

Our story world most reasonably and accurately transmits how nature works through mathematics whose 0-9 number sequence reflects the flawless sequence of the Unified Field. However, the use of mathematics is limited in relating to the Unified Field because

- The number one does not exist in Nature except in any single moment since all of nature is dancing, flowing, and changing moment by moment. Because there are no standard conditions in Nature, identifying "one" is not possible over time or in general.
- The number zero does not exist in nature since attraction bonds between things exist everywhere. Nowhere is there nothing in Nature. This means that objective science is based on mathematics that does not apply to Nature's ways.
- Objective science and technology are runaway destructively ~~runaway~~ because in any given moment their limits make our thinking omit the in-the-moment guiding energy and subjective sensory facts of our 53 natural attraction senses. Whenever objective reasoning omits the totality of our 54 natural sensibilities, it is unreasonable with respect to the welfare of the whole of life.

Einstein-54 works because learning to think and speak while connected to the attraction Dance of the Unified Field in any given moment helps us lovingly communicate with the non-storied whole of life and its eons of history. We can walk with Jesus or others in a natural area and bring their science and technology up to date. Dancing the Dance this way enables our stories and senses to increase well-being as our disorders transform into responsible, new Unified Field moments in peaceful balance with the whole of life now. This process transforms our nature disconnection into additional whole-life integrity. To not use it is like trying to stop our car by saying, "Whoa" and ending up with Earth overshoot misery.

> *I don't understand why when we destroy something created by man we call it vandalism, but when we destroy something created by nature we call it progress.*
> —Ed Begley, Jr., <u>Living Like Ed: One Man's Guide to Living an Environmentally Friendly Life, 2008</u>

Witness 19 Larry Singleton

Einstein-54 Testimony: *Personal Field Journal Report*

These exercises have been cathartic because to stop and reflect upon the more rewarding natural encounters was not only enjoyable but reflection upon them fed me in many unimaginable ways. Since returning to the larger United States, I have systematically grown further and further from the spectacular rawness of the rainforest. I have fought this disconnect daily, but now I have a daughter who has not been raised in the same nature-oriented manner that I was. This poses a dilemma for me. Being able consciously to connect to Nature as an Einstein-54 spirituality or religion that mimics the scientific approach towards non-literate relationships is affording me personal rejuvenation, a safe method, or place to share my unique background and will allow me to bridge the nature gap between my daughter's upbringing and my own. In this way, Einstein-54 stops my Freedom of Belief and Religion from unreasonable erosion by my return to the United States (*Peak Fact*, 2010).

The application of Einstein-54 on a wide scale could have major ramifications on the future of our planet. By using the process and learning to perceive nature in a more communicative mode, the individual receives numerous gifts, which include the ability to receive/hear one's own truth, to achieve a strong level of peace and balance, to recover from disorders, and to honor the environment. These gifts, if consistently appreciated and acted upon, would lead to less dependency on chemical substances, less conflict, less stress, less disorder, less resource use, less war, less environmental desecration. The world could achieve through the Einstein's unified field a loving state of balance that is the natural rhythm found in nature.

Without us using Einstein-54 our increasingly destructive frustrations due to our Nature-separated emotional deprivation reminds me of the most ferocious animal in the world, the "Tiglion." On one end, it is the head of a lion, the other end the head of a tiger. It is so ferocious because it cannot defecate.

A scientist lives with all reality. There is nothing better.
To know reality is to accept it, and eventually to love it.
—George Wald, Therefore Choose Life, 2017

Witness 20 Mary Fisher
Einstein-54 Testimony: *Philosophy of Critical Thinking*

Critical thinking is a core part of the hard science methodology that has produced our present lifestyle advantages and our technological advances. In considering the testimony already given, and no doubt presented, here as well as the workings of Einstein-54, I find that the only exception to all the information given to this jury is a few scientifically inaccurate, nature-disconnected, or mystical stories that deny the importance or rationale of Einstein-54.

A study published in *Skeptical Inquirer* magazine in 2006 showed that college seniors and grad students were more likely than freshmen to believe in non-evidence-based things such as psychics, telepathy and channeling, reincarnation, the "evil eye," astrology, communication with the dead, haunted houses, psychics, and ghostly encounters.

Contemporary people, on average, spend over 99% of their time engaged in felt-sense thinking and feeling that is neither in tune with or makes conscious sensory contact with Nature. We are using only 15% of our total ability to make sense by using Einstein-54 and this has produced our "unsolvable" Earth Overshoot deficit and its misery factors that violate civil and human rights.

Our unscientific, metaphysical, or mystical stories may be true in some other, presently unknown, or imaginary universe, but they are invalid in building our relationships on Earth until they become validated through scientific methodology. This is because when it is combined with 54-sense *attraction/love evidence,* Objective Science helps us feel-sense, think, and relate like the balanced and self-correcting life of the Big Bang Universe, being our Planet works and our having sent folks to the moon and back. Then we can think in the consensus of "con-senses" as we practice whole-life art and science.

By adding our 54 ECHN natural attraction senses to the accuracy of Objective Science, its runaway destructive powers become a Whole

Life Science that enlists Earth's self-organizing and purifying abilities to produce balance, healing, and peace instead of our present deficiencies in resources and reasonableness (Michael J Cohen, *Who, What or When is the Acronym NNIAAL?,* 2013).

The purpose of Einstein-54 is to offer guaranteed methods and materials that help people create moments that let Organism Earth/Gaia teach us what we need to know. The agencies responsible for making this possible have neglected doing this for 25 years. Their negligence violates the rights of a wide range of citizens and they are liable for their irresponsibility causing a wide range of damage to many aspects of people, places, and things. Critical thinking makes it evident that this is little different ~~than~~ from a terrorist attack on our people and our land by destructive ideas. Having not protected us from this assault, the Defense Department could also legally be a Defendant here.

> *The whole of science is nothing more than a refinement of everyday thinking.*
> —Albert Einstein, Physics and Reality, 1936

Witness 21 Peter Strand
Einstein-54 Testimony: *Personal Field Journal Report*

I immediately received a strong and positive connection that validated my right to privacy. My first attraction was to my sense of emotional place. I felt immediately as if the plants and nature in general not only gave me permission to connect but strongly wanted me to connect due to my current discomfort. I had a feeling of healing and nurturing emanating from all life forms, including a thin vine of poison ivy. I also noticed my aesthetic sense, as I noted how the weeds and grasses, struggled to grow in the fields, cluttered by man-made litter. Trees and bushes, even after having been hacked on and mutilated by humankind, still continued to bud and flourish. These two connections strengthened my sense of survival and healing as I felt nature pouring its wisdom and healing ways into me.

The interior landscape responds to the character and subtlety of the exterior landscape; the shape of the individual mind is affected by the land as it is by genes.
—Barry Lopez, Arctic Dreams, 1986

Witness 22 Michael J. Cohen
Einstein-54 Testimony: *Fundamentals of Einstein-54*

I am testifying to the excellence of the witnesses and the presentation of information to this Grand Jury and that I have been of assistance in assuring its and their quality. I, along with many others, have personally experienced the facts of the Einstein-54 and we hold its truths to be self-evident. I researched and developed it and I conceived ECHN at Project NatureConnect (Doherty, 2010; Cohen, 1993). Motivated by my elementary school's unjust and emotionally hurtful and destructive discipline to change my left-handed nature to right-handedness in 1936, I have dedicated my life to using Education and Counseling to protect Nature from harm, in and around others and myself. In this regard, I have identified and addressed the point source of our discontents. In so doing I have achieved several master's and doctoral degrees, published 11 books, directed environmental education and outdoor education accredited courses and degree programs for over 50 years as well as established many long-term "utopian community" expeditions in the process. I have been recognized as a Maverick Genius, received the Distinguished World Citizen award and experientially "solved" Albert Einstein's Unified Field Equation (Cohen, 2013). I warranty the accuracy of my work because it is based on empirical evidence (Michael J. Cohen, "Maverick Genius at Work," 2015; Michael J. Cohen, "Impossible Dream," 2011-2013).

In 1965, a transformational experience in the Grand Canyon scientifically convinced me that Earth acted homeostatically, like any living organism, and that acts of nature and humanity must be explained scientifically from this point of view. This led me to create the process of Expedition Education and the 1985 National Audubon Society International Symposium "Is the Earth a Living Organism." I hoped its outcome would verify "Organism Earth" that could then be protected under the Endangered Species Act as the only one of its kind.

I have established that by applying the sensory science of Einstein-54, human beings can enjoy part or all of themselves as being a unique personification of the Unified Field life dance of the Universe and its manifestation of itself as Organism Earth or Gaia. Each of its web-of-life dancer's attraction to live is violated by nature-disconnected stories that deteriorate the Dance, in and around us.

The heart of our troubles is our personal conflict. As unique personifications of the non-story Unified Field, we have invented and learned to communicate through stories. In and around us, the Field does not understand them so it cannot respond or deal with stories that separate us from it. This makes it and us vulnerable to their disconnectedness.

Human dancers relate with stories. When they trespass Earth it cannot complain with words so we do not understand it or what it shares with us. Einstein-54, also called the GreenWave Equation, is a Rosetta Stone for this catastrophe and its misery factors that violate the right to the life of our Planet and us. This sensory tool empowers any individual to speak with and for the Earth by creating moments in natural areas that let Earth teach us what we need to know. Earth accomplishes this through 54 sensory attraction/loves that its Unified Field invented to communicate with and balance its relationships with its life as us. (*The Hidden Organic Remedy,* 2013).

We are all in the same living planet boat, Earth, because we are it and when you tip one end, you rock the other. Although Objective Science helps us deal with the harmful effects of our tipping, it is also the runaway culprit doing the tipping. It needs Einstein-54 because this social technology enables Higher Education to transform the culprit into binding and blending with the *subjective* through 54 unified field natural attractions. This enables us to guide Objective Science into producing balanced, whole life relationships.

Objective Science won't accept that homeostasis works throughout Nature because in every time/space moment the life dance of the Universe in all things is attracted to be part of the central Unified

Field as well as simultaneously attracted to enter whatever new, diverse relationship is attractive in that moment. These two different attractions continually dance between and balance each other to produce the equilibrium of homeostasis.

We cannot win the battle to increase the well-being of the planet's life and ours, without strengthening our inborn ability to love all of life. As Einstein-54 enables our body, mind, and spirit to recognize itself as a unique personification of the Unified Field, we recover our missing 54 natural attraction/love sensory bonds with Nature, in and around us. They are our greatest hope in reversing Earth Overshoot because otherwise we do not give organism Earth the rights or opportunity to protect itself legally. We must fight to protect it and we seldom fight to save what we do not love enough. That fight is won by ferociously regenerating integrity through the substitution of Einstein-54 consensual relationships for destructive aspects of the factory whistle, the school bell, and non-organic authorities.

> *The senses, being the explorers of the world, open the way to knowledge.*
> —Maria Montessori, The Absorbent Mind, 1949

Witness 23 Margaret Nader
Einstein-54 Testimony: *Anthropology and Wilderness*

The historical cause of Overshoot and its violation of our rights is that the Unified Field loved humanity into a being designed to live in the tropics of organism Earth. There, extreme seasons did not exist, fur was unnecessary, and food and medicine were available in the wild year round. This geographical fact is the origin of the Garden of Eden story where Nature in the raw of its beauty and balance supported humanity.

As nomads wandered into non-tropical habitats, most discovered how to let Nature there support them in balance. Other groups invented and conveyed technological knowledge and stories that let them convert any non-tropical environment into a built environment that artificially provided tropic-like conditions. Survival became inventing, attaching to, and rewarding unbalanced survival stories and technologies along with the individuals who could best conquer and convert so-called hostile natural environments into fabricated indoor tropics. Our 54 natural attraction/love senses hurtfully disconnected from the Unified Field in natural areas, and bonded to stories and people who, by rewards and punishments, conquered nature, in and around us. This was accompanied by "lemon" stories that attached Nature's love for humanity to imaginary beings who existed in imaginary places elsewhere. They were, and remain, fantasies supporting our nature-disconnected thinking and relationships while soothing our stress and abandonment anxieties resulting from our excessive Planet Mother disconnection. These disconnected stories have caused our body, mind, and spirit to become more and more destructively addicted to profiting by creating artificiality. Our natures are disconnected from 54 senses; institutions, science, and technologies have advanced while eliminating the balancing controls that are found in all natural areas (Cohen 2011). Nature, in us, has responded to its continued abuse with our discontents that we tranquilize, stress about, or act out. It is as though the 911 Twin Tower catastrophe is a reprisal for centuries of our hi-tech, conquer-Nature story assaulting Nature in individuals and cultures. We cannot injure a life form that we are part of without us being injured, too. Einstein-54 reverses our runaway trespass of Nature, in and around us, by hands-on reconnecting our personhood to its origins and fulfillments in the unified field, backyard, or backcountry, and in each other. We develop a stalwart integrity that stops us from violating any individual's legal rights to life in balance. As an Anthropologist, I think Einstein-54 is essential because we still do not give legal rights to Nature itself, biologically or spiritually. Instead, construction after construction, the natural world becomes meat for our grinder instead of a protected outdoor cathedral that can bring our psyche and relationships into the equilibrium of wellness. Industrial society has become a cancer. Higher education illegally deprives us of our right to an education that addresses and prevents this cancer's cause and remedy.

The world is not to be put in order, the world is order.
It is for us to put ourselves in unison with this order.
—Henry Miller, Wisdom of the Heart, 1941

Witness 24 Sally Goodwin

Einstein-54 Testimony: *Personal Field Journal Report*

I was attracted at first to the field of flowers and noticed that while most of them had many flowers on one stem, one plant had only one yellow flower on it and I changed my direction because it attracted me. It brought to mind a situation in the past when I made a decision to take a new path, to change and let go of a situation where I was overly responsible and causing myself and others pain. I am now finding myself at a similar crossroad and yet my awareness has come very quickly, and transition is very rapid. In the past, I taught nursing on the Navajo reservation. I was cut off from sources of nourishment and support being 300 miles from the main campus and a worldview away. I experienced my ancestral trauma through the trauma of my students as they/we attempted without support to span the gap of what I would now describe as nature-connected vs. nature-separated thinking. I am now experiencing a cut-off of support in my present nursing practice where I suddenly do not feel safe, supported, or centered. Untrained staff, reimbursement issues, and chaos prevail. I keep habitually thinking if I were more…, patient, kind, understanding, smarter, faster, and so forth. Then I recognize this feeling of *aha!!* Here it is again—well, "thank you," to this field of plants and again to this process. You have freed me from habitual enslavement to putting energy toward my area of injury. Rather, I will put energy toward that which nourishes and supports me. I will, as the as the plant-one-blossom, expose the beauty of my one yellow flower—the pure and fragile essence of my true nature—only revealing this beauty to that which supports me and save further energy for continued growth and preparation as I follow alternate paths. I am grateful to the plants for the reminder of my freedom to focus inward, to seek intelligently through Einstein-54 natural love attractions that nourish and support me in fulfilling what life asks of me.

> *The greatest science in the world, in heaven and on earth, is love.*
>
> —Mother Teresa, A Simple Path, 1995

Witness 25 Toby Salvidore
Einstein-54 Testimony: *Prejudice against Nature Addiction*

In 1984, Dr. Cohen wrote that it was reasonable for our prejudice against nature to be identified for the prejudice, evisceration, or rape, that it was (Cohen, 1983). Sadly, he remembered a young child he knew at Camp Turkey Point in 1945, Michael Schwerner, who, as an adult, was one of the three civil rights workers murdered by the Ku Klux Klan in 1964. He felt that Michael did not risk putting his life on the line just to correct a misunderstanding or to complete incomplete information. Michael's rational passion called to him because racial prejudice was hurting the rights of human life, people of color were being hanged from trees. Cohen recognized that, similarly, our prejudice against nature had wounded or killed the web of life in the ongoing excessive nature and insensitive war that industrial society had, for profit, secretly declared against defenseless and non-literate nature. Unless people sensed the horror, unfairness, and pain inflicted by this war, they would remain desensitized and prejudiced. As the protectors of civil rights, peace, labor, equality, and social justice demonstrated, the correct word, *prejudice*, brought the passion of the heart into people's reasoning. Like "lemon memories," it motivated them to act especially to support and defend the lives of themselves and people, and things they loved.

In his 2015 Encyclical on Nature and elsewhere, Pope Francis has said that the violence that exists in the human heart is also manifest in the symptoms of illness that we see in the Earth, the water, the air, and in living things. If we destroy Creation, Creation will destroy us. The environment is intimately connected to our care for each other. We are faced with one complex crisis, which is both social and environmental. The rich and powerful shut themselves up within self-enclosed enclaves, compulsively consuming the latest goods to feed the emptiness within their hearts, while ignoring the plight of the poor. The poor are on the run from natural disasters and degraded habitats, shunted to the bottom of the world's pile of problems with decreasing access to its natural resources. The destruction of the Rainforest is a sin. Humanity has become enamored of another apple in the Garden of Eden, a forbidden fruit to innovative technology, but the sin remains the same: hubris. The earth, our home, is beginning to look more and more like an immense pile of filth.

Like the Pope, more and more authorities recognize the full story of equality, that humanity is part of nature and to harm one, harms the other. For centuries, authorities have held similar stories about the equality of individuals no matter their race, sex, religion or economic status. Advances have been made in honoring this equality, but sadly, to these come at Nature's cost as the advances further exploit it as a resource. This is caused by our Society's ultimate authority being the prejudice in our Nature-disconnected stories rather than their support of Einstein-54 contact with Nature's Unified Field.

Prejudice can be seen as an unreasonable pre-judging attitude that is, due to bonding, unusually resistant to rational influence and bonding can be addictive. Eintein-54 gives any individual the ability to discover and deal with the violence that results from authorities not recognizing that they are bonded to hold a cultural prejudice against nature that has painfully disconnected their and our mentality from the benefits of the Unified Field.

With respect to our higher education leaders and their prejudice against nature, we are, today, in real life, in far worse shape than were the subjects of the astonishing Milgram studies of 1961 (Milgram, 1974). In those studies, a supervisor committed the subjects to administer increasingly painful electrical shocks to people who answered meaningless questions incorrectly. The subjects could hear the shock-recipients in another room, but they could not see them. They were fully aware that they cried out in increasing pain, anguish, and protest as the experiment progressed and the shock voltage increased. Despite this, they sometimes applied the shocks even after they recognized that the recipient had died.

What the subjects did not know was the alleged recipients did not actually receive the shocks, that their cries were recordings.

What was not predicted was that although some subjects cringed and complained, most would not stop hurting the shock recipients as the voltage they applied and responding cries increased and the supervisor urged them to continue. The subjects, instead, responded to the authority of the supervisor. It was as if the subjects were insane. They could not act reasonably from their senses when they had the choice to disobey a voluntarily accepted authority. This experiment was recently repeated, and the results were the same.

We are in much greater trouble now than were the Milgram subjects and participants forty years ago. This is because today the authority phenomenon is not a study. It is real life and true to the lives of most contemporary people, especially young people; they are the most vulnerable. The life that our authorities have us shocking and hurting is the life of our Planet and Nature, in and around us. This is authentic. We know it full well and we see and feel the disastrous personal, social, and environmental effects of the traumatic stress it inflicts. However, we don't stop obeying our outer and inner authorities and our detrimental impact increases each year.

We are painfully aware that we are subject to stories from profit driven, nature-exploiting authorities, directives, and advertisements that unbalance us. They include the misguided information that induces, pays, applauds, or addicts us to excessively use products that secretly administer lethal shocks to the life of our Planet and Nature, in and about us, now and in the future. It begs two vital questions for each individual, "Who is the Boss of you? What disasters are you placing on your children?"

As part of Nature we suffer the pain we are goaded into inflicting on Nature while, be we administrator, scientist, or client in denial, our prejudice against Nature deceives us to say that we can't find a major way to stop doing this, even though Einstein-54 is available.

Our helplessness and its outrageous Earth Overshoot effects occur because our Society pays and promotes authorities to fire or admonish us for not doing their nature-disconnected biddings. In addition, these "bosses" encourage us not to believe what our 54 natural senses convey to us. Instead, the bosses say we must listen to their erroneous messages as well as spend over ninety-five percent of our time and felt-sense thinking and relating out of tune with how Nature's Unified Field works.

Due to our excessive disconnection from Nature we seldom hear, feel, or make sense of the pain and disorders we inflict on the natural world, in and about us. Instead, unhappily, we endure them or try to pass "band-aid" laws that forbid their continuance rather than Einstein-54 address and remove their point source.

We become so attuned to being attached to, or cultural-object subjects of, our authorities that part of our mentality subconsciously takes on their role. They become our inner authorities. We not only can't stop listening to real administrators, when they are absent, we listen to their images and instructions that we don't realize we have unconsciously fixed in our mind. Meanwhile our 54 senses scream, "Stop your shocking behavior. We are aware of what is happening to us and the whole of nature."

We can't realistically enjoy full trust and satisfactions from relationships when we know they are not honorable because we can see that they are not in balance. Even the best of researchers are not immune to this phenomenon. They can discover a truth and at the same time act as if it was not true. For example, although the faculties of most universities have the opportunity to add Einstien-54 to each of their disciplines, they choose not to while they address themselves as "honorable." Who is the boss of them? If you don't believe our crazy attachments to destructive authorities is addictive, just try and stop it.

> *My name is Chellis and I am in recovery from Western Civilization.*
> —Chellis Glendinning, My Name Is Chellis and I'm in Recovery from Western Civilization, 1994

I have seen where the connection of our 54 senses to their natural attraction origins in the Unified Field reasonably revives, restores and energizes them organically as well as frees them from their destructive attachments in Industrial Society. In Nature's Unified Field, mutually produced and attractive "Thank you for your love and care," good feeling fulfillments are always available. This connection reduces our prejudice against Nature. We become more sensible, healthy, and open to reasonable change. Our rights to our freedom from excessiveness, drug use, conflict, crime, stress, and illness increase as a result.

The Department of Justice can't enforce justice for Nature because the prejudice against Nature authority of the Constitution gives Nature no legal rights. Similarly, we are affected by the past and present prejudiced against Nature "Bosses" in our lives along with their violation of our rights and reasoning as demonstrated in the Milgram studies.

Our dilemma is that our addiction counselors are addicted to our nature-disconnecting stories. Bonding to Einstein-54 is not an addiction because its positive rather than negative effects produce whole life happiness, enlightenment, and relationships.

Einstein-54 is available as a counselor to help us make the Unified Field a wise, supportive, and trustable Boss instead of continuing to omit its contributions. How can any of us glue differing things together in beneficial unification if we don't learn how to open and use the can of glue that can do this?

It is obvious that each of us has a right to life that is being violated by our prejudiced-against-Nature stories. Through Einstein-54 their removal gives Earth's self-correcting abilities the time and space to recover and restore Earth.

This jury can promote the opportunity for the self-evident right to life-in-balance by us as well as by all other forms of life. Simply decide to let this issue go to trial. Be reasonable. Give the law a chance to reverse our prejudice against Nature by at least requiring higher education to make Einstein-54 skills a requirement for college admission, as are math and language skills now.

> *The Earth is our mother. Whatever befalls the earth, befalls the sons of the earth. If men spit upon the ground, they spit upon themselves.*

Humankind has not woven the web of life. We are but one thread within it. All things are bound together. All things connect.

The Earth does not belong to man; man belongs to Earth. What is man without the beasts? If all the beasts were gone, men would die from great loneliness of spirit, for whatever happens to the beasts also happens to the man.
—Chief Seattle / Ted Perry /
The Preacher King (Ecclesiastes 3:19 Revised Standard Version)

Witness 26 Lorie Flower
Einstein-54 Testimony: *Herbal Remedies*

My experience as an herbalist has led me down Nature's path. I am always looking for ways to enhance well-being and I have worked with groups of people, some in the professional sports world, as I explored adding Einstein-54 to complement my herbal remedies. A scientific study with weight loss provided a measured improvement in my clients' personal well-being as I found it did for others in depression, post-traumatic stress ~~syndrome~~ disorder, and physical injury. Attractions they discovered in Einstein-54 gave people wholeness with nature that led to better recuperation. Each person became more in touch with sensory connections that are vital to a whole body-whole earth consciousness and that process is a significant contribution to services provided by the herbal remedies profession. No other wide-ranged item appeared to be as effective for the array of measured recuperative changes. All beings have the ability to benefit from the Einstein-54 experience and people should be educated to enjoy this natural right.

No medicine can cure the damage caused by disregarding the inner intelligence with which we are gifted.
—Renu Chaudhary, Ayurveda to the Rescue - An Ancient Remedy for Modern Ailments, 2014

Witness 27 Steve Rector

Einstein-54 Testimony: *Meditation Expert Personal Field Journal Report*

While in a protected natural area beginning my first experience with Einstein-54, David, our mentor, introduced four of us to its equation by having us validate that whatever our senses experienced was an undeniable, self-evident fact for us that we did not need to defend. This included that we could sense that we had many more than five senses operating as we spoke and we identified some of them: hearing, distance, gravity, self, literacy, consciousness, aliveness, humor, and reason. It became obvious that the fact that we had only five senses was a distortion.

We recognized the truth that nowhere here or in our education could we find any evidence of Nature communicating through stories or labels. To help us know Nature as it knew its nameless self, we spent five minutes quietly in the woods identifying each thing that we became aware of there as "nameless" or "story-less." We then got together and shared what we sensed and felt from doing this. We discovered that by dropping our labels and stories what one person said they had experienced each of us sensed as well in this moment for we were still unified in the forest. This was reasonable because we realized that we were all part of Nature and each other.

We helped each other realize that our love or attraction to Nature was our 54 senses registering the Unified Higgs Boson Field bringing all things into attracted, connected belonging in the Universe's time and space of each new moment (A New Copernicun Revolution, 2012). Then, we spent the next five minutes by ourselves labeling everything we became aware of, including ourselves, as "Unified Field Attraction Love."

When we got together again as a group a stronger unifying ecstasy was present. Our senses of love, trust, place, community, and time were apparent. Folks shared how these same feelings of well-being had helped them and others when they were ill and that some folks had addicted to artificially producing them by using drugs or alcohol. These detached them from their stories but the relief they enjoyed was accompanied by detrimental aftereffect addictions. Einstein-54 was suggested as a healthy substitute for these questionable satisfactions because its aftereffects supported Nature. The things people sensed were

— how amazingly diverse Nature was,
— how they loved being aware of and in Nature,
— how each thing in a natural area was a unique individual, including each of them,
— how it felt good that everything was right there to experience in the moment,
— that they felt relieved by not having to label things "correctly" or at all,
— that they discovered many new things about Nature by removing the stories and labels that hid them thus feeling closer to Nature,
— that a "brightening" or vibrancy of things took place after we repeatedly called them "Nameless" thus hearing things we didn't hear moments earlier,
— feeling a greater belongingness when they called themselves "Nameless,"
— their habitual meditation processes benefitting from a new unifying dimension; and,
— calling human-built structures and effects "runaway blueprints" thus making them more in reasonable control of them.

We walked back to the beginning of the trail labeling things we experienced as "love," "attraction," or "unified field" and we felt much closer to each other than when we started. Then David had us pinch ourselves until it hurt so we stopped. We explored how the sense of pain was not a negative rather it was an attraction, Nature's attraction to signal us to find more satisfying and reasonable attractions.

We validated that moment-by-moment everything was attractively connected and as one as part of the Unified Field of the Universe throughout our walk. When we sensed that plants or we were alive, the Earth and Universe also had to be alive for everything was identical. We ended up looking at clouds as they moved across the sky into beautiful new shapes and we felt harmony and peace knowing we were doing the same with them and each other, no matter our cultural or genetic differences. We noted that people in the middle of a city could do this with clouds, parks or weeds as well. Then David distributed sheets with the 54 senses listed on them and activities we could do to strengthen them (Cohen, M. J., 2016).

What fascinated me was that using Einstein-54 we learned all this through trustable experiences in Nature, the real thing, in less than an hour because what we were learning we could sense and feel right there around and in us, not just from a book or lecture about it. We were helping our senses remember what they already knew as we connected them with it. At my school it would have taken a four-month science and philosophy course to get the same results if it was even possible. Can an indoor course ever substitute for learning how Nature works from authentic Nature, the fountainhead of authority in how it works?

The only source of knowledge is experience.
—Albert Einstein, Ideas and OpinionS,1954

Witness 28 Roger Elliot
Einstein-54 Testimony: *Political Implications*

I offer this jury that legal precedence has already been set to use Einstein-54 in the protection of the people's right to live reasonable and happy lives (Grange #966, 2015):

JUNE 3, 2015
A RESOLUTION CONCERNING THE OVERSHOOT OF EARTH'S CARRYING CAPACITY

WHEREAS, the Declaration of Purposes of the National Grange, adopted by the St. Louis session of the National Grange, February 11, 1874 stated, "We shall endeavor...to buy less and produce more, in order to make our farms self-sustaining; to diversify our crops and crop no more than we can cultivate; to condense the weight of our exports, selling less in the bushel and more on hoof and in fleece, less in lint and more in warp and woof;...; to discountenance the credit system, the mortgage system, the fashion system, and every other system tending to prodigality and bankruptcy" (National Grange, 1874); and

WHEREAS, many of the natural resources of Earth are finite, and are not being created at the rate they are being consumed; and

WHEREAS, many past civilizations have gone bankrupt and are no more, after overshooting the carrying capacities of their regions; and

WHEREAS, our current world-wide civilization is not immune to natural laws concerning the carrying capacity of Earth; and

WHEREAS, many of our current agricultural, industrial and financial activities tend toward "prodigality and bankruptcy" in regard to sustaining our civilization and our planet's life and integrity; and

WHEREAS, Scientists recognize Planet Earth is a living organism and that all members of its plant, animal, mineral and energy kingdoms are alive in balance;

THEREFORE, BE IT RESOLVED, that we must act as ambassadors of Earth to guide humanity away from its excesses which lead to an overshoot of Earth's ability to meet our material and emotional needs; and

BE IT FURTHER RESOLVED, that the San Juan Island Grange #966 offer the tools to accomplish this worthy goal to its members and to the public (The National Grange, 1874)

Passed Unanimously, June 3, 2015

SOURCE INFORMATION:

Earth, as a living organism, as understood through the application of Einstein's Unified Field NNIAAL Equation:

http://www.ecopsych.com/saneearth.html
www.mjcnow.info
www.ecopsych.com/zombie2.html
http://www.ecopsych.com/journalwarranty.html

The Declaration of Purposes of the National Grange, adopted by the St. Louis session of the National Grange, February 11, 1874: http://www.oocities.org/cannongrange/declaration_purposes.html

> *How few there are who have courage enough to own their faults, or resolution enough to mend them.*
> —Benjamin Franklin, Autobiography of Benjamin Franklin, 1791

Summation

Robert Goldwater, Prosecutor:
Before I read to you the key parts of Einstein-54 from its online GreenWave edition (Einstein, A., 2014-2016), I am going to describe for you what is at stake in this hearing and how you can help our present "justice for the few with power" become personal, social, and environmental justice for all. I again remind you that because we undeniably live in the time and space of our living planet, Earth, when negligence by some parts of society damage its health, they damage our health and they can be held legally responsible for their acts by those whose rights have been violated.

As Einstein-54 demonstrates, our living Planet and Universe is the self-correcting and pure foundation of our lives. We have excessively separated ourselves from it. Without its wisdom, process, and support as our foundation, we have corrupted ourselves as well as Nature at every level of relating. Einstein-54 can help us correct this corruption in our foundations as well as in incidents found throughout society.

Note that many people excessively profit from our corruption. They are against Einstein-54 because it is free and it gives us the tools and ability to correct the warp in the way we habitually felt-sense think and relate including the anti-nature warp that is the root of our troubles. However, as the witnesses claim, they would not be against it if they were engaged in it. Even this hearing is possibly corrupt. You do not know if or how many of the 23 of you have or will be approached by special interests to not let this complaint go to trial. It would be no surprise if you do not trust the Justice Department or even me in this regard, no less the trial by jury that you can sanction. Is it even possible for your sense of reason to make good sense of this grand jury hearing about how we have warped our 54 senses if your 54 senses are warped? What you can do is make the trial happen rather than not happen; significant potential for good is found whenever justice occurs especially justice for all including the web of life.

The Defendants are accused of illegally depriving us of the benefits of Einstein-54. To increase and strengthen fairness, the United States Department of Justice wants the Law to force the Defendants to make the Einstein-54 benefit available as well as pay for damages incurred from the Defendant's negligent omission of it that deprives us of many constitutional and human rights.

As the witnesses have just testified, by being educated to put on and wear Einstein-54 glasses we can relate to the world more realistically and harmoniously from the heart in the same way that the math-science of Copernicus helped us to benefit from the Sun, not the Earth, as the center of our solar system. Einstein-54 enables us to felt-sense think and relate to ourselves, each other, and the world simultaneously for what we actually are. We are, moment-by-moment, a singular, alive Organism Earth and the aliveness of its Universe that we also call Nature. It produces its own space and time and is held together each moment everywhere by natural attractions that include an attraction to expand or grow more attractive, an attraction that our 54 senses register and support.

As human beings we are each a unique personification of Organism Earth. We are all cells of it that hold in common our attractive genetic ability to build relationships through abstract stories. However, we are vulnerable to unreasonable "lemon story" inaccuracies and prejudices about our world. These stories mislead us to excessively separate from our planet, to habitually act destructively, and to suffer accordingly as does Earth as well. Our inaccurate stories that disintegrate the whole of life deprive us of our human rights as happy citizens of Organism Earth and the intelligence of its universal aliveness. As the witnesses have described:

> Our senses are the tools we use to register, believe, and relate to the world. When we lose or distort them what can be trusted?
>
> Our 54 natural senses normally attract our life to Earth's unconditional love of all things.
>
> We suffer our challenging problems because we learn to detach our senses from Nature's self-correcting ways and attach them instead to our artificial, Nature-disconnected stories and technologies.
>
> Our detachments emotionally tear our body, mind, and spirit from Earth's unifying 54 sense embrace, and it from ours.
>
> The pain and abandonment caused by our severance from Nature and its love deteriorates our collective and personal outlooks.
>
> Our destructive separation makes us want so we feel that there is never enough of anything, especially love.
>
> We addictively fill our love gap with material possessions and artificial relationships and can't stop even though we are aware that in the process our excessiveness is dismantling planet/person life and the support of its wholeness.
>
> Einstein-54 reverses our disorders by creating moments that let Nature's attraction/love help us produce whole life satisfactions, enlightenment, and relationships.

Our human rights include the rights and freedom of Nature, within us and as us, to be recognized as a person (PNC, 2007), to equality, to security, to public hearing, and to remedies by competent tribunal.

Our tribunal today can strengthen people's rights to love and be loved; to freedom of opinion, belief, and information; to get an education; to be considered innocent; to life, health, and freedom from degrading treatment.

Our inquest can reduce the huge economic costs along with the physical and mental pain we suffer from our attachments to nature-disconnected stories. They produce our racial, religious and gender prejudices, destructive stress, unfairness and inequality, mental illness, corruption, abusiveness, violence, addiction, rape, excessiveness, environmental degradation, and poverty. Each infringes upon our right to pursue happiness by deteriorating our ability and freedom to do so.

By requiring Einstein-54 in higher education this jury will give Nature in all of us personal rights that we can use to help protect Nature in the environment that our stories have given no rights. This will increase Justice for all members of the web of life, not just us, as well as reverse and heal the miseries we presently suffer from 150-400% Earth Overshoot.

Long-term happiness is the feeling that biologically comes into play whenever any of our 54 natural attraction senses are fulfilled in a reasonable way. The Declaration of Independence specifically states the right to the pursuit of the joy of life; the Constitution omits it. The Plaintiffs simply want the government to live up to the Declaration of Independence and the Constitution by legally giving them the knowledge of and access to Einstein-54 as part of government regulated education from pre-school on, no less High Education. This is the highest purpose of Higher Education and although higher education institutions acknowledge this, they are prejudiced to deprive us of the Einstein-54 tools we need to make it happen.

Tapping into the unified energy field of the Universe through Einstein-54 enables us to understand and act from who and where we are by removing the walls of alienation, environmental destruction, ignorance, and despair that result from our intellect's estrangement from our universal aliveness and its wisdom. Because Einstein-54 has ancient sensory roots in our planet and human experience as well as the frontiers of modern science, it helps us transform our discontents into the immense unifying powers of reasonable 54-sense love for life in balance and beauty.

For the reasons I have just stated I ask the 23 of you to find that the defendants must face the investigations, fairness, and decisions of a trial by judge and jury.

Conclusion

Readers of this Chapter are invited to become alternate members of its Grand Jury Metaphor and help it reach its conclusion by taking on the role of an alternate Juror or as an additional Witness. Simply read Einstein-54 at www.mjcnow.info, draw your own conclusions, and contact me at (360) 378-6313, or nature@interisland.net.

References

A new Copernican revolution. (2012). *Journal of Organic Psychology and Natural Attraction Ecology, 2.* Retrieved from http://www.ecopsych.com/journalcopernicus.html

Albert Einstein's unified field equation. (2014-2016). *Journal of Organic Psychology and Natural Attraction Ecology, 2.*

Retrieved from http://www.ecopsych.com/einsteinstart.html

Brown, N. (1990). *Love's body.* Oakland, CA: University of California Press.

Cohen, M. J. (1983). *Prejudice against nature.*

Retrieved from http://www.ecopsych.com/prejudicebigotry.html

Cohen, M. J. (1993). *The training ground of a nature-connected expert.* (2014). Retrieved from http://www.ecopsych.com/mjcohen.html

Cohen, M. J. (1995). Education and counseling with nature: A greening of psychotherapy. *The Interspsych Newsletter, 2*(4). Retrieved from http://www.ecopsych.com/counseling.html

Cohen, M. J. (2007a). *Thinking and feeling and relating through the joy of nature's perfection.* Retrieved from http://www.ecopsych.com/naturepath.html

Cohen, M. J. (2007b). *Whom am I? Who or what is your natural self?* Retrieved from http://www.ecopsych.com/thesisquote6.html

Cohen, M. J. (2008). *Educating, counseling, and healing with nature.* Illumina Retrieved from http://www.ecopsych.com/ksanity.html

Cohen, M. J. (2009a). *How to transform destructive thinking into constructive relationships.* Retrieved from http://www.ecopsych.com/transformation.html

Cohen, M. J. (2011). *The anatomy of institutions.* Retrieved from http://www.ecopsych.com/journalinstitution.html

Cohen, M. J. (2013). *The great sensory equation dance.* Retrieved from http://www.ecopsych.com/journalgut.html

Cohen, M. J. (2014). *Benefit from consciously registering your fifty-four natural senses.* Retrieved from http://www.ecopsych.com/insight53senses.html

Cohen, M. J. (2015). *A survey of nature-connected learning participants.* Retrieved from http://www.ecopsych.com/survey.html

Cohen, M. J. (2016). *Maverick genius walk.* Retrieved from http://www.ecopsych.com/MAKESENSEWALK.docx

Dewey, J. (1934). Individual psychology and education. *The Philosopher, 2.* Retrieved from http://www.ascd.org/ASCD/pdf/journals/ed_update/eu201207_infographic.pdf

Doherty, T. J. (2010). Michael Cohen: Ecopsychology interview. *Ecopsychology Journal, 2.* Retrieved from http://www.ecopsych.com/ecopsychologyjournal.html

Einstein, A., Cohen, M.J. (2014-2016)). Albert Einstein's unified field equation. *Journal of Organic Psychology and Natural Attraction Ecology, 2.*
Retrieved from http://www.ecopsych.com/einsteinstart.html Fishman, K. (1854). Chief Seattle's speech. *Wildwood Survival.* Retrieved from http://www.wildwoodsurvival.com/wildernessmind/chiefseattle.html

Grange [#966]. (2015). Resolutions.
Retrieved from http://www.sjigrange.wordpress.com/resolutions

Green, B. (2013). How the Higgs Boson was found. *Smithsonian Magazine.* Retrieved from http://www.smithsonianmag.com/science-nature/how-the-higgs-boson-was-fund-4723520/?cmd=ChdjYS1wdWItMjY0NDQyNTI0NTE5MDk0Nw&page=3

Hoke, P. (2015). Maverick genius at work. Retrieved from http://www.ecopsych.com/maverick-genius

Kluger, J. (2014). The sixth great extinction. *Time Magazine.* Retrieved from http://time.com/3035872/sixth-great-extinction/

Milgram, S. (1974). Obedience to authority: An experimental view. New York: Harper & Row. Retrieved from https://en.wikipedia.org/wiki/Milgram_experiment

Pascal, B. (1995). *Pensées*. (p. 312). Oxford University Press, USA: Penguin Books. Retrieved from http://www.naturalchild.org/jan_hunt/babyspeaks.html

International Astronomical Union. (2015). *Universe is dying.* Retrieved from http://news.discovery.com/space/galaxies/universe-is-dying-galactic-survey-shows-150810.htm

Natural attraction ecology. (2003). Retrieved from http://www.naturalattractionecology.com/index.html#anchoraxiom

Our living universe: Who is the boss of you? (2014). Retrieved from http://www.ecopsych.com/universealive.html

Peak fact: Whole life self evidence in action. (2010). *Journal of Organic Psychology and Natural Attraction Ecology, 2.* Retrieved from http://www.ecopsych.com/journalpeak.html

Project NatureConnect (PNC). (1997). *Reconnecting With Nature*, EcoPress. Retrieved from http://www.ecopsych.com/insight53senses.html

The hidden organic remedy: Nature as higher power. (2013). *Journal of Organic Psychology and Natural Attraction Ecology, 1.* Retrieved from http://www.ecopsych.com/nhpbook.html

The impossible dream: We ask you to be a part of it. (2011-2013). *Journal of Organic Psychology and Natural Attraction Ecology, 1.* Retrieved from http://www.ecopsych.com/journalwarranty.html

The magic of something from nothing. (2012). *Journal of Organic Psychology and Natural Attraction Ecology, 2.* Retrieved from http://www.ecopsych.com/journalessence.html

The National Grange. (1874, February 11). *The declaration of purposes of the National Grange.* Retrieved from http://www.oocities.org/cannongrange/declaration_purposes.html

The state of planet earth and us. (2001).
    Retrieved from http://www.ecopsych.com/zombie2.html

Thinking and learning with all nine legs. (2011).
    Retrieved from http://www.ecopsych.com/nineleg.html

Who, what or when is the acronym NNIAAL? (2013).
Retrieved from http://www.ecopsych.com/earthstories101.html

Searls, D. (2009). *The Journal of Henry David Thoreau, 1837-1861. 2.* [December 6 entry]. New York Review Books Classics. Retrieved from https://en.wikiquote.org/wiki/Henry_David_Thoreau

CHAPTER 4

How to Communicate Effectively to be a Successful Professional

Dr. Niranjan Ray
Akamai University

We talk to ourselves, to family members at home, to someone in the office or in public places. The key to success in life, in relationships, and in work depends on good communication skills. Effective communication sends or receives an unambiguous message that brings success in life. communicating makes the difference between success and failure. Language has the power to inspire, motivate, and entertain audiences. Your appearance, facial expression, and your voice all count for effective

Communication

Communication contains verbal and nonverbal messages. Verbal messages are clear and unambiguous most of the time. Nonverbal messages deal with body languages to communicate. Your body language can deliver more than your words can do. How effective you are in communication. Whether you are a leader or follower, you can empower ~~the~~ people ~~by~~ through effective communication. A successful professional almost always has an effective communication skill.

Reading, writing, speaking, and listening are four basic forms of communication. We spend years learning how to read and write. All forms of communication skills are important in life to succeed in our personal and professional life. When we speak, it is called sending a verbal message; we want to communicate with others. A verbal message consists of word tone, voice quality, pitch, volume, and emotion such as excitement/nervousness that we use to communicate and send messages to others.

Verbal Communication

Verbal communication and oral communication are similar but not the same forms of communication. Verbal means relating to the form of words. Verbal is used to describe things that can be put into words. Oral means spoken; sometimes verbal is used as a synonym for oral. People use the language to create influence and control either through verbal or oral communication. Oral communication relays a message using sounds and language. People use language to create a powerful or powerless impression. It depends on the power of the language they use to communicate.

Nonverbal Communication

A nonverbal message is called ~~the~~ body language. Body language (gestures) and facial expressions complete the message more meaningfully than verbal communication. In fact, we communicate more information by nonverbal signals, for example:

- Gestures—crossing arms, pointing fingers, and waving hands.
- Posture—the way people sit or stand up.
- Facial expressions—eye contact, smiling during interviews, crying when you hear some bad news, and frowning when

somebody is accusing you unnecessarily without knowing the facts.

People communicate in two ways, sending and receiving verbal messages and nonverbal messages. Even though they don't know it, they use both forms of communication all the time. When your friend is telling you something, notice his body language (nonverbal communication) is also talking to you. If verbal and nonverbal communications sound the same message, it is called an effective communication. That means there is no ambiguity of the message sent.

In day-to-day life, effective verbal communication skills can help you establish and promote better relationships with your coworkers, managers and maintain a large networking contact that you may need in future when necessary.

- **Example 1:**
  In love affairs, when two people fall in love with each other, first they communicate through their eyes (nonverbal communication). Then comes the verbal communication to build and continue the relationship.
- **Example 2:**
  At the time of a job interview, the employer looks for both verbal and nonverbal messages to interpret that you are really interested in the position for which you are being interviewed.
- **Example 3:**
  By nature, I talk to people in a bit of a loud voice. When my daughter was 6 years old, I was talking to her about her homework and why it was not done on time. She started to cry as she was not used to hearing a loud voice. She prefers a low tone of voice. Now she is used to my voice.
- **Example 4:** My son and I attended a conference with his Spanish teacher at a parent-teacher conference night at his high school. As I was talking to the teacher in a bit of a louder voice about the academic progress of my son, the teacher walked out of the classroom.

I did not say anything bad about her class. Why did she walk out of the classroom? The reason was that she was not used to hearing a loud voice from a demanding parent like me. I was able to settle this issue in another conference with the same teacher in the presence of a school counselor.

Mass Communication

Mass communication combines both verbal and nonverbal forms of communication by transmitting information to people through mass media. Examples of mass media are newspapers, radio, television, books, movies, magazines, film, and websites that transmit information to the common public. Mass media channels play an important role for mass communication. It is a one-way process with mostly no feedback from the audiences. Internet websites are is an exception where people are allowed to provide feedback.

Retrieved from https://www.communications-major.com/mass communications/

Listening

In today's world, listening is a part of the communication exchange between two persons. Listening builds relationships, resolves conflicts, and saves time through better understanding between two individuals or two parties. Effective listening at work helps minimize errors, lessens wasted time, solves problems, promotes friendships and careers.

At home, listening enhances the relationship between husband and wife, and their relationship with their kids. Kids thus become self-reliant in solving their problems in day-to-day life.

Listening is an Art

Listening skills can open the door to opportunities like improving productivity of the employees, boosting revenue, enhancing customer service. Everyone has the chance to improve their listening skills and become better listeners. Mastering the art of listening will make you a leader in your professional field. Professional and business people and leaders, all listen carefully to their peers, to their staffs, to their friends, and to their family members.

> "We have two ears and one tongue so that we would listen more and talk less."
>
> –Diogenes

Diogenes. (n.d.). AZQuotes.com. Retrieved May 08, 2018, from AZQuotes.com Web site: http://www.azquotes.com/quote/79010

Tips on developing effective listening skills:

1. **Be Silent:** When you are attending a lecture session, be quiet. This is a message to the speaker that you are listening to him or her. Listen attentively to what the speaker is saying.
2. **Be Understanding:** Focus your mind toward the speaker and try to understand the contents of the topic that the speaker wants to convey to his audience. The speaker should be given a chance to say everything he would like to say without any interruption. When somebody interrupts the speaker, it looks like he isn't listening, even though he is listening.
3. **Main ideas:** You may wonder what the speaker will say next. Listen for the main idea. The speaker may mention the main idea at the beginning or at the end of a talk, and he may repeat it many times to get it across to the audience.
4. **Feedback:** During the lecture session, keep eye contact with the speaker, nod sometimes to show that you understand. At right points, you may laugh, smile, and be silent to connect to the speaker. At the end of the lecture i.e., during a question-answer session, the speaker asks for questions from the audience. Ask appropriate questions and give feedback related to the lecture topic or add some valuable points to the lecture. The speaker will be happy to answer the questions from the audience.

5. **Feel the speaker's feeling:** Listen to the words the speaker is saying. When he talks about sadness, or joyful events, you should reflect those feelings by your words and facial expressions to ensure your effectiveness as a listener. You need to put yourself in somebody's situation and feel yourself what the speaker is feeling. This connects the speaker to foster a relationship further.

Negotiation and Conflict Management

In our day-to-day life we all negotiate with our family members, friends, car sellers, bank managers, and salespersons of retail stores. Interpersonal and communication skills are the key components of negotiation skills. Interpersonal skills are the skills we use when engaged in face-to-face communication with one or more other people. For any business success, negotiation plays an important role. You need to set up a strategy on how to negotiate effectively. You also have to know ahead the strength and weakness of your opponent(s) or competitor(s). This will help you to negotiate with your competitors to come to an acceptable solution of to the problem.

When does negotiation happen? When two individuals or parties disagree with the solution of to a problem or a contract, the negotiation is the effective way to solve the problem that brings two parties or individuals to a common point for mutually acceptable agreement. The results of negotiation are: lose-win (one loses more or less and the other wins), compromise for both parties, or win-win situations for both parties depending on the conflict. And lose-lose situation happens when both parties do not achieve the results they desire.

Use the right words at the right time during the negotiation process to create a friendly environment with your opponents. You need to consider multiple options (like option 1, option 2, option 3, etc.) to make an acceptable solution of to the problem. If option 1 does not work, go for option 2, or go for option 3, etc. until you know where the other party's bottom line is and then make a mutually acceptable deal.

Negotiation is a give and take condition, it is a compromise deal where both parties win in some way and lose in another way.

Tips on effective negotiation

1. Create a common ground with your opponent
2. Try to know the strengths and weaknesses of the other party
3. Apply friendly approach to start the negotiation.
4. Be flexible and make concessions as needed to make a deal.

An example of negotiation

We had four partners and formed a LLC company to do business. The LLC Company borrowed money to start a 3-star hotel business. I was a 10% loan guarantor of a $1.0 M commercial loan. The loan was taken from a government agency (i.e. it is a secondary government loan). My loan guarantor portion is $100,000.00 (10% of $1.0 M). Due to a recession the monthly revenue was reduced by 30% and the hotel was foreclosed and was taken over by the primary lender.

How did I apply negotiation skills to settle the loan guaranty of $100,000.00? It took more than 5 years to resolve this loan issue. As per government requirements, I submitted my financial status i.e. my income and my wife's income, bank balances, and other assets. Initially the government agency wanted the full guarantor money $100,000.00 from me. I started the negotiation with the government agency offering 10% i.e. 10% x 100,000.00 = $10,000.00, then 15% i.e. $15000.00, $20,000.00 and so on up to 30% i.e. $30,000.00. When I offered $30,000.00, the government agency rejected it. It took 5 years to negotiate and ultimately, they accepted 30% i.e. $30,000 and they released me from the loan guarantor's obligations.

What negotiation technique did I apply to come to a conclusion? Initially in the year 2010, I lost lots of money in other businesses due to the economic recession, when I submitted my financial to the agency, offering them to accept $10,000.00 (1% of loan $1.0 M). The agency rejected my compromised offer. In 2014, I offered them 30% i.e.

$30,000.00, using the tool that I will be retiring soon and am talking to attorney to do bankruptcy. If I declare bankruptcy based on my current financial situation, the agency will not get any penny. They took months to think and accepted my compromised offer of $30,000.00.

Cross Cultural Negotiation

As business deals at the International level cross borders, so they cross cultures too. Culture dominates how people foresee, behave, and communicate. It also influences the kinds of transactions they make and lead the way they negotiate them.

Knowing any foreign language is helpful to face and solve the problem. The cluster of codes in language can be used in communication to build credibility that helps cross cultural negotiation.

Cultural differences influence different aspects of negotiation. Knowledge of foreign language and culture help reach the goal of business negotiation. It may be a great outcome for Americans business or a long-lasting business relationship for Japanese.

Retrieved from Cross Cultural Negotiation: https://www.pon.harvard.edu/daily/conflict-resolution/a- cross-cultural-negotiation-example-how-to-overcome-cultural-barriers/

Language barriers and body language influence how we meet-and-greet business delegates that may have an impact on our negotiations.

To succeed, probably you need to do a reality check on cross cultural negotiation before you make your plan.

Retrieved from Cross Cultural Negotiation: https://www.pon.harvard.edu/daily/conflict-resolution/a- cross-cultural-negotiation-example-how-to-overcome-cultural-barriers/

Presentation

In almost every field, in school, office, to compete for election process or to start a business, you have to have effective presentation skills.

Presentation is a method of communication such as talking to a group or addressing a meeting or a team. To get your message across to the audiences or listeners, you need to prepare, use method and means to present the information. Get to know your audience and their expectations before the presentation. When you are on the stage, all the eyes of the audiences are on you. Your attire, your appearance, your body language, every word you mention, the tone of your voice, the presentation method and the material, all will be watched and evaluated by your audiences. So, try to know the perspective and expectation of the audiences before delivering the presentation.

The following are tips on presentation skills:

- Try to know your audience and their perspective.
- Research and document the information.
- Write the presentable speech.
- Prepare the power point slides.
- Prepare yourself by rehearsal.
- Introduce yourself and objective of the presentation.
- Present the material, use pauses as needed.
- Engage your audience.
- Question and answer.

Other BASIC TIPS

Non-Verbal

- Dress up smartly. You look nice and professional.
- Standing up straight.
- Smile as needed with respect to the context. Be confident and enthusiastic.
- Smile when greeting the audience.
- Speak clearly, and confidently. Check whether back sitters can hear you.

- Eye contact with some of audience from time to time, trying to involve everyone.
- Walk from side to side, showing hand gesture.
- Use silence to stress points. Use pauses as needed.
- Involve audience by asking them a question.
- Keep presentation/talk within the time limit.

VOICE

- Clear, calm
- Slow/fast depending on speech context
- Vary voice as needed.
- Use ~~of~~ humor as needed.

CONTENT

- Structured well and in a logical sequence
- Should have an introduction and conclusion
- Speaker should be well prepared.
- Speaker should be enthusiastic, and confident
- Make speech material interesting
- Key points notes may be used
- Speaker should interact with and involve the audience
- Do not read the slide. Explain the contents of the slide, and do not read word for word.

VISUAL AIDS

- Power Point slides, flip chart, graphs, logos and picture
- Demonstrations, hands on involvement with quick activities are also great way to involve your audiences and grab their attentions.

Interview

Tips on best Job interview:

1. Research about the Job Opportunity and the Employer [5]:
2. Do the homework about the employer and the type of industry you are getting ready for interview questions. You need to learn about the employer from the organization's Website, your network of contacts, and the requirements of the job you applied for. Get to know the interviewer's name before the interview date. Collect the background information about the interviewers in LinkedIn and have some ideas about the questions interviewers will ask you during interview.
3. 2. Dress up, get ready and be on time
Make sure your dress is neat, clean, pressed and appropriate for the company
4. and you look like Professional. Carry copies of your resume and a list of
5. references. Have a pen and paper handy for note taking.
6. Try to reach the interview location 15 minutes early. Report to the reception for
7. Your attendance, take a company's batch. Use the rest room, check up your tie
8. and brush your hair. Turn off your cell phone. Wait for the interviewer to come
9. and greet you. Shake hands firmly, if a hand is offered by the interviewer first.
10. Face the interview confidently
    - During the interview, be confident to answer to the questions.
    - Listen attentively. Appreciate all questions, even the difficult one.
    - Have a smile on the face.
    - Keep eye contact.
    - Watch when you talk, your body language also talks.

- Make sure your response is short and to the point.
- Be honest and answer directly.
- The interview is about to get the job. Showcase your skills and experiences as you are the best candidate for the job.
- Mention good examples of the problem-solutions and your accomplishments to add value to the process, products and services.

11. *Set Good impressions to end Interview for Success*
    - Create good impressions, conveying warm greetings every interviewer you meet, smile, and get eye contact and handshake firmly.
    - Be motivated to sell your skills and experiences to the employer, showcasing yourself that you are the best fit for the job.
    - Ask if there will be additional interviews.
    - Mention when the hiring manager is planning to make decision.
    - Be polite until the end of interview.
    - Thank interviewers in person or by email.

Conclusion

To be a successful communicator, we need to develop inter personal communication skills, verbal and non-verbal skills, listening skills, negotiation skills, presentation skills and interview skills. We need to know when to talk, what to talk, where to talk and what not to talk. As we communicate with friends, family members, co-workers, employers, and everyone around us, we should be attentive to our surroundings, so that no one gets hurt or have misunderstandings during the process of exchanging messages through the communication.

References:

Difference between verbal and oral communication: https://www.quora.com/What-are-the-differences-between-verbal-and-non-verbal-communication

Mass Communication: https://www.communications-major.com/mass communications/

Quote says: http://www.azquotes.com/quote/79010

Cross Cultural Negotiation: https://www.pon.harvard.edu/daily/conflict-resolution/a- cross-cultural-negotiation-example-how-to-overcome-cultural-barriers/

Research about the Job Opportunity and the Employer: https://www.livecareer.com/career/advice/interview/job-interview-tips

CHAPTER 5

Neo-Platonism, its influences in the Italian Renaissance and Connection to the Advancement of the Human Condition

Sandra L.M. Kolbl (Koelbl) Holman Ph.D.
Akamai University

Overview

Not too long ago, I remember Dr. Leo Ferrari (Philosopher Extraordinaire) at Saint Thomas University in New Brunswick, Canada debating with me whether the Earth is flat and why and inviting me repeatedly to join The Flat Earth Society. And Dr. Ferrari's logic reminds me that the world has evolved, but many of the classical and Neo-Platonic themes recur throughout time or perhaps never vanish, thereby continuing to influence and shape future directions of thinking. In fact, as I was writing this chapter, I was thinking of a patient of mine who is pagan and practices the mythological world of fairies with her young family still to this day. It is interesting to note that as we seek further definition of the human condition, both its advancement and betterment, that we need to understand the narratives of the past in order to design our future.

This chapter addresses Neo-Platonism and its influences in the Italian Renaissance period, discusses the life of master artist Piero di Cosimo, including new documentation that contradicts some of Vasari's accounts of this artist (Waldman, 2014), and presents a dialogue regarding *The Visitation with Saints Nicholas and Anthony Abbot*.

The setting is Florence, Italy. The change movement is humanist. The prevailing thought movement was to define and understand what it means to be human in terms of art, music, literature, mathematics, knowledge, medicine and philosophy. An individual was faced with the following, regardless of the status of being intellectual or not intellectual, as follows: (1) a complex political environment in Florence and surrounding regions, (2) scholars fleeing to Florence from other parts of Europe and the Turks, (3) the recurrent cycles of the Black Death, (4) poor hygiene and sanitation, (5) the leaders of the Roman Catholic Church religious zealousness and obsession with the concepts of eternal salvation and perdition, (6) the return to the magical and mythological, (7) humanism and the neo-platonic rise to the imperfect physical reality as an extension to the spiritual realms, (8) the darkness of fear, death, violence, the unknown and literally darkness with no electricity, (9) laws and rules that held restrictive gender roles, (10) societal class distinctions fading within the philosophy of equalities of humanism, but still thriving, (11) heavy taxation, (12) pre-scientific thought and confusion of the absolute and relative, (13) severe justice and trials with public executions, (14) warring factions and greed, (15) chronic psychological impacts brought to the forefront by the plague, major change and cultural fabric destabilization, and (16) four different time keeping conventions to measure the beginning and the end of a day(Waldman, 2015) - and the list goes on to present a society in stressful flux looking for answers with often very Christian, Neo-Platonist influences as philosophical mechanisms of the humanistic perspective. And the violent nature of the Renaissance culture is easily voiced by Vasari, according to Peter Schjeldahl of the New Yorker Art World (2015), where Schjeldahl notes that Vasari comments: *"Piero regarded public execution as an enviable way to die – under an open sky, with a big audience"*.

Despite all the chaos and change, these societal shifts within the Renaissance provided the means to artistic freedom. Piero di Cosimo crashed the barriers of artistic treatments and renditions with his Renaissance uncategorized style, his portrayals of the rise and struggle of humans from the lowest realms of beast-like behaviors towards the spiritual realms and borrowed mythological images strategically placed within his compositions. Additionally, his giftedness for painting sacred religious stories, while occasionally transcending his images to a time that can exist in both the present and the future have challenged the readers of his paintings to understand Piero the Artist.

Piero di Cosimo (Piero di Lorenzo Ubaldini), called Pierus Lauerenti Pieri (born 1462-died 1522) – Old and New Speculations towards Understanding his Paintings

Piero, as demonstrated in scholarly archival evidence, was an artist of mystery who filled his paintings with the mystical, Christian allegory, poetry, symbolism, surrealism, piety and neo-platonic leanings. He was an artist who Andre Breton named "the spiritual ancestor of modern surrealism" (Online, 2015. Washington Post.), and presented mostly an atypical, although sometimes typical, expectation seen in Italian Renaissance painting. Piero envisioned an imperfect world and his life exemplified an imperfect world full of contradictions and strange visions. Vasari stated, as it reads in the text on the National Gallery of Art website (2015), that Piero epitomized *"the strangeness of his brain, and his constant seeking after difficulties."* Piero continued to baffle with his choices of artistic content, that encompassed, the sacred and serene, as well as mythological and/or scenes invented from his imagination. As a painter, I have often wondered what is happening in the mind of the artist that is able to create or re-create violent and grotesque narratives often with great detail and vividness.

Art and Architecture critic Phillip Kennicott asks the question in his Washington Post (2015) article *what makes a Piero a Piero*? I would suggest that his uniqueness, his intellectual genius, his use of bright hues, his courageousness of building themes through complicated/

mixed scenes or his direction towards serenity and sacredness, and his challenge to the viewer to see the symbolism and questions asked within the context of his paintings. Kennicott addresses this same question by referring to Elizabeth Walmsey and infrared and scientific analysis. He answers this question by referencing Piero's painting techniques, *"the sharp contrast in his use of highlights"*, and his use of his fingers to paint or to manipulate the paint.

Piero's life history details are much like his paintings, always leaving the viewer on the edge of their seat, like an unending 'I Spy' game to find the allegory, symbolism and intellect within each of his distinctive creations. It was thought for a long time, according to Vasarai and many scholars, that Piero lived alone in an anti-social cocoon with bouts of irritability and chronic ill health. Also, Piero was believed to not be able to tolerate loud noises such as the cries of children or bells ringing, and his gardens were left unattended and his sustenance was composed almost solely of hard-boiled eggs, because of his phobia of fire (including lightning).

Perhaps, to some extent, that is what Piero wanted us to believe? New documents illustrate a different story. Some of Vasari's accounts regarding the biography of Piero are confirmed and other parts are doubted (Waldman, 2014). Waldman recounts the following:

> *"Piero's adoption of a surname later in life, following the practice of many artisans at this period, indicates that he possessed a degree of social self-awareness and even pretension, as well as a sense of kinship, such as Lives never have led us to expect…at least, Piero will never be quite so solitary again."*

Furthermore, new documents (Waldman, 2014) confirm that: Piero owned a significant amount of real estate, he had an assistant painter reside with him later in life, there existed support and help received from his neighbor Giovan Simone throughout his life, and Piero died not from his palsy or his chronic health afflictions, but rather assuredly from the plague. It seems Piero's neighbor Giovan Simone provided food, clothing and financial assistance, for which Simone was later reimbursed posthumously. And it is theorized the Madonna and Child with Saint John, Two Angels, Saint Margaret and Saint Martin, dated around circa 1515-1520, a painting completed much later in Piero's life, may include the strokes of another painter (Waldman, 2014).

The Visitation of Saints Nicholas and Anthony Abbot

The Visitation of Saint Nicholas and Anthony Abbot, circa 1489/1490 is a stunning and brilliantly offered presentation of Piero's story-telling style, pious themes, and Neo-Platonism at work. This painting was commissioned by the Capponi family as an altarpiece for the chapel within the Church Santo Spirito in Florence, Italy. Santo Spirito is *"the church of the Augustinian friars that was the last and purest masterpiece of the Renaissance architect Brunelleschi"* (Online, 2015. Catholic Herald). Piero used oil paint on wood panel. The overall dimensions of the painting are 184.2 cm x 188.6 cm or approximately a somewhat modified square of 6ft. (72.5") x 6ft. (74.25"). A detailed description of each of the sections is provided in images two through ten, as quoted from the National Gallery of Art website, that show written details that would be otherwise potentially missed by the viewer exploring a general view from a discussion post. Forty-four (44) of Piero's paintings are now on display at the National Gallery of Art in Washington, D.C. as part of the exhibition (February 1st, 2015 – May 3rd, 2015) Piero di Cosimo: The Poetry of Painting in Renaissance Florence.

The Visitation of Saint Nicholas and Anthony Abbot (referred to as 'The Visitation') is comprised of a central scene and three other scenes. The style of this composition appears to be influenced by Piero's studies of Flemish art, and the works of Leonardo da Vinci. The central scene meets in the middle of the painting. This scene is composed of three focuses. The central focus is the young Virgin Mary, mother of Jesus Christ, and an older in her late 60's or 70's Saint Elizabeth, mother of John the Baptist. The two women meet together and at the center of the meeting figures, as well as the exact center of the painting, is their clasping of hands. An interesting point is through technical analyses of the painting, small nail holes have been placed around the perimeter and along the central axis. These small nail holes meet upon the union of the clasped hands. According to the Catholic Herald (2015), this convergence is *"a magnificent homage to the dignity of the unborn child"* and acknowledges their pregnancies.

Within the context and focuses of the central scene is *Saint Nicholas seated on the left* and *Saint Anthony Abbot seated on the right* of the two women figures. Saint Nicholas, seated to the left, is identified by the placement of the three gold balls near the base of his garment, symbolizing his act of charity of *"magically"* providing for the three daughters of an impoverished nobleman (Southgate, T. 2002). If you take a closer look and further peer into the hidden meaning of the three gold balls, you can see what appears to be reflections of the interior of the Santo Spirito, according to my research. Saint Anthony, to the right, is identified by the requisite cane and pig. These three focuses within the central scene seem to form a triangle with an apex and base.

The atmospheric perspective in the background frames three other scenes within this composition. In the right background is the *Annunciation*, where Gabriel announces the pregnancy to the Virgin Mary. In the left background, above Saint Nicholas' head is the *Nativity and Adoration of the Shepherds*. And centrally located to the right behind Saint Elizabeth is the Massacre of the Innocents, an illustration of the call to violence by King Herod to kill all infants in the search to kill the baby Jesus.

I believe the *Visitation* tells a story of imperfection and the suffering of humankind, as humankind tries to reconcile the needs of the earthly and spiritual worlds. This composition speaks to serving both the material and spiritual realms. It is a meeting of both through the connections of time, and two female figures clasping their hands together. Both the Virgin Mary and Saint Elizabeth symbolize the convergence of the earthly and spiritual kingdoms. This composition is filled with many meanings and symbols which could be the source of analyses for decades, including the central positioning of the sprig of flower to the monkey scattering along the railing.

However, two major points within the *Visitation* stand out for my brief analysis. The Virgin Mary and Saint Elizabeth met almost 1.5 thousand years before Piero's time. The architecture in the background is that of Florence, which stages the scenes through breaking the boundaries of time and brings the theme current and applicable to the Italian Renaissance. It seems that Piero is stating the moment of the conceptions changed the current moment in Florence, including the direction of the Catholic Church. I think Piero's intellect would have been capable of this kind of insight.

The figure of Saint Anthony Abbot is based upon a Saint Athanasius (circa 296-273), who is considered the founder of organized Christian monasticism. In my thinking, Saint Anthony mirrors Piero's life of mostly solitude, having only two friends for fifteen years (Piero had two friends in his old age, his assistant and neighbor), and both were afflicted with an ailing imperfect human body that were destined to be returned to perfection in the spiritual existence, after their resurrection from death. I feel Saint Anthony could be a symbolic depiction of Piero. Although my research did not turn up this comparison, I would theorize there is merit to this idea, and it should be explored more.

Conclusion

I chose to write this exploratory chapter about Piero and the *Visitation*, because of his constant struggle within himself. His works and life are a disguised, complex matter. Piero appears to me as an autistic-like genius with a hypersensitivity to outside sounds and distractions. But then again, we are left with the conundrum of the unanswered through his artworks, that appear to have manifested themselves as brush strokes of an overachieving complicated genius, while attempting to maintain the salvation of his soul within Catholic rewarding parameters of the day. He brought magic and sacred subjects to life. He mixed content, the real and the imaginative. His unattended ways of his garden, vines and weeds remind me of the progressive transition of a philosophy directed towards nature, the imperfection within nature and humankind, and Neo-platonic perspectives of thinking.

Perhaps he was not a man who lived in abject squalor after all, as Vasari describes Piero? Perhaps Piero was ahead of his time, because he would fit well within the Eco-psychological nature trends of today? Or perhaps he just fooled us all with his compositions, and we always be left reading his art looking for answers?

References

1. Online (2015)
   http://www.blatner.com/adam/consctransf/renaissance/neoplatonism/neoplatonism.html

2. Online (2015)
   http://www.wsj.com/articles/review-of-piero-di-cosimo-the-poetry-of-painting-in-renaissance-florence-at-the-national-gallery-of-art-1424734750

3. Online (2015)
   http://catholicherald.com/stories/Piero-di-Cosimos-Visitation-a-pilgrimage-in-a-painting,28385

4. Online (2015)
   http://www.newadvent.org/cathen/01553d.htm

5. Online (2015)
   http://www.newyorker.com/magazine/2015/02/09/change-artist

6. Online (2015)
   http://www.nga.gov/content/ngaweb/features/piero-di-cosimo/the-visitation.html

7. Online (2015)

- http://www.washingtonpost.com/entertainment/museums/piero-di-cosimo-a-misunderstood-master-at-the-national-gallery-of-art/2015/01/29/ecb016da-a635-11e4-a06b-9df2002b86a0_story.html

8. Southgate, T. (2002)
   The Visitation of St.Nicholas and St.Anthony Abbot. JAMA Network. Dec., 2002. Vol. 288. No.2.

9. Waldman (2014)
   Fact, Fiction, Hearsay: notes on Vasari's Life of Piero di Cosimo. The Art Bulletin.92:1. 171-179.

CHAPTER 6

The Foundations of eCampus Excellence

Khoo Voon Ching
Akamai University

According to Bruton (2007), "Technology can be defined as the process of changing inputs into outputs and the application of knowledge to performance work", that is, theoretical and practical knowledge, skill, and the manufactured article, which can be used to develop products and their production and delivery system. The term "technical" refers to the use of people to improve their surroundings, the application of science, especially to attain industrial and commercial objectives, and the entire body of methods and materials used to achieve such objectives (Bruton, 2007).

Technology management is important to the development and management of online resources, and improvement of efficiency of operations, and may be defined according to Wikipedia:

> *Technology management is a set of management disciplines that enable organizations to manage their technological fundamentals to create competitive advantage. The typical concepts used in technology management are technology strategy (a logic or role of technology in organization), technology forecasting*

(identification of possible relevant technologies for the organization possibly through technology scouting), technology roadmap (mapping technologies to business and market needs), technology project portfolio (a set of projects under development), and technology portfolio (a set of technologies in use). The role of technology management in an organization is to understand the value of certain technologies for the organization. Therefore, a continuous development of technology is valuable as long as value is created for customers and its function in an organization is able to decide when to invest on technology development and when to withdraw (http://en.wikipedia.org/wiki/Technology_management; Cited: 6 Oct 2013).

Technology management can also be defined as the integrated planning, design, optimization, operation, and control of technological products, processes, and services (Thamhain, 2005). It refers to the use of technology by management for the people's advantage, for example, using an e-education system to improve the efficiency of a study process. The other aspect is point-to-point transportation, which has improved by changing the type of vehicle used, from a conventional bicycle to car, motorbike, train, and even airplane, to shorten the time it takes one to reach his/her destination. As for the industry, it improves productivity by replacing the worker with high-technology equipment.

It is important to understand that technology is not only computer and information technology but a wider array of technology such as the manufacturing machine, the transportation vehicle etc (Thamhain, 2005). The main goal of technological management is to direct an event using technology, either with a computer, efficient vehicle, or high-technology equipment, to improve efficiency and thus reducing time and cost, the defining factors of profit margin. Return on investment (ROI) is perhaps one of the most popular measures for determining the efficiency of technology management. ROI involves revenue, cost, and investment. Revenue and cost are the main variables of profit margin in profit theory (Thamhain, 2005).

The principle of management is to reduce costs by improving the efficiency of administration and operations (Kamaluddin et al, 2011). The cost is affected by the efficiency of productivity. The theory of the firm based on the average cost theory holds that cost will only be reduced if the productivity efficiency is improved to produce more output, which is equal to the total cost (includes the fixed and variable costs) divided by the output (Samuelson, 2001). Fixed cost includes the operation, facility, and building costs. For the current research, fixed cost is the daily operational cost of the university, including building and labor costs.

In summary, technology management is a management model that uses technology to improve the efficiency of productivity. In this research, the technology used is the e-campus and the productivity that needs to be measured is the quality of output of the distance learning education. The following section discusses previous studies on distance learning.

Distance learning

Distance learning or distance education is a mode of delivering education and instruction, often on an individual basis, to students who are not physically present in a traditional setting, such as a classroom. Distance learning provides access to learning when the source of information and the learners are separated by time or distance or both. Distance education courses that require on-site presence are referred to as hybrid or blended courses (http://en.wikipedia.org/wiki/distance_ education, cited: 1 Dec 2013). The following are distance education theories that have been proposed.

According to Holmberg (1995), the "basic general assumption is that real learning is primarily an individual activity and is attained only through an internalizing process" (p. 47). Unmistakably, Holmberg focused on the learner and the learner's learning responsibility. Nevertheless, a learner's accountability is not unilateral and finds its full expression in relation to the teacher's contribution to the process of education.

Holmberg called the learner–teacher relationship as a "guided didactic conversation." He presented seven postulates and emphasized the importance of a "personal relation" between learner and teacher. However, this theme is often lost in the midst of the discussion of the current lay views on distance education, where it is represented more as a "delivery system" or a "technology" or in some other similarly misguided way.

The independence of the learner is the conceptual attractor for seminal thinkers in the field, including Wedemeyer (1981), an American theorist. He recognized the independence of the learner and posited that such independence would be afforded to learner by a variety of means and strategies, including anytime and anywhere learning and learner control over the learning process. Wedemeyer also acknowledged the necessity for the learner to take more responsibility for learning, freeing the instructor of the "custodial" duties of teaching. However, the real effect of Wedemeyer's contribution to the theory and practice of distance education is yet to be realized.

For Wedemeyer (1981), distance education is a distinct "nontraditional" type of education. In his book *Learning at the Back Door*, he stated, "As Moore pointed out, learning apart (physically separated) from a teacher by means of communications through print, mechanical, or electronic devices implies quite a different concept of learning from that acquired in school" (p. 111). Thus, he put into motion an essential concept for a revolutionary approach to learning that is only beginning to be noticed by administrators and program planners in higher education, as well as those in government, business, and industry.

Building on Wedemeyer's concept, Moore (1983) introduced "transactional distance," which precisely defines the relationship between the instructor and the learner. According to Moore, "There is now a distance between learner and teacher which is not merely geographic, but educational and psychological as well. It is a distance in the relationship of the two partners in the educational enterprise. Therefore, it is a 'transactional distance'" (p. 155).

Moore's concept of transactional distance is important because it is grounded on the concept of distance in education in a social science framework and not in its usual physical science interpretation. It is a significant paradigm shift of the kind described by Kuhn (1970).

As significant as the individual learner is to distance education, this type of education invariably involves institutional structures. The structure of institutional concepts in distance education is reviewed in the next section.

Peters (1994) recognized the industrialization of education: the use of technology to reach a mass audience. It has been a feature of distance education for several years. In fact, distance education is difficult to imagine without some elements of industrialization. Correspondence education relies on the mass production of instructional materials and involves a division of labor. Therefore, it is an industrial enterprise. As originally conceptualized by the British Open University, the course team is another example of the division of labor in distance education.

Keegan (1993) presented a typology of "distance teaching systems." He classified the organizational structures of institutions involved in the field and presented two general categories, namely, autonomous and mixed institutions. Autonomous institutions, which are free-standing organizations, encompass (a) public and private correspondence schools and (b) distance teaching universities. Mixed institutions encompass (a) independent study divisions of extension colleges (mostly found in the United States and Canada); (b) consultation systems in which students are assigned both to a distant university or college from which they receive their degree and to a nearby "consultation" institution from which they receive instructional services (mostly found in Europe); and (c) integrated systems in which an academic department, supported by administrative staff, provides the same curriculum to both on-campus and remote students (first established in Australia).

The picture of distance education that has emerged thus far in this review is of a complex set of relationships between learners and teachers within various types of industrially structured organizations. The virtual campus is discussed in the following section.

Virtual campus

The author has reviewed previous studies on virtual campus. Virtual teams and organizations have been studied and discussed to define virtuality (Chudoba et al, 2007). One major aspect of virtuality is geographical separation (Shekhar, 2006). For distance education, this means teachers and learners are not geographically co-located but interact at a distance. The author has located research studies about virtual universities dating back to the onset of conventional distance education. Educators were quite familiar with distance education before the concept of the virtual university was introduced. The United Kingdom's Open University is one of the first groups to successfully conduct distance learning programs.

According to Van Dusen (1997), the term "virtual campus" is a metaphor for the electronic teaching, learning, and research environment created by the convergence of powerful new information and instructional technologies. The current education context calls for technology to provide expanded higher education opportunities to a wide spectrum of present and potential clientele (Van Dusen 1997).

A number of academic authors have defined the "virtual campus" as an environment that uses the metaphor of a university, and one that provides users with a range of different tools for learning. A growing number of universities have introduced virtual representations of themselves in the form of virtual campuses for supporting a wide range of educational activities, as considered by Fominykh et al (2008) in their study about the meaning of the virtual campus. Collaborative virtual workshop (CVW) was one of the tools mentioned in their study. CVW was introduced as an innovative resource in the context of a virtual campus. In certain respects, CVW supports collaborative work among instructors and learner's using three-dimensional (3D) educational content, and shares and reuses such content. It combines the features of both virtual campuses and museums to take the advantages of both approaches. (Fominykh et al, 2008)

According to Vygotsky (1978) socializing among students is an essential element for learning, and thus it needs to be maintained within the learning environment. Vygotsky (1978) stated that a shift of concepts has occurred from the well-defined, clear, and 100% online static virtual campus to virtual mobility. Traditional universities have opened their borders, collaborated across institutions, and often internationally, allowing non-traditional students to participate through e-learning. Vygotsky (1978) feels scholars neither has nor yet provided a strict definition of the virtual campus. To him, every campus can become a virtual campus. Most schools show interest in a blended model of classroom-based and virtual. According to Vygotsky (1978), that the virtual campus should be redefined to be applicable to the current educational needs. This author finds this concept highly relevant to this research project.

The virtual campus can also be explored with a focus upon its system for implementation. With this understanding the quest for a single absolute definition of virtual campus can be discarded. Instead, a more improved definition can be valued against the degree of viability, such as in the case of:

- Context (instructed lessons verses self-paced study),
- Target group (the learner new to college and the graduate student),
- Different goals (technical training verses professional training),
- And technology, such as video verses eClassroom dialogue and so on
- And the context may vary, such as between; the learner new to college and the graduate student.

To establish a new meaning of virtual campus, several major factors should be considered. One such implication is that of a paradigm shift from a professor-centered system to a student-centered learning. This shift has particular importance for the teaching profession in the future.

Another factor is a recommitment to creating an ideal learning environment for students and using new technologies to address variances from the traditional style. Additionally, for the college faculties there is a shift from traditional roles and classroom responsibilities to new ones, such as one-on-one mentorship, individualization of learning, instructor as facilitator (Capogrossi, 2002).

According to Barr and Tagg (1995), the transition from lecturer to facilitator does not occur overnight and must be accompanied by institutional and professional commitment to incorporate research findings into professional development activities. Beyond merely providing technical training in the latest (and soon obsolete) technology, professional development activities will need to focus on crucial classroom variables that will ultimately determine the level of productive interaction and intellectual engagement apropos to the individual and group (Barr & Tagg, 1995). Faculty instructors to be effective in the future eClassroom educational environment must a solid understanding of the technology and usefulness of the eClassroom software. Otherwise, in the absence of well-informed instructors, the software alone would be totally non-functional.

Learning in the virtual campus has differences from the traditional residential environment. With time and distance removed as constraints, colleges and universities are empowered to serve a more heterogeneous clientele. This allows for service of more diverse educational backgrounds, locations, and needs. According to Plater (1994):

"These new century students confront us with the possibility that a postsecondary educational system designed to manage enrolment growth by weeding out unprepared or uncommitted students may no longer be appropriate or economically defensible" (Plater 1994 p. 9).

The most obvious difference between learning in the traditional and virtual campus is the manner and extent of interaction. In traditional classrooms, the potential for learner–instructor and learner–learner interactions is high, but instructors have largely ignored this mandate for change and continue to use the lecture mode as the predominant method of instruction. By contrast, technology supports other educational processes in virtual classrooms, such as collaborative learning, heterogeneous groupings, problem-solving, and higher-order thinking skills (Brindley et al, 2008).

Fominykh et al. (2011) found that virtual education environments (virtual worlds) represent real educational institutions based on the metaphor of a university and provide users with different and equally viable learning tools. What is more interesting is the idea of integrating a virtual campus into the context of a virtual city, permitting easy interaction and user understanding within the online environment. This familiar concept reflects close similarities for on-campus students, related to where they live and work, and it extends the possibilities of a virtual campus in supporting learning and socializing in a manner that is already known to them. Fominykh et al. (2011) has provided a set of guidelines for designing a effective virtual campus in a virtual city format. Fominykh (2011) related that the virtual campus is an important concept in the field of education, but a theoretical framework has yet to be generally accepted by researchers and that a contemporary definition should be developed. Bacsich et al. (2010) collated definitions for the theoretical framework of the virtual campus from more than ten European countries. Similar to the work of Stoof et al. (2002), they also reflect upon the boundary approach for virtual campuses, as an aid to support e-learning stakeholders in understanding the virtual campus concept.

Cesarini et al. (2004) argued that virtual campus leverages both the reusability of existing courses while building new ones and the customization that enables the adaption of existing courses to different situations. To achieve course and material content reusability, they developed a model based on metadata. This model enables the storing, classifying, and browsing of didactical materials, making them available for flexible learning paths. A run-time infrastructure was developed that could drive a student along a learning path previously designed by the teacher. A workflow management system manages each student's state of advance, allowing path customization. A set of monitoring tools assists students during their learning activities by providing them with suggestions and feedback to teachers. Isolated and cooperative work sessions, tutored and untutored participation by students, virtual and "real" presence in an extended or restricted study group, and synchronous and asynchronous communications were studied for testing the global system.

Fominykh et al. (2011) focused on one type of educational virtual world, that is, the virtual campus. Specifically, they suggested placing a virtual campus in the context of a virtual city. A virtual campus can be defined as an environment that uses the metaphor of a university and provides users with a range of different tools for learning. A growing number of universities have introduced virtual representations of themselves in the form of virtual campuses to support a wide range of educational activities. However, Vygotsky (1978) argued that socializing is essential for learning and thus needs to be maintained.

Virtual campuses have substantial potential in terms of attracting new students (Fominykh et al., 2008) by providing information through different media, enabling prospective foreign students and other users to learn about the local culture, architecture, and history.

The next section provides an overview of existing virtual campuses and cities, their features, and their current weaknesses. According to Prasolova-Førland et al. (2006), the virtual campus provides users with different sets of possibilities, ranging from web-based systems (e.g., http://vu.org/) to immersive 3D worlds. For example, virtual campuses such as the Nanyang Technological University in Singapore (Prasolova-Førland et al., 2006) are based on blaxxun technology (www.blaxxun.com). Such virtual campuses provide a realistic, photographic resemblance of the corresponding physical campus, with offices and classrooms. Different tools for consultations, lectures, and practical exercises, especially in computer graphics, are also available for students (Prasolova-Førland et al., 2006)

The current most widely used platform is Second Life (SL), although it has certain disadvantages as a learning environment (Helmer, 2007). According to Helmer (2007) over 500 universities and colleges are present in SL, a 3D virtual world opened to the public in 2003. Today, SL is inhabited by millions of "residents" from around the globe. Major universities are part of SL, including California State University, Harvard University, Ohio State University, University of Hertfordshire, and University of Sussex, to mention a few (Fominykh et al., 2009). The presence of institutions working in SL varies broadly, from full-scale, highly realistic campuses to less realistic "digital interpretations" and individual classes taught in common areas. For example, Northern Illinois University supplements both credit and non-credit courses with SL classes in art, computer science, education, and communication (Kelton, 2007). In the virtual campus of Ohio State University, visitors can take several courses, gain access to learning materials, and visit art installation, music centers, and other places. Harvard Law School offered a course in SL called "CyberOne: Law in the Court of Public Opinion" (Jennings & Collins, 2008). Virtual campuses that attempt to create a "familiar" atmosphere for the students are common. These campuses often provide a clear association with the real educational institutions they represent, conveying their "spirit" and atmosphere by different means, including a realistic outlook, informational resources, and contact information of the representatives of the educational institutions, among others (Fominykh et al., 2012)

Fominykh et al. (2008) presented an initial set of requirements for a virtual campus, and it includes the appearance of a virtual campus, which should be as authentic as possible to create a familiar atmosphere and aid navigation. They also suggested the selling of commodities that the students might need. The design of certain places for various educational, social, fun, or other activities could have a limited reality resemblance to serve specific goals in the best possible way, such as auditoriums, buildings representing courses and faculties, and private houses and educational spaces that can be built by the students and teachers within the major structure of the campus/city (Fominykh et al., 2009). In their research they did explained that the exteriors of certain buildings could be scaled down to facilitate the easy mobility of users, whereas the interiors could be expanded to provide more space for activities.

Accordingly to Prasolova-Førland et al. (2010) informational resources should also be an essential part of virtual campus, they argued that the virtual campus is not only a space but also a framework of educational content, learning activities, associated tools, and resources. In this context, Collaborative Virtual Workshop (CVW) is one of the main tools of the virtual campus based on student feedback. Prasolova-Førland et al. (2010) focused on two case studies conducted in a virtual campus of the Norwegian University of Science and Technology (NTNU). The virtual campus was a venue for guest lectures and collaborative 3D educational visualizations and cross-cultural interaction. According to their study, virtual campus should have some realistic buildings to convey the spirit of the NTNU, but at the same time, it should be engaging, user-friendly, and have realistic features/designs necessary for an enhanced and more efficient educational experience. While discussing the proposal of the project gallery/CVW and how it should appear, the students considered support for information sharing and meetings, and a creative and fun atmosphere as important. As some unrealistic designs (e.g., small rooms and auditoriums) were criticized as not being user-friendly, the CVW exterior should preferably resemble an existing university building, and the interior should have a realistic appearance for best possible performance (Prasolova-Førland et al., 2010).

Regarding the structure, Prasolova-Førland et al. (2010) case study also suggested that the overall structure of the NTNU virtual campus should be well-organized and resemble the structure of the physical campus to a certain degree. The structure should have a varying degree of flexibility to allow for modifications from the users while maintaining consistency in the overall structure at the same time. Realistic buildings and places should be used for social activities and as representative areas that hold various informational resources about the university and its life. At the same time, the virtual campus should have workplaces for conducting educational activities. CVW is considered a tool in a virtual campus context with a complex structure, which integrates several places in one framework. The design of CVW is based on previous research and on three suggestions from the participants of the case studies. First, more support should be provided for constructing processes. Second, support should be provided for project presentation and awareness. Third, a library of resources should be provided. Accordingly, CVW will have a virtual workplace equipped with building tutorials and tools. This workplace should also be linked to a library with ready-to-use objects, textures, and scripts, as well as university-related resources (Prasolova-Førland et al., 2010). A virtual stage equipped with corresponding facilities, such as a projection screen, a space to present 3D constructions, and public seats, should provide support for project presentations. This stage should be surrounded by a virtual gallery that can store and exhibit student constructions (e.g., those made in the second case study). Gallery exhibits can be implemented as posters with the capability of extracting any project to the virtual stage.

Prasolova-Førland et al. (2010) also highlighted the role of the NTNU virtual campus in serving as an arena for work and learning in a 3D virtual environment. Various virtual places in the campus should have a number of secondary roles, such as providing support for specific educational or social activities, providing information about the university, and attracting more students.

Chen (2010) identified six major characteristics of virtual university: purpose, mission, tools, organizational models, financing sources, and instructional language. He then selected and compared six virtual university cases from different countries based on the six characteristics. Chen (2010) found that 1) virtual university exhibits national differences in stakeholders and organizational structures, and 2) the choices of tool or platform for virtual university vary between developed and developing countries.

Summary

Technology management is a set of management disciplines that uses the latest technologies to improve the daily work efficiency of humans, including planning, design, optimization, operation, and control of productivity. However, technology management is not only limited to information technology, but it also includes transportation and manufacturing, among others, as long as the management event involves a particular technology. The main goal of technology management is to improve the productivity and ultimately to reduce cost.

Technology management is important in distance learning education because it can improve the efficiency of the conventional distance learning approach. Holmberg (1995) pointed out that a learner or student should be placed at the center. In other words, the study material and the distance learning support staff should be student centric to ensure their successful completion of the program. Therefore, the distance learning support staff can operate in the manner of industrialization in which the economic concept of division of labor can be implemented. Keegan (1993) classified the organizational structure of distance learning institutions into two types, namely, autonomous and mixed institutions. Distance education can be construed as a complex set of relationships between learners and teachers within a framework of various types of industrially structured organization.

The virtual campus approach was implemented to incorporate technology management into the distance learning environment to improve the operational efficiency of the study; in this context, virtual means geographically separated (Shekhar, 2006). Virtual campus is a metaphor for the electronic teaching, learning, and research environment created by the convergence of powerful new information and instructional technologies (Van Dusen & Gerald, 1997), such as CVW. An effective virtual campus should be immersed in the 3D world to simulate the real campus enrollment (Prasolova-Førland et al., 2006). The simulation is necessary to store, classify, and browse didactical study materials to make them available to flexible learning paths. A run-time infrastructure is also needed to drive students along their learning path, and monitoring tools are required to assist them during their learning activities by providing suggestions to the students and feedback to teachers. According to Vygotsky (1978), aside from the learning features, the socializing features are also essential for learning, which should be maintained.

Prasolova-Førland et al. (2010) proposed that a virtual campus should not only have workplaces to conduct educational activities but also have supporting features, such as a library, a virtual gallery to store students' projects, and a place for presentations (virtual stage), which are equipped with corresponding facilities such as a projection screen.

http://www.akamai-ecampus.com/ecampus.htm

CHAPTER 7

Teaching And Learning For Working Adult Students (WASs)

Prof. Dr. Lee Karling, PhD
Akamai University

Overview

Changing demographics, technologies and dynamism of today's globalized world has led to a shift in the teaching and learning methodologies in institutions of higher learning. Such a shift has also led to more working adults returning to school or to higher education institutions (HEIs) to pursue an additional qualification or enhance on the existing skills in order to meet the upcoming challenges of the future work place. These working adult students (WASs) are classified as non-traditional students, and although many HEIs do not see the importance of understanding and catering to their learning needs, progressive HEIs have been increasingly focused on bringing in these WASs to strengthen the HEIs as global student enrollment drops.

Rationale for understanding teaching and learning for working adult students (WASs)

The number non-traditional students enrolling in various courses has been on increasing steadily after the mid 2000 (Newbold, Mehta & Forbus, 2010). These students are technically characterized as being over 25 years of age, working full time, and often having dependents to support (Gale, 2011), although the actual definition may differ slightly as provided further into the chapter. Many of these non-traditional students return to attend college or universities on a part time basis as they are working full time. Between 1996 and 2006, the number of non-traditional undergraduate college students in the United States (US) increased from 30% to 50% (Bye, Pushkar, & Conway, 2007). The National Center for Education reported that 73% of all students have some characteristics of the non-traditional student (Compton, Cox, & Laanan, 2006). These WASs bring with forth desires and needs that are different from the traditional counterparts while on campus (Newbold, Mehta & Forbus, 2009). The shifting campus population toward non-traditional students necessitates that colleges and universities understand and adapt to these changing student needs in order to improve the overall student satisfaction and engagement for a holistic education experience as these WASs embark on as journey to acquire a degree or qualification.

Many universities globally are increasingly paying attention to this group of non-traditional student by developing a framework for assessing the university's ability and capacity to meet the needs of the WASs or non-traditional students and to prepare the university to cater to the needs and requirements of these non-traditional students. Unfortunately, many traditional universities are reluctant to acknowledge that there are differences between the traditional and non-traditional students and has thus, made decisions to maintain the pedagogic teaching and learning methodologies to cater to these non-traditional students. This is not a wise move as the wake of returning WASs or non-traditional students to colleges or universities is taking HEIs by storm and a failure to address the non-traditional students' teaching and learning styles will lead to a loss for the HEIs in the near future.

It is now pertinent for universities to re-examine the programs and methods for informing and working with these WASs in order to facilitate learning and to ensure that the needs and requirements of the WASs or non-traditional students is catered for to ensure academic success.

Challenges of WASs

Choosing to return to school, college or university can be a life-changing decision, whether it has been one year since graduation or a decade since one has sat in the classroom. There are significant challenges posed to working adults who decide to pursue further education after having worked for a few years. The good news is that these challenges are recognize by many HEIs globally, and non-traditional educational opportunities are becoming more widely available across the nations. School, colleges, and universities are increasing being made aware of the need to make learning accessible to everyone and are, consequently, offering more flexible options for the non-traditional students to pursue long-kept education dreams. Many HEIs now offer evening and weekend classes, as well as online or distance education options. There are also HEIs that offers cross-border education for the WASs who would like to acquire a global mindset and to learn and travel at the same time. Bursaries and grants serve as lure to the WASs or non-traditional student to assist with the costs of tuition and books. For example, in Malaysia, the government has instituted an initiative known as MyBrain15 that allowed WASs to pursue postgraduate education on a part-time basis via a subsidy or RM10, 000 per WAS. Although many may say that the subsidy does not constitute a huge sum, the additional subsidy is definitely a cost saving for many WASs as the money saved is able to be used by the WAS or non-traditional student for the family. As more working adults return to college or university, more services and resources become available to assist with this challenging but worthwhile endeavor.

Fundamentally, there are three (3) major challenges that WASs face commonly as follows (Caschera, 2015):

1. *Accessibility*

   A major challenge facing WASs is accessibility to classes. Many a times, getting to class is the biggest challenge! This is because many WASs have extensive time commitments such as meetings at the work place, sudden workload to shoulder, family engagement and commitment, and other commitments. Regardless of the nature of the commitment imposed on the WASs, it can lead to difficulty of succeeding at the college or university or even a reluctance to return to study at colleges or universities. This could impede the growth of the nation as the higher education the populace, the more likely the country will grow and prosper.

2. *Cost*

   The rising cost of education can be challenging for everyone, regardless of status. Tuition fees, books, supplies — it all adds up. For the WAS or non-traditional student, there may be added daycare costs or mortgage payments and the cost of pursuing an education as a WASs can thus become very prohibitive. In the case of Malaysia, there is subsidy for tuition fee as well as tax exemptions, the overall cost of education is still extensive, and WASs would often need to consider carefully before making the investment in education for personal growth and advancement.

3. *Balancing between life and study responsibilities*

   As any postsecondary student can attest, going to college or university is a huge time commitment. The WAS or non-traditional student needs to attend class as well as spend time preparing for class and complete essays, assignments and other homework or assessments. The time needed for study is already challenging for traditional students, whereupon, for WASs who are returning to study at HEIs, they face additional demands from employers and family members. This could cause the WAS or non-traditional student to experience higher level of stress as the WAS attempts to juggle all the different priorities, including own study.

Many of these WASs are pursuing the college or university education while still working full time, and many still have families and family obligations. This means less time is available for college or university-related activities. These additional responsibilities can lead to stress and frustration for the WASs and thus colleges and universities need to keep this in view when designing programs or modules for the WASs

Cercone (2008) also stipulated that WASs are different from traditional students as many have responsibilities (for example: family and work) and other situations (for example: mobility, children care, domestic violence and the need to get an income) that may interfere in the learning process. Although many of these WASs enter into educational programs voluntarily and will often adapt the classes to work around family, work, and other responsibilities, it is still a difficult balancing act that WASs find challenging.

Definition and characteristics of WASs

Technically, a 24-year-old who is pursuing university studies, according to the law is an adult, and is consider as a young person from the pedagogic point of view as long as the 24-year-old has never left the educational system. University students, although legally considered adults, in the collective imaginary are young people, and thus, for the purpose of this chapter, will not classify as a working adult student (WAS). A university student is pedagogically an adult only IF the person had gone back into the education system after having left it before. This is the case of many students of distance universities. Two examples:

- A 17-year-old person, who is not an adult according to the law, can enroll into the university, and they actually are, to adult

educational centers. This means that a person is considered an adult for education purposes even when they are not legally such.
- Being an adult, for a pedagogue who has to deal with life processes and developments; it is not possible to have it defined based on the age or biological factors; it also has cultural, economic, and historical implications as well that have to take into account (Fernández et al., 2009).

The WASs is describe as one who has already acquired a complexity of life experiences, and who is self-motivated and independent in decision-making when faced with different situations and needs. Among the needs of the WASs is the need for an authentic ability to learn and to cultivate a specific focal area of interest to ensure that the WASs have life-long learning.

According to Pappas (2013), WASs display eight (8) common traits concerning learning. These are as follows:

1. Self-direction
Generally, working adult learners feel the need to take responsibility for own lives and decisions and this is why it is important to have control over the learning for the WASs. Therefore, self-assessment, a peer relationship with the instructor, multiple options and initial, yet subtle support are all imperative to provide support for the WASs self-learning.

2. Practical and results-oriented
Adult learners are usually practical, resent theory, need information that has immediate application to the work or professional needs, and prefer practical knowledge that will improve skills, facilitate work and boost confidence vis-à-vis extensive theoretical discourses. This is why it is important to create a course that will allow the facilitator to cater to individual needs and have a more utilitarian content.

3. Less open-minded and therefore more resistant to change.

Maturity and profound life experiences usually lead to rigidity, which is the enemy of learning. Thus, instructional designers need to provide the "why" behind the change, new concepts that can be linked to already established ones, and promote the need to explore. This will help the WASs to leverage on past experiences to absorb the new knowledge learnt

4. Slower learning, yet more integrative knowledge
Aging does affect learning, and thus a WAS tended to learn slower than the traditional student. However, the depth of learning tends to increase over time, navigating knowledge and skills to unprecedented personal levels. Therefore, it is imperative for the facilitator to help the WASs to internalize and integrate the new knowledge learnt once learning had taken place. This will ensure permanence for the WASs.

5. Use personal experience as a resource
WASs have lived longer, seen and done more, and thus have the tendency to link past experiences to new theories, concepts and practices and to validate new concepts based on prior learning. It is thus crucial to organize a class with WASs or non-traditional students that share similar life experience level in order to encourage discussions and sharing. This will then create a learning community that consists of people that can profoundly interact at a deeper professional level.

6. Motivation
Learning in adulthood is usually voluntary, as it is often a personal choice to attend college or university after being away from the education system for some time in order to improve job skills and achieve professional growth. This motivation is the driving force behind learning and this is why it is crucial to tap into a learner's intrinsic impetus with the right thought-provoking material that will question conventional wisdom and stimulate the mind to think at different planes

7. Multi-level responsibilities

    Fundamentally, WASs have a lot to juggle: family, friends, work, and the need for personal quality time. This is why it is more difficult for an adult to make room for learning. Therefore, the WAS or non-traditional student needs to learn how to prioritize if he or she wishes to succeed in the learning. If the WAS life is too demanding, then, the learning outcomes will be compromised. With the above constrain in mind, an instructional designer needs to create a flexible program, accommodate busy schedules, and accept the fact that personal obligations might obstruct the learning process. At times, it is necessary to adopt relevant technologies to provide the needed flexibility to facilitate the learning of WAS or non-traditional student.

8. High expectations

    WASs often have high expectations, and expect to learn things that will be useful to their work, have immediate results, and thus, is likely to seek for a course that will be worth working on and not be a waste of time or money for the WASs. It is important thus, to create a course or program that will be able to leverage on the WAS or non-traditional student's inherent advantages in order to meet the individual needs of the WAS as well as to address all the learning challenges faced.

Therefore, it can be surmised that working adult students (WASs) are self- motivated and self-directed to learn but, have to learn to juggle the pressures of work, family, friends, and other obligations and commitment in order to have a fruitful learning experience. Apart from that, it is imperative to highlight that WASs are more demanding and have higher expectations, and prefer to learn things in a pragmatic manner instead to discoursing about theories, concepts, and models. By understanding the characteristics of the WASs, colleges and universities will be better able to design instructional design and delivery strategies that cater to the needs, characteristics and desires of the WASs.

Apart from the above, it is of value to have an understanding of the differences between the WAS and the traditional student. The table below provides a summation of the traits, profiles, and characteristics of both the traditional students and the non-traditional students (WASs):

Table 1. Similarities and Differences between traditional students and WASs

Feature	Similarities	Differences
Attitude	- completing the course of study is important and will have an impact on the future benefits to be reap	- Traditional students take for granted that the instructor is right (the sage on the stage); WAS questions, challenges and may even voice a differing opinion based on experience.
Prior Knowledge	- in general, both WA and traditional students have a high school education on which to build upon for the higher education level study	- WASs have more extensive knowledge of work (that is, work-related experience) than traditional students, which they bring into the course - WASs may have better communication skills (having extensive practice from the work environment) than traditional students, which allow them to engage better with the course content and the instructor - although both WASs and traditional students have been a high school student, easy access to that knowledge may be more difficult for WASs because it may have been years since WASs have had to use this knowledge (e.g., a WAS may have more difficulty retrieving math skills for completing a course in statistics).

Needs	- affirmation (as a competent learner) - respect	- WASs and traditional students may have different motivations for obtaining the degree (job advancement vs. just getting a first job, pay raise, status, etc.) - quick degree completion (WASs may need to complete in time to apply for upcoming opportunity for promotion; whereas traditional students may have a more relaxed attitude about completion because pre-degree years are for partying . . . besides, parents are paying so why rush) - traditional students need more guidance in general (e.g., developing good study habits, knowing what is relevant, how to apply knowledge, practical problem-solving, etc.), whereas WASs are more focused and conscientious as many are paying for their study
Expectations	- will gain new knowledge - that effort expended in studies will pay off with a degree at the end of the journey	- WASs want knowledge and skills which can immediately be used in their job or for advancement; traditional students acquire knowledge and skills for future application - WASs have a better idea of what knowledge and skills they want to get out of the course (to help them do their job or advance in their career) – more likely to be active learners - traditional students are more pliable and accepting of being told what to learn, hence, are more likely to be passive learners

Source: adapted from Adult Learning (2014); Booth and Schwartz (2012); Pappas (2013)

Andragogy VS Pedagogy

Knowles (1988) proposed the Andragogic framework for the teaching and learning of the WASs, whereby the six principles of adult learning is as follows:

- Adults are internally motivated and self-directed
- Adults bring life experiences and knowledge to learning experiences
- Adults are goal oriented
- Adults are relevancy oriented
- Adults are practical
- Adult learners like to be respected

As a whole, it can said that the Pedagogist prepares for the "afterwards", while the Andragogist prepares for "today", and even at times the "tomorrow"; that is to say, to attain immediate personal, intellectual, and economic goals for promotions and to internalize the knowledge learnt for use in subsequent career progression.

Motivation is different for the young, traditional student as compared to the WAS. Consequently, the methodologies adopted for teaching and learning needs to differ. However, although the focus of this chapter is on approaching the way in which Andragogy sees the working adult student, it is important to bear in mind that Pedagogy also provides help in the analysis of this kind of student, albeit in a different manner from that of the traditional student.

Although Andragogy has been widely debated by scholars who noted the situational variables that influence the degree to which working adults exhibit these characteristics, the Andragogy framework is one of the most enduring and widely cited theories of adult learning (Merriam, 2001). Other adult learning theories center on self-directed learning (SDL), a key assumption of andragogy that posited that educational goals within formal education could be supported by using teaching methods and assignments designed to increase learner control of the learning process relative to that of instructors (Candy, 1991). On the other hand, self-directed learning can also be situational whereby the manifestation can be at different levels among traditional students of various ages as different learning environments could lead to such manifestations.

In the past twenty years, transformative learning (TL) has become one of the most prominent and debated theories in adult learning research, with the version of TL proposed by Mezirow (2000) receiving perhaps the greatest attention. Mezirow and others view transformational learning as involving fundamental transformation of the adults' core frames of reference, often in response to disorienting dilemmas—situations that challenge adults' previous ways of thinking about the world and prompt them to reflect critically on previously held assumptions. While much of the research on transformational learned has focused on TL that occurred both in higher education and naturally as an outgrowth of adult life situations, some have also proposed that educators can help stimulate transformative learning by using teaching methods that foster critical reflection (Cranton, 1994).

Despite all the different adult learning theories that are prevalent in today's HEIs learning environment, the debate is still ongoing as there has not been any concrete conclusion.

Towards the end of the twentieth century, there was a body of research that suggested that adults learn differently from children and that "Andragogy" was a better term for this process than "Pedagogy". The key difference between adults and children is that adults are motivated to learn in a very different manner as compared to the children. Although the arguments no longer seem quite so clear, the line described by Knowles (Knowles et al., 2005) was that adult learners differ from child learners in six respects:

(1.) The need to know (Why do I need to know this?)
(2.) The learners' self-concept (I am responsible for my own decisions)
(3.) The role of the learners' experiences (I have experiences that I value, and you should respect)

(4.) Readiness to learn (I need to learn because my circumstances are changing)
(5.) Orientation to learning (Learning will help me deal with the situation in which I find myself)
(6.) Motivation (I learn because I want to)

These observations, when linked and associated with Kolb's experiential learning model (Kolb 1984) as shown in Figure 1 have allowed the consideration of learning and teaching strategies that are deemed to be appropriate for adult learners. In Kolb's scheme, the learner has a concrete experience, upon which the WASs will reflect, and then through the reflection, the WASs are able to formulate abstract concepts, and make appropriate generalizations. Once the validation of the generalization is completed, the WASs will then consolidate the learning and understanding by testing the implications of the knowledge in new situations, which is often the work place. This then provides the WASs with a concrete experience, and the cycle continues.

Therefore, the conclusion is that the WAS learn more pragmatically than the traditional student, whereby concrete experience is critical for WASs as compared to the traditional students. The following is a table to illustrate the key differences between Andragogy and Pedagogy as the debate continues on how working adult learners at HEIs learn.

Table 2. Differences between Andragogy and Pedagogy

Key Factors	Andragogy	Pedagogy
Learner characteristics	Self-directed learner who is focused and motivated. Self-evaluation of learning is common as the learner is responsible for own learning	Dependent learner that needs constant guidance and instructions. Evaluation is often carried out by the teacher whereby the teacher is also responsible for the learning

Learner's experiences	The learner brings in work and life experiences that serve as shared resources for tapping into by other WAS learners. Diversity of experiences lead to richness in learning that are shared to promote and strengthen self-identity	The learner has minimum or no work experiences to be shared and relies on the instructor's experiences to facilitate learning
Readiness to learn	Self-motivated and eager to learn as WAS is usually self-funded Assesses gaps to strengthen learning	Traditional students are told what to learn, when to learn it, and how the content is learnt.
Approach to learning	Subject matter must be relevant and useful to the learner The purpose of learning is to help solve a problem, perform a task or to support decision making Learning has to be organized around work or life situations and not in accordance to the subject matter sequence	To learn about the prescribed subject matter and to learn the content in a systematic, structured and sequential manner
Motivation to learn	Internally motivated: focused on enhancing self-esteem, better quality of life, recognition, self-confidence and self-actualization	Usually motivated by external forces such as parents and society Competes for grades and often fears the consequences of failure

Source: adapted from Adult Learning (2014); Herbold (2011); and Taylor and Hamdy (2013)

Complicating the ongoing debate between Andragogy and Pedagogy is a new terminology that focuses on WAS known as "Heutagogy"!

So, what exactly is "Heutagogy"?

Heutagogy refers to a system of self-determined learning aimed at challenging ideas about teaching and learning that still prevail in teacher-centered learning (Hase & Kenyon, 2000) and the need for "knowledge sharing" rather than "knowledge hoarding" which is inherent in the teacher-centered teaching and learning model. However, it is not totally unlike the student-centered teaching and learning whereby the focus is on facilitating students' learning rather than being the "teacher" that instructs, and insist on the students' learning (teacher-centered model). Accordingly, Heutagogy is able to empower the learners to acquire the needed skills for subsequent lifelong learning (Blaschke, 2012). The table below provides an overview of the key differences between Andragogy and Heutagogy.

Table 3. Comparison between Andragogy and Heutagogy

Andragogy (Self-directed)	Heutagogy (Self-determined)
Single loop learning that focuses on the problem, actions taken and the outcomes	Double loop learning that integrates beliefs, values and actions with problem and outcomes
Develops competencies	Strengthens capacity
Linear learning approach that relates to work and life	Non-linear learning approach – multi-facet and multi-dimensional
Still need an instructor to facilitate	Self-determined – what to learn, when to learn, how to learn, where to learn
Self-directed and motivated to learn the required content	Focuses on how to learn as well as how to unlearn and re-learn when needed

Source: adapted from Blaschke (2012); Hase and Kenyon (2000); McKeown (2013)

In conclusion, it is interesting to note the development of adult learning models and framework as more and more WASs return to colleges and universities to pursue the eluded educational dreams. Consequently, for the HEIs, there is much more to learn, adopt, absorb, and assess before the HEIs could truly appreciate and understand the WASs within the HEIs learning environment. Future researches could focus on the WAS from the perspective of andragogy as well as heutagogy as these concepts differ from the traditional pedagogy methodologies.

Designing Programs for the WASs

For the WASs, the multiple roles and commitments increased the likelihood that the WASs will actively seek out degree and certificate programs that can provide time flexibility and appropriate locations to support course completion and for access to critical student services, such as the library. In recent decades, a number of HEIs in the United States (US) have started to design programs around the needs of the WASs such as the Empire State University, Fielding Institute, Regis University, and, more recently, the University of Phoenix and many other institutions in the for-profit sector. As the demand for higher education continues to grow globally amongst the WASs, universities and colleges will need to adapt to the shift in teaching and learning technologies and methodologies to cater to the non-traditional students. The design of programs for the WAS cannot be the same as for the traditional students are the characteristics, learning preferences and focus differs.

The innovative student support and learning strategies described in this chapter is not evident in traditional university programs. Therefore, there is a need for HEIs to use these information to adapt the existing programs to cater to the WAS or non-traditional student accordingly. One example of this type of program is Empire State's faculty mentor model, which allows students to develop highly individualized programs of study. Other innovative adult learning practices—such as distance learning, accelerated course formats, and prior learning assessment—were previously uncommon in mainstream institutions or departments, but are increasingly commonplace today in traditional universities that range from small liberal arts institutions to large comprehensive and doctoral institutions (Ross-Gordon, 2011).

Distance Education

NCES reported in 2008 that at least two-thirds of two-year and four-year Title IV degree-granting institutions offered online courses, blended/hybrid courses, or courses offered in other distance education formats for college-level credit (Parsad & Lewis, 2008). In the case of Malaysia, a public university has already been running the distance education program for WASs since the early 2000, and the response have been tremendous as many WASs who earlier had no opportunity to continue with higher education, now has the chance to fulfill the education dream. However, during the early days, without the advancement of technology, only videos, uploaded materials on the university's website, and teleconferencing were the sources of interactions between the facilitator and the WASs. Despite the technologically challenged constrained of those early days, many WASs throughout Malaysia benefitted and many moved on to become key personnel within the organization that they worked in.

Prior Learning Assessment

A 2006 study by the Council on Adult Experiential Learning (CAEL) on the use of assessment of prior college-level learning as a means of acquiring college credit found that 87 percent of responding HEIs accepted College-Level Examination Program (CLEP) exams, whereupon another 84 percent accepted the Advanced Placement credits, with 70 percent accepting credit for corporate or military training (evaluated by the American Council on Education), and 66 percent made provisions for faculty evaluation of student portfolios demonstrating prior college level learning (Klein-Collins & Hein 2009).

However, generally, a more structured form of PLA is recommended to ensure that there is consistency and standardization across the board and to ascertain that no particular WAS has been disadvantaged.

A more recent CAEL report of Prior Learning Assessment and Adult Student Outcomes (Klein-Collins, 2010), addressed faculty concerns about adult students getting "credit for life experience" by focusing on a study conducted by CAEL on student outcomes. Based on over 62,000 academic records of adult students from a geographically diverse HEIs sample from forty-six percent of public HEIs, the study showed that 50 percent private of non-profit institutions and 4 percent of for-profit institutions describe several positive outcomes for students who earned credit through prior learning assessment, when compared with students who did not make use of PLA.

Although the above report provided the information that WASs with PLA performed better academically, there is a need for more in-depth study and research on this area to ensure that PLA recognition of work-life experiences do contribute to effective WASs learning at the HEIs as such a research would definitely benefit the HEIs community in general, and aspiring WASs specifically!

Accelerated Course Formats

Courses, certificates, and degrees designed to be completed in a shorter period, and in which either the course duration or contact hours may be modified are learning formats that tend to be more responsive to adult learners' lives (Wlodkowski, 2003). Although these intensive learning experiences are sometimes criticized as formats that prioritize convenience over rigor and sacrifice breadth and depth, a number of studies indicated that adult learning in accelerated courses is comparable to or better than that of younger students enrolled in conventional courses. The criticism on such formats for WASs is often base on the traditional students programs' mindset, and thus, many are still not receptive of the newer form of programs that catered specifically to WASs. In Lee (2013), a research conducted on cross-border bi-lingual WASs education indicated that the accelerated course format with interspersed residential periods supported by online learning not only helped the WASs within the ASEAN and Asian region to obtain a desired qualification, but had also contributed effectively to the career advancement of the WAS upon completion of the program. The accelerated course format fundamentally does not lack the depth and breathe inherent in traditional college or university programs offered to the traditional students. In fact, in many circumstances, the accelerated course formats supported by online learning management systems (LMS) had provided more insights and depth to the WASs to allow integrative and transformative learning to occur simultaneously. Furthermore, the adoption of online LMS meets the needs of the WAS as the LMS platform encourages collaboration, discussions, sharing of experiences that facilitates the scaffolding of knowledge for the WAS. This makes the content more relevant and useful for the WAS, thereby improving the motivation to learn as well as the study success of the WAS or non-traditional student.

Teaching and Learning Strategies for the WASs

Monts (2000) found that faculty tended to have a more positive perception of the WASs as compared to the traditional students, especially in recent years with the enrolment of the Gen Y traditional students who were viewed as lazy and unmotivated (Lee, 2011) whereas the WASs were seen as motivated, independent learners and possess strong self-direction (Monts, 2000).

Teaching Strategies for WASs

As WASs are generally motivated, independent, self-directed learners, the teacher served more like a facilitator to facilitate the WASs learning, as opposed to being an instructor that imparts knowledge. Therefore, according to Strang (2014), the following are a few teaching strategies that had been extracted from Davis (2012) for helping teachers in HEIs understand the strategies and to determine the most appropriate strategies to adopt when facilitating the WASs learning:

- *Use the WAS work and life experiences and knowledge as a basis from which to teach.* Knowledge and information shared with the WASs becomes more relevant to the adult learner if it relates to either general or specific life experiences. Furthermore, the more matured WASs' accumulated knowledge can be tapped into to lend credence to the WAS career goals and to show the link between the learning and the WASs' career aspirations. This will help to drive the learning in WASs. It is also important to incorporate the adult learner's valuable practical experience and knowledge into each lesson to illustrate the relevance of the topic to the work and other experiences during discussions
- *Shows a WAS how the class will help them attain their goals.*
Generally, WASs appreciate a class directed toward helping the WASs achieve career or life goals—in this case, the college or university degree or qualification. By illustrating how the information in the class leads the WASs in the desired direction, the adult learners will be more cognizance on how the program or course will benefit in the long term.
- *Makes all course and text material practical and relevant to the WAS*
WASs need to relate the course information directly to the work place and careers; therefore, all course material must focus on the WAS work and career. For WASs, information must carry very practical and applicable purpose and the facilitator is required to communicate to the WASs exactly how the material and information will be useful on the job. For examples, exercises, metaphors, and analogies shared and integrated into relevant theories need to be career relevant, familiar, and timely.
- *Shows WAS the respect they deserve.*
WAS possesses a wealth of experiences and tacit knowledge gained from the work place, and thus, such knowledge should be honored and respected. Be courteous toward WAS by treating the WAS as equals and to allow for the voicing of opinions without judgment or censorship.
- *Adjusts teaching speed to meet the needs of the WAS*

As WAS learn differently from younger students, be conscious of the rate at which the facilitator presents the material or content. Be careful not to offer too much information too fast and to constantly check and regulate the flow of information accordingly. In a mixed class where the presence of traditional students is evident, pace the delivery accordingly and provide room for the WASs to ponder, reflect, relate, and internalize the materials delivered

- *Motivate WAS to learn new information.*
  Through such techniques as positive reinforcement, motivate adult learners to learn and retain new information as a means to recognize the relevance of information to future careers and achieve their goals. Relate how the new information is able to strengthen the WASs future career direction and progression and the WASs will be motivated to remain in the education system and to continuously absorb and learn new knowledge and information.

Doherty (2012) on the other hand, provided more insights into how to further engage and motivate the WASs to learn more effectively via the tips provided:

Treat them like the adults they are.

WAS or non-traditional student is often more sophisticated and experienced than the younger traditional counterparts and thus, would benefit from realistic examples of skills that can use in "real life." Fundamentally, WASs enjoyed the group discussions that allowed for brainstorming and sharing of experiences and ideas based on a theory proposed. Thus, facilitators must be able to draw out the work and life experiences of the WASs to further engage the WAS in learning. WASs dislike it when facilitators "talk down" to them as though the adult learners are young, fresh-faced juniors. Facilitators need to be more discussive and adopt an open mind when working with WASs

Be aware that their classroom skills may be "rusty."

To a certain extent, stepping into a classroom after 20 or 30 years can be disconcerting and "Scary" for some WASs. The facilitator needs to remind the WAS of basic rules and etiquette required in a classroom setting, such as raising a hand to ask a question or listening to others' views before sharing as the WAS is used to work place habits that may differ from classrooms.

At the same time, it is important to re-assure the WASs that as the facilitator, the role is to facilitate and not be judgmental of life experiences or perspectives, and the WAS should not be evaluated solely on the mastery of the content in accordance to academic guidelines. Be generous when it comes to formatting issues such as APA writing guidelines, and allow leeway for the WAS to make mistakes at the beginning as he or she adapts to the academic learning environment. Being too "academic" in insisting on formats and style could hamper the WASs' learning. It will be more effective if the facilitator is able to gauge the WASs "audience" during the first class in order to ascertain the level of "academic" standard required. For example, when I work with group of entrepreneurs, I would normally be more relaxed on the formatting and APA guidelines although specific academic writing principles still needs to be maintain.

Consider and acknowledge the technology gap.

For some of the more matured WASs, technology could be a challenge when compared with those 18 or even 30 year olds. Assess each WAS's level of proficiency as it relates to class requirements and compensate. If necessary, the facilitator needs to be patient and to "teach" the more matured WASs on how to navigate through the technologies. For examples, many matured WASs find it difficult to understand how to access the learning management system (LMS) such as, Blackboard, and thus, the facilitator could spend time to support the WASs to overcome the fear of technologies and to work on improving the grasp of today's many disruptive technologies. On the other hand, the more matured WASs are better able to concentrate on complex material without feeling "withdrawal" from a technology device as compared to the younger WASs or the traditional students. My experience working with WASs indicated that even for some of the younger WASs, when it comes to the LMS, there is still some resistance as the WASs are unfamiliar with the system. Therefore, it is prudent for facilitators to help the WASs to adjust to the LMS and to obtain maximum benefit from the LMS to enhance learning.

Be efficient with lessons and activities.

It is important that facilitators understand that WASs do not like to waste time, and thus, it is imperative that the lesson flows appropriately and delivers the required content within the stipulated time or lesson. The facilitator needs to adopt an approach of "Strict Flexibility" to factor in the WASs commitment to work, family, and other obligations. Build in safety nets that allow a limited number of late assignments to maintain flexibility, accountability and expectations of excellent work. On the other hand, WASs or non-traditional students often work hard to meet the dateline, but will always appreciate extension where necessary or required.

Be creative:

Use the unique vibe or personality of each class to teach the lesson and choose activities that engage, and even entertain to some degree. Pair highly motivated students with those less skilled on projects to create peer encouragement and mentoring. Inject games and fun sharing into the session to keep WASs motivated, excited, and eager to continue learning despite all the work and life pressures!

Learning Strategies for WASs

As WASs are independent, self-directed learners, it is important that the WASs acquire the necessary skills for learning effectively when enrolled in a HEI. The following are some suggestions for WASs to learn more effectively:

Be proactive in planning, mapping out the learning, and reviewing and evaluating the education goals consistently to ensure alignment

Discard preconceived notions about the disadvantages of being back to "school" and strive to be free to absorb the learning experience offered. This will enrich the WASs' life *Choose subjects and courses* that are most relevant to the WAS's job or profession or personal life that are offered within the program. This will help to sustain the interest and keep the WASs motivated

Apart from the above strategies for the WASs to adopt for effective HEI learning, the following pointers are also useful to ease the WASs back into the education system:

1. *Write out the career and educational goals and expected time commitments*
   It is important for WASs to stay focused, to know the direction to take and thus, WASs need to set clear career and education goals, and to relate these goals with each other in order to know the commitment required in achieving these goals.
2. *Establish a good rapport with the instructors or facilitators of the courses undertaken*
   This will be helpful in negotiating optional learning projects that have more relevance to the WASs' specific situation and goals. Furthermore, when there are work or family pressures and constrains, having a good rapport with the instructors or facilitators will better allow the WASs to negotiate for extension of dateline and other support.
3. *Develop an awareness of the learning styles*
   When the WASs is able to understand learning styles better, it will help the WASs to learn in the most productive manner and to alert the WASs as to the study areas where support or help is required to succeed or excel (for example: speaking, writing, math, testing, etc.)

A Learning Styles Inventory was developed by Honey and Mumford (2000) that focuses on the WAS. The Inventory is very useful for WASs to understand the personal learning style and to seek to individualize the learning to match the learning style preferences. For the facilitators, it is also very useful to know the learning styles of each of the WASs in the class (virtual or physical classroom) in order to design materials that could cater to all the different styles. However, as learning technologies evolved, the WAS learning styles will also change. Younger WAS prefers to learn in a mobile manner instead of being confine to a physical classroom. By using a mobile phone, a WAS can learn, collaborate, share experiences with like-minded individuals across the world while earning a much needed qualification.

Consequently, for the WASs, the teaching and learning strategies need to focus on the following areas in order to cater to the needs of these adult learners:

- Be adaptable and flexibility to suit the WASs audience and the needs of the adult learners
- Allow WASs to collaborate and work with each other via the adoption of self-organized teams or groups to facilitate sharing, brainstorming and collaborative learning
- To design the curricula in a manner that WASs could draw upon the work and life experiences to be integrated into the theories, concepts and models taught
- Focused and emphasized on the relevance of subject matter taught and the WASs career and educational goals and aspirations
- Assist the WASs to transform from working adult to students, and back to working adult with enhanced knowledge, skills, capability, and competencies
- Provide the WASs with the opportunity to interact and network amongst themselves as well as with other corporate personalities to expand portfolio and career advancement opportunities

Strategies for HEIs to Engage with WASs

Based on the Adult Learning Focused Institute's principles, a set of principles to better cater to the needs of the WAS is as below (Klein-Collins, 2011):

Outreach: The HEI conducts its outreach to adult learners by overcoming barriers of time, place, and tradition in order to create lifelong access to educational opportunities. Outreach initiatives could take many forms and could involve minimal or extensive investments in technologies or physical structures or to collaborate with specific partners for the outsourcing of outreach initiatives and services to support the WAS.

Life and Career Planning: The HEIs need to address the adult learners' life and career goals before or at the onset of enrolment in order to assess and align its capacities to help WASs learners reach established learning and career goals. This is because the purpose of the WASs to embark on studies at HEIs was to pursue specific career goals, and thus, HEIs could support the WASs accordingly to help WASs realize the potential and goals.

Financing: The HEI needs to promote choice using an array of payment options for WASs learners in order to expand equity and financial flexibility. Soft loans, if possible can be arrange via collaborations with financial institutions would greatly support and assist the WASs in financing HEI education. For Malaysians, WASs are able to request to withdraw a specified amount of money from the Employee Provident Fund to finance HEI education, and this has helped to encourage many WASs in Malaysia to pursue higher education after working for a few years.

Assessment of Learning Outcomes: The HEI is required to define and assess the knowledge, skills, and competencies acquired by the WAS learners both from the curriculum and from life/work experience in order to assign credit and confer degrees with rigor. PLA must effectively integrate into the system via standardization, to provide clarity and alignment for the assessment of Prior Learning Assessment

(PLA) in order to provide work-life experience credit to the WASs in accordance to the level of attainment.

Teaching–Learning Process: The HEI faculty should adopt multiple methods of instruction (including experiential and problem-based methods) for WASs in order to connect curricular concepts to useful knowledge and skills that the WASs could bring back and apply to the work place to enhance performance. If the curricular become too focus on the employ of theoretical discourses without pragmatic, hands-on applications, the WASs would not be able to find value from the learning at the HEI.

Student Support Systems: The HEI would also need to assists adult learners using comprehensive academic and student support systems in order to enhance students' capacities to become self-directed, lifelong learners. The provision of various WASs centered student services will allow WASs to feel more motivated to remain in the course or program.

Technology: It is imperative that in this age of disruptive technologies, HEI also uses information technology to provide relevant and timely information to WASs and to enhance the holistic learning experience. Technologies that support collaborative, integrative, and transformative learning will motivate WASs to remain within the education system for subsequent learning enhancements

Strategic Partnerships: For HEIs to serve WAS more effectively is to engage WASs in strategic relationships, partnerships, and collaborations with employers and other organizations in order to develop and improve educational opportunities for adult learners. These collaborations could also be extended to traditional students by leveraging on the WASs work connections and networks.

Transitions: HEIs need to support guided pathways that lead into and from its programs and services in order to ensure that the WASs learners will have a smooth transition from the work place to the study environment and vice versa.

HEIs can help WASs persist and succeed in the higher education studies by explicitly

Recognizing the connections between the current educational experiences its antecedents and consequences. More importantly, HEIs need to keep an open mind when serving the WASs as each and every WASs is unique as the background, work, and life experiences of each and every WAS differs.

Conclusion

The WASs or the "re-entry" students (Ross-Gordon, 2011) appear to be a student population that is here to stay for many HEIs. Increasingly, HEIs have attempted to create programs and services that are responsive to adults' life and learning preferences, and such effort has challenged college faculty and administrators to think beyond traditional ways of teaching and delivering educational programs. A large number of HEIs or program units have a long history of adaptation to the adult learner student population. For other HEIs or programs, this effort is more recent. Yet we can learn much from the existing program's experiences with various modes of distance learning, prior learning assessment, and intensive or accelerated format courses, via the examples highlighted in this chapter. Faculty can play an important role as change agents in creating supportive learning environments for the WASs learners by incorporating theory and research on WAS into their own classrooms and by advocating for adult-oriented programs and services on the college or universities' respective campuses (Blair, 2010). The design and delivery of these programs are key to a successful undergraduate and postgraduate holistic learning experience for re-entry adult students (Ross-Gordon, 2011) and such experiences will most definitely serve to enrich and enhance the life and career of these WASs.

CHAPTER 8

Power of Service Healing Hearts and Following Dreams: Complementary and Alternative Medicine as a Positive Force for Love, Renewing, and Revitalizing Health

Dr. Mary Jo Bulbrook, RN, CEMP/S/I
Akamai Univerity

From serving individuals, a theory emerged titled, "Healing from Within and Without" (HFWW), first presented professionally at the International Nursing Diagnosis in Calgary, Alberta, Canada in 1985 and more recently at the International Association for the Study of Subtle Energy and Energy Medicine in Kansas, June 2015 as a single subject research development; and lastly, at the International Kinesiology College in September 2015 at Banff, Canada with a presentation of soul healing-one aspect of the theory. This chapter will focus on both the evolution of soul healing as well as HFWW where it is housed. Since 1985, the theory has evolved from single subject research into an international training program that has helped heal hearts, support individuals in following their dreams and life purpose, spanning over 30 years of serving clients and training individuals throughout the USA, Canada, Australia, Peru, South Africa, Chile, and New Zealand.

Lives have been changed. Paths have been reshaped and contributions made that have set a new course for not only the individual but have spearheaded positive change and affirmations to a rewarding life and social change in a culturally relevant base. Explore how HFWW, now changed in name to "Transform Your Life Through Energy Medicine" (TYLEM), became an international force that has transformed the human condition and has inspired others to follow in its footsteps. HFWW served as a foundation for health and healing modeled with complementary and alternative medicine (in partnerships with traditional healers. An offspring of the work is The CAM Academy which is an international framework to support growth and create a collegial force for change focusing on the energy system that surrounds and connects all things and all people. Woven together, the work has led to the CAM Program at Akamai University dedicated to supporting others to do the same and create their own theory of practice, education, or service to reshape lives for the betterment of the world.

Outline: Historical roots, theory described, force for change in individuals' lives, transformed educational model in partnerships with traditional health and healing, honoring cultural perspectives

Origins of Dr. Bulbrook's Theory including Soul Healing

The original foundation for soul healing is based on the holistic nursing theory first introduced at the International Nursing Diagnosis Conference held in Calgary, Alberta in 1985. The theory was born from an analysis of three cases from my private practice in family centered holistic care that paralleled my university teaching at Memorial University, St. John's, Newfoundland, Canada.

The theory has survived the course of time and been expanded by additions that have added clarity to the work. My model of soul healing has been enriched by focusing on multiple single-subject clinical cases from 1970 to the present time, covering a 40-year time span of practicing, teaching, and researching CAM in multiple countries: USA, Canada, Australia, New Zealand, Peru, South Africa, and Chile.

Soul healing revitalizes the soul and includes: energy centers (chakras), energy tracts (meridians), energy field (aura), central power current, core star, integrating fragmented energies, and clearing unwanted energies.

The theoretical model includes physical, emotional, mental, and spiritual focus to *transform your life through energy medicine* (TYLEM).

Soul healing focuses on the spiritual aspect of the person and includes the following:

- Hara alignment (connecting with our intentionality and core being),
- Earth star (anchoring our energy to this planet and time frame); and
- Soul star (holding our energetic template between lifetimes).

Soul Healing Intervention through Spiritual Clearing, Renewal, and Revitalization

The following are the ABC's of doing soul healing:

Part A: What I notice

Meditate. Change comes from *within. Focus your attention and intention* to accomplish what you desire, need, or dream. Move into spirit and connect with a knowing that I *can* do or *be* what needs to happen. *Inspiration* is moving into spirit and fully connecting with the *divine.*

The following questions focus on *attention* and *intention* from your inner space. Become aware, register what you are aware of, and then assess each aspect using the following formula.

As I look within, I am aware of
1. Soul essence (*My divine energy is. . .*),

2. Soul memory (*What comes to me are the following memories. . .*); and
3. Soul karma (*I came into this lifetime with this to* address. . .).

We come into life as a divine essence and move into the ego. Our essence is spiritual and the state of all that is possible.

Outcome of questioning: Record your *intention* in some way to anchor-in the progress you made using words, movement, color, pictures, affirmations, or painting.

Part B: Energetic assessment

Energetic assessment is conducted through a muscle test, pendulum, or inner reflection to determine where in your spirit healing is needed. Check the following to see what needs your attention.

Time orientation
- Present-7 inches around the body
- Past-back of the body
- Future-front of the body

Location where issues are evident
- Top-visions
- Bottom-grounding
- Left side-emotions, female
- Right side-mental or male

Energetic aspect
- Energy tracts-Energy centers-Energy fields
- Core elements: Hara-Core star-Earth star-Soul star

Fragmented energies
- Part of your energy leaves

Interfering energies
- Another's energy gets in the way

Part C: Record your findings

Intention and intervention for revitalization. Set your intention and attention to drive energy to what needs to change. As you focus inward on the area you have identified, notice what comes into awareness-thought, image, feeling, picture, or word.

Intervention. Once identified, set your intention through prayer to clear, heal, integrate, or renew your energy.

Reassess your energy. Give appreciation and gratitude to source. Record your intention in some way to anchor-in the progress you made using words, movement, color, pictures, affirmations, or painting.

Lee Lawrence's work on *The Science of the Soul* inspired Dr. Bulbrook to renew her primary goal to focus on spiritual work. Lee's gifts developed from a near-death experience. Over the years he became a master practitioner and teacher of the science of the soul. Lee presented his work at the Energy Medicine Partnerships International and Akamai University Congress in Durham, NC in 2014 which parallels my original soul work from 1985 and first presented in Calgary in 1985.

Transform Your Life™
Energy Medicine

Since that time the theory has been advanced to this new level synthesized from the extensive application of the work worldwide within multiple cultural settings, different illness conditions, and health challenges for all ages. The current version of soul healing had been presented at the American Holistic Nurses Association as an all-day preconference workshop that was well received in June 2014.

The original theory title, *healing from within and without*, was later changed to *transform your life through energy medicine* (TYLEM). It includes 3 dimensions (parts) outlining the journey of the person using a psycho-spiritual orientation grounded in practice. Part I is physical, Part 2 is emotional and mental, and Part 3 is spiritual. The spiritual parts which I will include in this paper identify: soul essence, soul memory, and soul karma. The time frame is beyond time and space and includes concepts listed below that are shown in pictures (based on the teaching from Brennan, B. A., 1993, *Light Emerging*) illustrating these concepts:

1. Energy field – Connect the past with the future through the subtle body
2. Energy center – Exchanging between and among levels of consciousness
3. Energy tracts - Flowing through and beyond the physical body
4. Central power current – Hara line
5. Core star – Divine essence
6. Fragmented energies – Part of your energy becomes disconnected from the core

7. Unwanted energies – Spirits or other energy can become attached and influence all aspects of life depending on the severity of the attachment and completeness of the source.

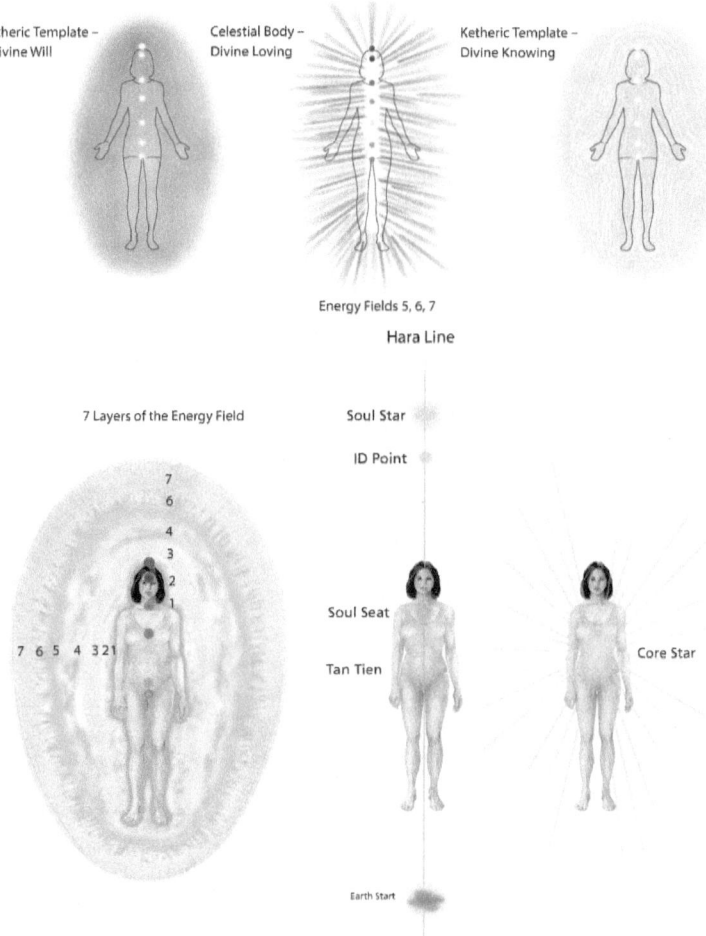

Acknowledging Barbara Brennan for her descriptions of the Hara Alignment and Core Star in *Light Emerging*, 1993, Bantam Books, pages 287-305.

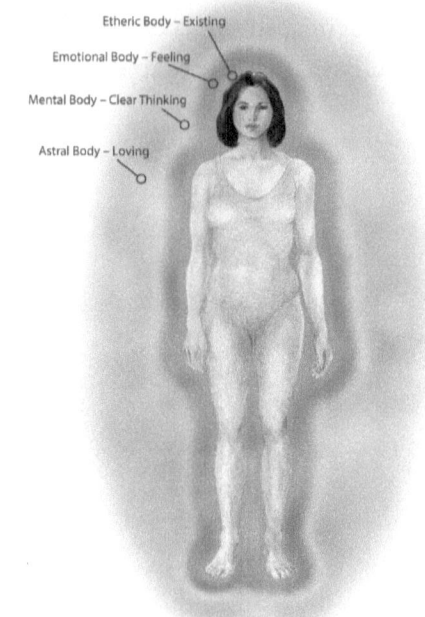

Energy Fields (4 of 7)

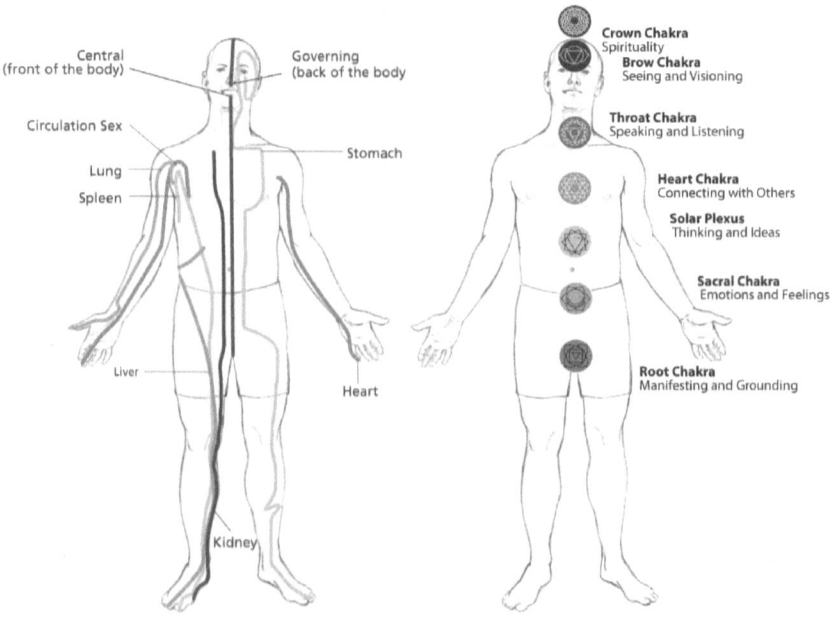

Energy Tracts   Energy Centers

Original 3 Case Studies of the Theory: Healing from Within and Without

1. **Presenting story:** *I have been having reoccurring thoughts about something that happened a long time ago and I don't know what to do about it.*

Outcome Summary: The inner environment of unresolved issues of abuse affected her outer behavior (arm pain) and created a dynamic similar to unresolved anger in childhood traumas triggered by anger with men.

2. **Presenting story:** *Can you teach me some ways to deal with my chronic back pain? I have been through extensive medical workouts and am on a lot of drugs for pain.*

Outcome Summary: From multiple psychiatric diagnosis he became addicted to medications prescribed by health care professionals. Moved into treatment center to detox from drugs and learn how to balance energy through simple interventions. On discharge he said "For the first time in my life I am drug-free and pain free. I don't know who I am or how to live."

3. **Presenting story:** *I have been diagnosed with lymphoma and the psychiatrist referred me to you for help.*

Outcome Summary: Energy flow of communication to physical disease and intention clearly linked together. Alive and thriving after 30 years.

Current Clinical Single Subject Case Studies

May 2015 Clients

1. **Presenting story:** *30-nine-year-old with several months of left leg pain that moves around*
   Findings: Gall bladder meridian tied into emotional anger at personal life situation
   Intervention: Channeled energy into leg and showed him how to clear GB meridian
2. **Presenting story:** *40-year-old woman who described herself as being all over the place*
   Findings: *Energy like an amoeba*
   Intervention: Put her in an energetic (visualized metal-like) support to hold that energy
3. **Presenting story:** *60-year-old female experiencing multiple spirits in her home*
   Findings: Unable to protect the self
   Intervention: Built the energy system with golden light meditation
4. **Presenting story:** *50+ oncology surgeon with 6 month history of pain up and down the outside of both legs treated originally in Western medicine*
   Findings: Blocked energy in large intestine meridian due to sadness
   Intervention: Taught him to release sadness, tap on the meridian, and do neuro-lymphatic release.

As you can tell from these brief summaries a range of interventions were incorporated to support the healing process. My research has spanned four decades and over this time additional data has been collected that serves to support the client using a range of interventions that are directed by the soul's pathway for this life time.

Theory Elements Summary from 1995:

- Present, past, and future are linked together with emotional, mental, physical, and spiritual health.
- Life is a spiritual journey and includes interaction with the self, others and the environment in a given context.
- Who we are radiates into the environment and affects all our interactions and transactions.
- Process of change is facilitated by the synergistic blending of the caregiver and receiver allowing a sacred space to be created in which the personal dynamic world of the individual is activated to release, renew, and recreate hope, health, and healing.
- The person is held in a dynamic, flowing, energetic system that reflects the relationship to others.
- An individual's health and healing is intimately related to the health of their environment.
- The individual represents the whole, a holographic representation of all that is and can be.
- The earth has chakras and an energy system that interacts with and influences you.
- The world and everything in it is interconnected-each influences the other.
- Health and healing in the future includes these dimensions in an integrated way honoring the culture.
- The essence of life revolves around soul evolution and healing.
- Soul healing includes living life fully embraced by divine light and love.
- Clearing our path is needed to find a new perspective and to enrich your life to the fullest while walking your path

Over the years, teaching and practicing complementary and alternative medicine in a variety of countries has been a lifetime commitment of service following spiritual guidance. From working with clients in a variety of settings with a range of health / illness conditions, it has been a magical journey of discovery of finding out what helps a person grow and heal and to become more fully human.

The impetus to become more fully human was the motto and influence of Virginia Satir. She was my mentor throughout my life path as an educator and clinician. Virginia rose above existing paradigms of teaching and practicing mental health and connected at a heart and soul level with those she served. I, too, followed her lead as my personal mentor and teacher for over 40 years. This experience dramatically influenced the soul healing part of my theory the became my Model for Social Change as it wove the elements of the self in relationship to others to the context of one/s life journey-all three elements influence one's life.

Following in Virginia's footsteps has expanded service to others enriched by the evolution of what makes us uniquely human and well connected to others to achieve peace within, peace between, and peace among. A graphic for this statement is best illustrated by the original flame of Avanta Network the teaching arm of Virginia Satir that I helped shape.

VIRGINIA SATIR
PEACE WITHIN
PEACE BETWEEN
PEACE AMONG

Soul healing vision is to achieve peace. Life is filled with stress and concerns that shape who we are and all of our relationships. How we deal with stress is what makes the difference in life. As we learn to accept what life has to offer, to forgive and move forward with the energy of love and service not only will our lives be changed but the contribution of the self will evolve to fully express the human condition to become all that we can be. This change is the flame of eternal life as exemplified by this universal truth of the oneness of all things.

References

Bulbrook, M. J. (1987). Holistic health care and decision making. In Hannah, K., Reimer, M., Mills, W., & Letournear, S., *Clinical Judgment and Decision Making: The Future with Nursing Diagnosis*. Brisbane: John Wiley & Sons.

Bulbrook, M. J. (1995, April). Healing from within and without: A holistic nursing theory illustrating the role of the inner and outer environment on health. [Foundational roots]. *Australian Journal of Holistic Nursing*, *2*(1), pp. 4-12.

Bulbrook, M. J. (1991). *Holistic approaches to stress relief and pain management*. North Carolina, NC Center for Healing Touch. Retrieved from http://www.energymedicinepartnerships.com

Brennan, B. A. (1987). *Hands of light*. New York: Pleiades.

Brennan, B. A. (1993). *Light emerging: The journey of personal healing*. New York: Bantam Books.

Bruyere, R. (1989). *Wheels of light: Chakras, auras and the healing energy of the body*. New York: Simon & Schuster.

Coon, R. (1993). *Spheres of destiny: The Shaftesbury prophecy-a planetary vision for the 21st century*. UK: Glastonbury Circle.

Dale, C. (1997). *New chakra healing: The revolutionary 32 center energy system*. Minnesota: Llewellyn Publications.

Gerber, R. (1988). *Vibrational medicine*. New Mexico: Bear & Company.

Judith, A. (1996). *Eastern body, Western mind: Psychology & the chakra system as a path to the self*. CA: Celestial Arts.

Judith, A. & Vega, S. (1993). *The sevenfold journey: Reclaiming mind, body and spirit through the chakras*. CA: The Crossing Press, Freedom.

Leslie, M., Bulbrook, M. J. (2016, June 24). Widening our lens, deepening our practice: An exploration of energy within the context of the teachings of Virginia Satir. [Presented at the *Becoming More Fully Human: The Evolution, A Conference Celebrating 100 Years the Life and Legacy of Virginia Satir*]

Myss, C. (2001) *Sacred contracts: Awakening your divine potential*. New York: Harmony Works.

Mentgen, J., & Trapp Bulbrook, M. J. (2000). *Healing touch level I notebook*. North Carolina: North Carolina Center for Healing Touch.

Redfield, J. (1993). *The celestine prophecy*. AL: Satori.

Thie, J., & Thie, M. (2012). *Touch for health: The complete edition*. CA: DeVorss & Co.

Satir, V. (1988), The new peoplemaking, CA: Science & Behavior Books.

Zukav, G. (1989). *The seat of the soul*. New York: Simon & Schuster.

CHAPTER 9

Video as a Medium for Online and Social Media-centric Education

Dr Seamus Phan
Akamai University

Abstract

The notion that professional-quality video or films can only be produced by expensive and bulky cameras and finished on expensive post-production systems is over.

Today, even a smartphone has been successfully used by professional filmmakers to make feature films, while tiny point-of-view (POV) cameras are used for second camera footage (or B camera) in feature films, including 4K resolution footage.

The advent of 4K-capable DSLRs and mirrorless cameras have put professional quality in the hands of many people. Though a good quality film or video has less to do with the price or features of equipment, but more to do with a well-written story and an expressive cast, it is gratifying to know that equipment is no longer the inhibitor to the average person seeking to communicate through motion video. The success of online video streaming platforms such as YouTube or Vimeo means that more people are spending time watching video, rather than reading long blocks of text, or books.

Education is the same. It is difficult to engage students in a class unless an educator is exceptionally charismatic. It is far easier to present a good-quality video or film and discuss the salient points thereafter.

Let us explore some of the options of equipment, software, and techniques that are now more easily available to educators, and how best to think as a filmmaker and storyteller when approaching an educational topic.

Introduction

Video is a medium that has consistently been a contender for education and training since the early days of non-linear editing (NLE), with suites such as Adobe Premiere 1.0 and AVID Media Suite Pro (MSP) on RISC-powered Macintoshes in the late 1990s.

More than a decade ago, video was recorded on magnetic tapes (VHS-C, VHS, MiniDV, Betacam SP, etc) and then the footage was digitized via FireWire connections. Digitizing the tapes into a digital format suitable for non-linear editing, editing them digitally on a computer, and then rendering the finished edit back to tape, were a test of patience, as computers were underpowered compared to today's computers. Digital video that could be played back on computers directly was not high resolution either, as playback on client computers demanded far more computational power than most desktop computers could provide.

Therefore, video as a training or educational medium was confined to analog video tapes that had to be manually played and paused during discussions or mastered onto proprietary and expensive laserdiscs.

Video became much more usable in both footage acquisition, editing, and playback, with the H.264 encoding algorithm, which eventually became pervasive on computers, smartphones, tablets, video cameras, and IP cameras (Internet protocol).

Today, hybrid cameras are capable of acquiring both still images and video, such as the Panasonic Lumix GH4, Sony A7, and Olympus OM-D E-M5 Mark II. Filmmaking has also become more affordable, with digital film cameras such as the Blackmagicdesign Pocket Cinema (BMPCC) and Digital Bolex, providing film-quality footage with high dynamic range that afford much flexibility to filmmakers and editors during the video editing and color grading stage. Even smartphones today are capable of capturing full HD (1920x1080p) quality, with some smartphones achieving 4K cinematic quality.

At the same time, the delivery platform has become much more sophisticated, with Google's YouTube leading the way to populate video as the primary medium for social communication today, followed by other video platforms such as VIMEO, Instagram, Vine, Wistia, and so on.

According to a Cisco study (source: 2011), mobile video accounted for more than 271 million users and is slated to reach 1.6 billion users by 2016. Even in 2011, online video already accounted for more than 50% of Internet traffic, partly because video is a data type that takes up a lot of storage compared to textual or audio content, and demands even more from Internet connectivity.

For example, in July 2012, a virtually unknown Korean singer, Psy, suddenly became the global YouTube phenomenon with his Korean popular song (K-pop) "Gangnam Style". Between July 15, 2012 to December 21, 2012, just a matter of months, his official music video on YouTube accumulated more than 1 billion views. And by April 2015, his official music video has accumulated more the 2.2 billion views. There were also many parodies to his song from all corners of the world, with many cover versions in various local languages.

[Video]: https://www.youtube.com/watch?v=9bZkp7q19f0

To get an idea of some of the most viewed YouTube videos compiled as a list, visit: http://en.wikipedia.org/wiki/List_of_most_viewed_YouTube_videos.

In 2011, a radio DJ Hooman Khalili and Patrick Gilles used a Nokia N8 mobile phone to shoot a full-length family film "Olive" (2011, Reference: http://www.imdb.com/title/tt2125574/). The film was a poignant and delicate portrayal of a young girl who did not speak at all, but helped a few people transform their lives through her mysterious powers. Although the mobile phone was rigged to some professional attachments and rigs, the efforts of the "Olive" team showed that filmmaking has truly leaped forward, and that everyday smartphones and affordable hybrid cameras have brought good quality storytelling through the video medium not just a possibility, but a reality.

[Video Trailer]: https://www.youtube.com/watch?v=er03vp8QCvI

The Guardian newspaper reviewed how the film "Olive" was produced on a smartphone (2011, http://www.theguardian.com/film/2011/dec/02/olive-film-shot-on-smartphone).

Understanding video formats

In the early years of video, whether analog or digital, the predominant resolution was the VCD format, which when translated to pixels, measures 352 horizontal pixels. The later DVD format measures either 704 or 720 horizontal pixels (source: http://en.wikipedia.org/wiki/DVD-Video).

Moving up, the HD (high definition) format is split into 2 formats, HD, and full HD. The HD resolution is 720p, or 1,280 horizontal pixels by 720 vertical pixels. The full HD resolution is 1080p, or 1,920 horizontal pixels by 1,080 vertical pixels.

Larger video formats are intended for cinema applications, such as 2K (2,048 horizontal pixels by 1,536 vertical pixels in the 16 mm format), and 4K (4,096 horizontal pixels by 2,214 vertical pixels in the 35 mm 1.33 aspect ratio format) (2004, Reference: http://www.videotechnology.com/0904/formats.html).

Understanding polar patterns of microphones

For audio acquisition, we need to understand microphone polar patterns, namely: omnidirectional, cardioid, and figure-8 (or bi-directional) (Reference: http://ehomerecordingstudio.com/microphone-polar-patterns/).

If you like to record video for a live event, such as a round-table discussion where your microphone has to pick up multiple voices or audio in all directions, or live large room performances (such as an orchestra), then you can use a recording microphone with an omnidirectional polar pattern.

If you like to record video for a stage performance where the main voices and audio come from a more concentrated source, or rooms with poor acoustics (such as concrete rooms with no audio-softening materials such as thick curtains or carpets), then a microphone with a cardioid polar pattern would work.

If you want even more audio isolation and thereby shutting more ambient noise while using a microphone at a distance, then a microphone with a figure-8 polar pattern would work. Remember that the figure-8 microphone (usually known as a "shotgun" microphone) does pick up audio in the opposing direction (usually towards you, the user), and so you must reduce noise from you the camera or audio handler.

Some omnidirectional microphones, despite having audio pickup in all directions, may actually work well to isolate vocals from the ambient noise. These specific microphones are Lavalier microphones which are often used by broadcasters, and can be wired, or wireless. They can work in environments with ambient noise simply because their proximity to our voice is very close, and therefore the signal-to-noise ratio (SNR) is manageable enough for us to pick up sufficient vocals despite the background noises.

Understanding depth-of-field

In an educational context, the notion of focus may be important.

For example, if we want to illustrate the assembly of a smartphone through video, then our visual focus should zoom in to smartphone being assembled, rather than on the background or the foreground. The technique to "blur out" the background from the subject or object in question, is often achieved with a shallow depth-of-field (DoF).

A typical removable lens on a hybrid camera has 2 sets of adjustable attributes, the distance (which determines focus), and the aperture (which is expressed in f-stops).

So, a lens may show f-stop values from 2, 2.8, 4, 5.6, 8, 11, 16, and 22.

If an image is acquired at F2, the background will be blurred against a sharp foreground subject or object. This is due to a shallow depth-of-field (DoF) at F2.

Conversely, if the lens is at at F22, the aperture becomes very small, and invariably not only the foreground will be in focus, the background will likely to be in focus too. In this scenario, since both the foreground and the background are both in focus, then the viewer may be more distracted because of the background.

Therefore, whenever possible, it is ideal to have as shallow a DoF as possible, and this often means using a prime lens, rather than a zoom lens. If the location is large, then it may be possible to use a prime lens that is more telescopic. If the location is small, then a wide-angle to normal lens may be more suitable.

Basic video equipment for on-demand use

What kind of equipment should an educator choose when producing video content for on-demand use?

Remember, it is not about having expensive gear, but how we tell a story well.

Typically, a hybrid camera, such as a mirror-less interchangeable lens camera, such as the Panasonic Lumix GH4, Olympus OM-D E-M5 Mark II, would be best. There is little reason to go for more expensive (though more capable) cameras since both of these cameras produce very good still images and video. Both these cameras are capable of accepting external audio through a 3.5mm audio jack, which means that you can plug in powered microphones, including wireless lavalier microphones, for much higher audio quality otherwise unobtainable through the on-board microphones. The Panasonic Lumix GH4 also features a headphone jack so that you can monitor the audio you are recording, while the Olympus E-M5 Mark II requires an additional HLD-8G external grip to get a headphone jack for monitoring audio. The Panasonic Lumix GH4 trumps the Olympus E-M5 Mark II by shooting 4K resolution as well. If you want to shoot in a "run-and-gun" format where you are moving with your camera and the camera is not mounted on a tripod, then the Olympus E-M5 offers a 5-axis image stabilization technology that can provide you with very steady footage. The Panasonic GH4 requires stabilized lenses which can be more limiting.

However, it is entirely possible to go for bridge cameras, which have zoom lenses but these lenses are not interchangeable. For example, the Panasonic Lumix FZ1000 or the Sony RX10 are good choices. Both of these bridge cameras, also feature 3.5mm audio jacks for you to plug external powered microphones into. Both the Lumix FZ1000 and the RX10 are image stabilized bridge cameras.

If however, you intend to use a smartphone as your image acquisition device, then the Microsoft Lumia 1520 and Lumia 930 (Reference: http://www.microsoft.com/en/mobile/phones/all/) are good smartphones that offer very good small-sensor cameras for video, since these smartphones have built-in optical image stabilization. The Sony Xperia Z3 and LG G3 offer very good optics with optical image stabilization too, running the Android operating system. The Apple iPhone 6 and 6Plus are good for portable video acquisition too, with what Apple terms as "Cinematic Video Stabilization," some form of software-based video cropping and stabilization algorithm that works very well too.

If your camera or smartphone does not feature built-in image stabilization (either by software or hardware/optical), then you may need to mechanically stabilize your camera or smartphone. This is typically achieved by mounting your camera or smartphone onto a tripod. A smartphone typically does not have a tripod mount, and you may need a small adapter that allows your smartphone to be mounted onto your tripod. There is typically no need for a heavy-duty tripod as you are likely to use a consumer or prosumer camera, or a smartphone for video acquisition.

While most cameras today feature HD video, and even smartphones today feature HD or even 4K video, the weakest link is often the audio.

In most consumer or prosumer cameras and smartphones, the onboard microphone is typically of average or below-average quality, and will not offer you a good signal-to-noise ratio that brings out the vocals in your video.

Therefore, some kind of external microphone should be linked to your camera or smartphone.

The caveat is that not all consumer cameras have an input port for audio (a 3.5mm audio-in jack). It is advisable to select only consumer or prosumer cameras that have audio-in capabilities. Smartphones typically have an audio jack that can be used as a microphone-in jack.

For most purposes, a powered microphone is required, as unpowered microphones typically have very weak audio signals. A good "shotgun" microphone is best for our purposes, to record vocals of trainers or professors.

Next, we will need to find a way to import our video footage into a computer, and then use a non-linear editor (NLE) software to edit the footage into a completed video. For educational purposes, we do not need to use the NLE to have special effects or extensive editing - just "cuts-only" videos will do.

Once we complete the editing of our video, we can output the finished video to industry-standard formats, such as MP4 (MPEG 4). Most online video hosting platforms such as YouTube or VIMEO will accept MP4 formats.

Going further with live streaming

Some educational video content can be streamed live to audiences around the world. With YouTube and other comparable live streaming options, live streaming of video content is now within reach.

First, for live streaming of video, the camera must offer a clean HDMI-out signal. Some prosumer cameras offer a HDMI-out port, but cannot output clean HDMI signals. A clean HDMI signal is one where the video signal is directly output through the HDMI output port without going through the internal compression-decompression (codec), usually providing a higher quality video signal. This signal is usually streamed to a HDMI encoder that is wirelessly connected to the Internet, and the video feed is then compressed "live" by the hardware encoder to a remote web server that can interpret the live video signal, and then presented to audiences using the RTMP streaming protocol (realtime messaging protocol) with a web browser (which can be viewed on the desktop, tablets, or smartphones).

Usually, the HDMI encoder is connected to the Internet via WiFi, although there are some encoders capable of connecting to the Internet via 3G/4G LTE cellular networks.

For smartphones, there may be no necessity to use a HDMI hardware encoder, as most smartphones allow live streaming directly via its own built-in WiFi or through 3G/4G LTE networks. Although the video feed may not be as adjustable as a good quality camera, the smartphone may suffice for most educators.

Conclusions

The emergence of advanced and increasingly miniaturized smartphones and cameras capable of acquiring good quality video has hastened and heightened the empowerment of everyday people, including educators. It is no longer necessary to rely on expensive equipment, or large crew, to acquire and stream video content to learners.

The pace of improvement of such equipment is quickening, while the costs are decreasing. The shift from learners merely reading textual content to viewing video to a large extent, means that educators have to adapt to a changed learners' world, where video will be key.

References

https://www.youtube.com/watch?v=9bZkp7q19f0

http://en.wikipedia.org/wiki/List_of_most_viewed_YouTube_videos.

DJ Hooman Khalili and Patrick Gilles (2011, Reference: http://www.imdb.com/title/tt2125574/) https://www.youtube.com/watch?v=er03vp8QCvI

(2011, http://www.theguardian.com/film/2011/dec/02/olive-film-shot-on-smartphone).

http://www.videotechnology.com/0904/formats.html)

http://ehomerecordingstudio.com/microphone-polar-patterns/).

http://www.microsoft.com/en/mobile/phones/all/)

CHAPTER 10

Neoliberal Transformation of Education in Turkey: Political and Ideological Analysis of Educational Reforms in the Last Decade

Dr Kemal Yildirim
Akamai Univerity

Abstract

I will concentrate on a well-theorized, and biting evaluation of the neoliberal-cum-Islamo-conservative reformation & reformulation of schooling and education in Turkey over the last 15 years. And most part of this chapter will examine Political and Ideological Analysis of Educational Reforms in the Age of the Justice and Development Party (AKP) in power. As known to many people the Neoliberal policies have had an impact on educational systems globally. So this chapter will thus provide a detailed and critical analysis of neoliberal transformation of educational policies and reforms in Turkey by focusing on the Justice and Development Party's reform efforts over the last fifteen years.

Its wide-reaching and trenchant analysis in which it makes a clear picture on the importance of understanding and critiquing the neoliberal and neoconservative assault on public services, and related sector workers, and education globally. However, it exposes the Islamicization of education and society in Turkey under the AKP government, belying Western approbation of Turkey's supposed 'moderate Islam.'" "This chapter will be an important part of this book that deserves serious attention, especially at this precipitous historical moment of the crisis of neoliberal capitalism of today. Frankly, what exists currently in Turkey is a global problem that requires a certain global solution: Probably the struggle for a socialist alternative to transnational capitalism."

Keynotes : Neoliberal, reforms, education, transformation

This chapter mainly concentrates on the neoliberal and neoconservative transformation of the educational system in Turkey during the last decade which covers most of the period where Justice and Development Party (AKP) is in power, whose educational policies were based on several reforms to change the educational philosophy of the country since early 2002's and thereafter. It's main goal was to build a powerful neoliberal and neoconservative agenda in Turkey. These reforms include making students and their parents pay in every stage of education, increasing the number of the exams for enrollment to any school, putting individualization at the center of education, and increasing the number of Quran courses. and opening premises for five times pray at scholl buildings and Allowing students at all levels of education to veil their heads and wear islamic clothes. The main reforms made by conservative decision makers within the Government and through its ally organizations such as the pro islamic union for education called EĞITIM BIR-SEN and TÜRGEV (Türkiye Gençlik ve Eğitime Hizmet Vakfı) so called Youth of Turkey and eductaional services Foundation, A charity NGO counting Turkish PM's son as a board member which involves several number of AKP front Parliamentarians as wel as Government Ministers such as Mustafa Açıkalın, Hilmi Güler, İdris Naim Şahin and Prof. Dr. İzzet Özgenç, Prof. Dr. Adem Baştürk, Necmettin Üçyıldız, Ahmet Ergün ve Ali İbiş

"From the examinations of the records it appeared that individual and institutional donations to TÜRGEV from Aug. 27, 2008, from within Turkey totals 29,666,533 Turkish Liras and from abroad $99,999,990," the statement released by Deputy prime minister Arınç quoted. He also indicted that the declaration related to the donations for 2013 was not available yet. TÜRGEV has been under fire since the Dec. 17, 2013 graft probes, as many allegations dealt with the activities of the foundation.

The Directorate of Foundations is an independent institution under the Deputy Prime Minister Arınç's responsibility.

Leader of the main opposition Republican People's Party (CHP) Kemal KILICDAROGLU has maintained that the Foundation of Youth and Education in Turkey so called the charity (TÜRGEV), Foundation of Youth and Education in Turkey of which Prime

Minister Recep Tayyip Erdoğan's son Bilal Erdoğan is an executive board member, served as a center where bribes were transferred by businessmen whose companies were thus granted public tenders,

As part of a far-reaching graft probe that became public in December involving four former cabinet ministers and others, Bilal Erdoğan was sent a summons by one of the prosecutors leading the graft probe to give a statement regarding corruption allegations in which he is allegedly involved. But the prime minister's son is under the protection of his father and did not respect the prosecutor's call.

"[TÜRGEV] **Foundation of Youth and Education in Turkey** is a center where bribes were collected against public tenders," CHP leader Kemal Kılıçdaroğlu told the daily, maintaining that money acquired would be used to set up a parallel, alternative structure in the education system[1]

Kılıçdaroğlu, The chair of People's Republican party believesthe fact that Erdoğan has tampered with every state institution to cover up possible leaks about new corruption cases, the amount of corruption in the government was therefore so big that it would not be possible to cover it up. "Sooner or later The opposition party CHP would make new announcements [about the corruption] so as to show The prime minister thus to continue watch them," the CHP leader also indicated. As part of a far-reaching graft probe that became public in late December involving four former cabinet ministers and others, Bilal Erdoğan was sent a summons by one of the prosecutors leading the graft probe to give a statement regarding corruption allegations in which he is allegedly involved. But the prime minister's son is under the protection of his father and did not respect the prosecutor's call. In the party's group parliamentary meeting in the past week, Kemal Kılıçdaroğlu the leader of CHP (People's republic party) demanded to know if $99,999,990 was deposited into an account that TÜRGEV had at a public bank on April 26, 2013.

Noting that he has not yet received a response from President Erdoğan regarding his claim about TÜRGEV, Kılıçdaroğlu said: "Prime Minister Erdoğan closely follows the money being transferred to the foundation; he personally provides financing [for the foundation].

He is presenting this [transfer of money to the foundation] as charity. No charity is conducted with ill-gotten money.

Kılıcdaroglu believes that they know very well why this money is being collected. Because They want to establish a new structure [in Turkish education system]. Finally it is very well known that son of Erdogan so called Bilal Erdoğan meets with officials from the Ministry of Education from time to time. One feels the need to ask: 'What does Bilal Erdoğan have to do with civil servants? Why do they come together? They want to set up a parallel structure in the area of education."

In a previous news report that appeared in the Cumhuriyet daily on Wednesday, the bank account number Kılıçdaroğlu made reference to in his speech in the CHP group meeting was the first account TÜRGEV had in Vakıfbank, a public bank. The $99,999,990 deposited in this account was later transferred to another account in the same bank, the daily noted.

Nearly a month later, $50 million of the money was transferred back to the original account and four months later, $28 million more, according to Cumhuriyet. The report in Cumhuriyet provided no answers about to whom, from which account number and for what in return the wire transfers were made. But a large sum of money was withdrawn on Sept. 26, 2012, from the money deposited in the original account and TL 50 million ($21,800,000) was paid from this account to purchase the Fatih Cultural Center in a joint venture between the Ensar Foundation and TÜRGEV. Nearly TL 50 million of the money was, after being deposited in various accounts, deposited on July 2, 2012, into an account in Albaraka Türk.

Nowdays many appointments of ministry of education high officials to educational departments are first reviewed by Bilal Erdogan and then are approved by ministry.

İt is interesting that the charity receives aid from AKP municipalities as well. even on direct channels For instance, **The Küçükçekmece Municipality in İstanbul, which is run by the ruling Justice and Development Party (AK Party), recently donated two of its buildings to a foundation that is known to have close ties with** the Foundation of Youth and Education in Turkey (TÜRGEV), of which President Recep Tayyip Erdoğan's son, Bilal Erdoğan, is an executive board member.

"It is likely that noone can understand what is going on because they [municipal officials] do not have an understanding of transparent governance," because It is not the first time the Küçükçekmece Municipality has donated buildings and plots of land to TÜRGEV and other foundations close to the government. In 2011, The mayor Yeniay donated a public school to the civil religious movement İlim Yayma Cemiyeti. which is a pro Islamic organization in connection with Government and where Government choose their high officials suchas governors, rectors, judges etc from among members of this organization.

Previously, ownership of a $2.7 million student dormitory built with public funds by the Antalya Metropolitan Municipality and a youth center was also transferred to TÜRGEV. Students and activists protested in early September in front of the Children and Youngsters' House Social Facilities building against the conveyance of the two buildings to TÜRGEV in Antalya.[2]

One of the important innovation among the reform In Turkey by AKP government on educational projects was to increase and promote number of, an Imam Hatip school (Turkish: *İmam Hatip Lisesi*, 'hatip' coming from Arabic 'khatib', meaning *the one who delivers the "khutba"* (Friday sermon) is a secondary education institution. As the name suggests, they were originally founded in lieu of a vocational school to train government employed imams; after madrasasin Turkey were abolished by the Unification of Education Act (Turkish: *Tevhid-i Tedrisat Kanunu*) as a part of Atatürk's reforms. are now in question and they were restored again as the number of these schools increased during AKP governance and The Government made several changes in schooling system to open borders for pupils to attend these schools after they graduate of their four years basic education. and so many schools were changed as Imam Hatip schools.

Research suggests that between the years of 1993 and 2000, prospective students registered at Imam Hatip high schools primarily to receive religious tutoring alongside a more general education. In addition, research shows enrolment at Imam Hatip high schools was based solely on the student's decision. The third proposed factor in the rise in popularity of Imam Hatip schools is the admission of female students in 1976. By 1998, almost 100,000 females attended Imam Hatip high schools, making up almost half of all students. This statistic is particularly revealing because women are not eligible to become either priests or ministers[3]

On 1 November 1928 Law no 1353 introduced a new <u>Latin</u>-based <u>alphabet</u>was accepted. In 1931, the Turkish Association of History, and in 1932, the Turkish Language Association were established to protect Turkish from influences of foreign languages, improve it as science suggests and prevent misuse of the Turkish language[4]

Political and Ideological Analysis of Educational Reforms

The new system: 4+4+4

In March 2012 the <u>Grand National Assembly</u> passed new legislation on primary and secondary education usually termed as "4+4+4" (4 years primary education, first level, 4 years primary education, second level and 4 years secondary education). Children will begin their primary education in the first month of September following their sixth birthdays and will come to a close during the school year in which students turn 14 years old.[5]

The primary education stages, which includes the first two stages of four years' education each, will entail four years of mandatory elementary education, followed by an additional mandatory four years of middle school education, in which students will be able to choose whether they want to study at a general education middle school or a religious vocational middle school, which are referred to as Imam Hatip schools. The new legislation includes the reopening of Imam Hatip middle schools. Primary education establishments will be set up separately as independent elementary schools and middle schools.[6]

When the <u>Justice and Development Party</u> (AKP) come to power in 2002 only about 2 percent of eligible children attended clerical schools.

Since then, the AKP has been determined to undo the effects of the 1997 reform. The idea is to revitalize middle schools and allow children to take a large number of elective options: in some cases, plumbing; in others, religious studies.⁷

4+4+4 system and the future of Turkey

To many intellectuals The 4+4+4 process is likely to draw a very pessimistic picture about the future of Turkey in terms of development of democracy and the transformation of the education system. Education, an area which interests everyone and which should be constructed on the basis of scientific findings, has witnessed a transformation within one month, which turned the whole system upside down, without any research or impact assessment processes. Opinions of non-governmental organizations and the major universities of the country were substantially ignored. Incidents that have nothing to do with democracy took place under the roof of the Parliament. Unfortunately, it was proven once again that the most important factor to pass a bill is the leader's ownership.

As they move quickly towards the 2012-2013 education year, the major problem facing the system is the uncertainty of how the amendments will be implemented. Because Neither public schools nor private ones have any idea or information about which course programs will be taught next year, whether they will serve as a primary or a middle school, how the transition from grade 4 to 5 will happen and, on top of everything else, how the FATIH Project, through which all students will be given tablet computers will be implemented. Beyond all these, the reforms promoting individual development – i.e. strengthening the services provided in basic education according to the needs of the students, postponing and improving vocational education, personal development oriented restructuring of middle school education, freeing the education system from the suppression of central examinations etc - are losing ground. What sticks in our minds is the question of whether it is possible to reflect upon the economic incentive package that was declared only days after the adoption of 4+4+4 by the Parliament, and the statement of "the South-East will become the China of Turkey" separately from the 4+4+4 issue.

I think "Courses delivered generally outside the school hours which require an extra effort from the student for participation. Here, the student does not select from among different options, but makes an extra request to school management to take this course." The same publication defines elective courses as follows: "Courses chosen by the student from a set of options and delivered during the normal school hours." However, the recent law stipulates that the courses related to religious education ("Koran" and "Life of Mohammed, the Prophet") are "voluntary optional courses". This provision, of course, reinforces the uncertainties. The Government uses religion as an instrument to show itself in symphaty with the local supporters so programs are entirely designed based on religious agenda.

The idea behind new system: 4+4+4

Actually it looks that The Law 6287, which made history as the "4+4+4" formula, is likely to bring forward many changes in the educational system of the country. There are lots of obstacles with the new law ammendment For instance, One of the main uncertainties lies in the age of starting school.

The Ministry of National Education announced that the age of starting primary school is brought forward one year. Previously, children who turned 72 months in the same calendar year as the school year were allowed to start school. Thus, those who were born in 2006 were going to start school in the 2012-2013 school period.

The new law however, says that 5 year-old children can start school. There is no regulation as to how the age will be calculated; therefore it is not clear whether turning 5 means turning 60 months or 72 months. If those who turn 60 months are allowed in school, primary schools will have to host almost two times at may students as they normally do. According to teachers, neither they, nor the curriculum, nor the physical conditions at schools are ready for accepting the 60-month-olds. Making children start primary education one year earlier can also have a deep impact on pre-school education, about which great efforts have been made in Turkey in the recent years. Participation in pre-school for five-year-olds (60-72 months) has increased very quickly: two out of every three 5-year-old children were enrolled to a pre-school program. However, this trend may come to a halt when they start to accept five-year -olds in the primary schools. Pre-school education may be overshadowed as the priority of the educational bureaucracy will be to implement the new regulations, and families (just like in the past) may be reluctant to send their 4-year-olds to pre-schools. Turkey may not be able to see the promised benefits of the pre-school education.

How students will be separated in different schools and programs remains unclear. Imam hatip middle schools will be opened for sure. But it is still uncertain whether permission will be granted to open vocational middle schools or middle schools under prestigious high schools. Even slight differentiations between schools may result in the introduction of competitive exams for placement as well as competition among parents and students who believe that the number is too low for good quality high schools and universities. If this happens, students in Turkey will have to pass a central examination at the age of 9. Even though placement will not depend on a central exam, the questions of how to decide which middle school to attend and how to make sure that the socio-economic status of the family will not affect this decision still remain unanswered.

Another fear is the possibility that the transition to middle school at the end of the 4th grade may turn into an excuse to pull disadvantaged children, especially girls and children with disabilities, out of school. In that case, despite the efforts from the central government, schools may not be able to provide a friendly environment for children with disabilities. As the transition to middle school is an important breaking point, children with disabilities may be discouraged to continue school. The same risk is also valid for girls, for whom, even before this law, the schooling rate towards the end of primary education had been dropping despite all the gains of the eight-year compulsory schooling. Research results have also shown that with the eight-year compulsory schooling, there was a significant drop in the phenomena of "child brides" and "teenage mothers". If the risks in question materialize, this falling trend may reverse and the number of child brides and teenage mothers may increase again.

It is still not yet known to Public what kind of different programs, schools and elective courses (apart from religious education) will be introduced in middle schools. It is also not fair whether these courses and school types will be classified as vocational education programs. Uncertainty prevails over other issues, such as whether courses related to religious education will be delivered during or outside of school hours, whether these courses will be "voluntary" or "elective", how schools will ensure freedom of faith and thought, or how they will guarantee an environment free of discrimination. The international statistics suggests that the Turkish education system ranks 34th among the 40 European and Asian countries

Similarly, the 2012 report of the Programme for International Student Assessment (PISA) stated that Turkey's students lag far behind those of most member countries of the Organisation for Economic Co-operation and Development (OECD). According to this report, Turkey ranks 34th out of 44 countries.

The main idea behind new system: 4+4+4 is to train more religious students and increase the growth of the religious population to destroy finally secularism in the country is likely to be one of the main objective goal of the AKP government.

I think according to the Government In general, the new 4+4+4 educational system has a positive goal on the effects increasing subject quality of education by guiding students and giving students more opportunities to pick different subject for their future plans, leveling the education, and putting same aged students into same buildings. For the applicability of the system and a more supportive system, some important suggestions are given as below.

1. Passing necessary legislations suitable to new system
2. Providing physical needs of the schools urgently
3. Supporting schools related to their physical infrastructures caused changes of the system

4. Considering playgrounds and places for physical activities during construction of the new schools, similar to
5. the places constructed worldwide
6. Getting necessary number of teachers for the second 4 in the system, and assigning teachers to get rid of
7. unskilled teachers from out of subjects
8. Assigning teachers to demanded areas for elective classes in order to avoid selecting teachers depending on
9. norm positions
10. Decreasing number of hours weekly in the schedule
11. Preparations to increase the motivation of the unmotivated teachers, or to allay teachers from negative impact
12. Increasing the number of school buses in central schools
13. Taking the necessary actions in order not to cause any unwanted disciplinary situation emerged with the new
14. mandatory high school education
15. Giving seminars and orientations to teachers and administrators of the high schools about the age level of students because of combining middle and high school

These all are basic and simple asumptions because the main target is to open borders to clerical school after first four years of education where the syylabus is entirely based on a religious agenda

Religious education
De-establishment of schooling system

In 1927, all courses concerning religion were excluded from the curriculum of primary, secondary, and high schools on the basis that non-Muslims also live in Turkey. Between 1927 and1949, religious instruction was not permitted in schools. In 1949, the Ministry of Education allowed a course on religion in 4th and 5th grades of primary school.

Re-establishment of schooling system

In 1956, as a result of multi-party democracy, a new government was established. Being more sympathetic towards the religious sentiments of society, this new government introduced a religion course into secondary schools. This time, if the parents wanted to exempt their children from the course, they had to apply to the school with a written request. After nearly ten years, in 1967, the religion course was introduced to the 1st and 2nd grades of high school. Students, however, were enrolled for the course with the written request of their parents. In 1975, the course was extended to the third (last) grade of the high schools. And, finally, following the military coup in 1980, the religion course became schools was also constitutionally secured. The exact title of the course was, "The Culture of Religion and Knowledge of Ethics."

In 1985, the Institute for Creation Research, a United States creationist group, helped advise Turkey's education minister Vehbi Dinçerler on how to introduce creationism in high schools. Turkish academics have stated that the resulting ignorance of evolution led to Turkey coming last in a survey that measured knowledge of evolution in 34 industrialised nations[8]

Currently, religious education courses begin at the 4th grade of primary school and continues throughout secondary and high schools. From the 4th to the 8th grade, classes consist of two hours per week. At the high school level, there is one hour of class per week Thus, a student who has graduated from high school receives 8 continuous years of religion courses. There are no fixed books for the course. Rather, each school decides which book to follow—provided that the book for each level is approved by the Ministry of Education. Nearly half of the content of these courses concerns religion and Islam (whom majority are Muslims) with remaining topics ranging from secularism to humanism and from ethical values to etiquette. The major world religions such as Judaism, Christianity, Hinduism and Buddhism are included in the content of the course.[9]

Criticism on <u>Turkish</u>: İmam Hatip Lisesi, so called clerical schools

Since their creation in the 1950s, Imam Hatip schools all have been controversial in the debate about Turkey's secular state[10] Kenan Cayir, assistant professor of sociology at Istanbul's <u>Bilgi University</u>, says the schools can have a positive impact so that religion and modernity can be together.[4] An objection to the free choice of Imam Hatip graduates came from TÜSIAD (<u>Turkish Industrialists' and Businessmen's Association</u>. According to their research conducted in 1988, approximately 32% of graduates of Imam Hatip schools picked faculties of law as their first choice in university entrance exams, proving more popular than religious based alternatives. The report concluded that, due to fundamental differences in their upbringing, Imam Hatip graduates were rendered unsuitable for public office. Politicians tended not to agree with TÜSIAD's position. For example, the then Minister of National Education, Avni Akyol, criticised the report in terms of human rights, claiming such proposals undermined the principle of equal opportunity in education.[11]

Following the reforms of March 2012 that extended compulsory education to 12 years and allowed for Imam Hatip schools to be opened and "middle school" level (second term of four years) experts warned that the possible increase in the number of Imam Hatip schools was not in line with people's expectations and described it as a "top-down" process. Critics noted that the new education system seemed to be a revenge being taken for Imam Hatip schools that were shut down after 1997.[12] A survey conducted by the Turkey İmam-Hatip Alumni Foundation (TİMAV), revealed that the majority of Turks hold positive views about Imam Hatip schools. The survey, titled "Perception of İmam-Hatip High Schools and İmam-Hatip Students in Turkey," was conducted between April 24 and May 18, 2012 with 2,689 people in 26 provinces. Most of the respondents were not Imam Hatip graduates.

The bill of March 2012 was written without public debate — or even discussion in the education ministry's own consultative body, the National Education Council — and it did not figure in the government's 2011 election manifesto. According to education specialists, the new measures would undermine educational standards and deepen social inequalities.[3] The education faculties of most of Turkey's leading universities — including Sabanci University, Bosphorus University, Middle East Technical University and Koç University all issued press statements describing the reforms of 2012 as hastily conceived, retrograde and out of step with current thinking[13]

To me, Turkey appears once again to be headed for turmoil. In this 700-year old country of 70 million Muslims, the seven-decade old military government is at war with Islam, imposing western secularism under the boots of Mustafa Kemal's generals. While some of the battlefields in this ongoing conflict are conventional in the military sense, many are not. A major site in the struggle for the hearts and minds of Turkish Muslims is the system of educational institutions.

By this Fall, the Pro Kemalist Generals have vowed to implement a number of new policies and restructuring programmes aimed at Muslim majority in Turkish schools and universities. While hijab was already banned in a number of Turkish universities before AKP government change the law so, new policies were set to extend that ban countrywide. In addition, semi-autonomous religious schools would come under tighter government control, in a wide ranging programme designed to prevent practising Muslims, women in particular, from achieving the high level of success they are known for in Turkey's educational system. Following weeks of protest and lawsuits, a Turkish court ruled some proposals unconstitutional, enforcing the ruling is more precarious and the future thus remains uncertain.

Education has been contested terrain for most of modern Turkish history. After the collapse of the Ottoman Empire, General Mustafa Kemal (ata 'Ataturk', meaning the father of Turks) thus tried to implement a series of anti-Islamic policies, the nature and scope of which are well known and need no repetition here. Upon Mustapha Kemal's death in Nov 10. 1938, the military establishment which he entrenched, became the enforcer of secularism in so called secular Turkey but to me Turkey has never been a Secular governing state.

Ottoman sultans had introduced western educational policies into the Empire, under Kemalism State schools and universities were pressed into service to teach the new secular religion, forbidding or severely circumscribing all vestiges of Turkey's Islamic heritage, and enforcing a uniform dress code banning hijab for women and beards or turbans for men. There have been several waves of Islamic resurgence since then, notably during the presidency of Adnan Menderes in the 1950s when the Arabic adhan was restored, but secular educational policies have remained stringent.

The government attempted to monitor a growing Islamic movement by opening a network of State sponsored Muslim schools in late 1960s, the Imam Hatip Lisesi so called The clerical schooling system, which would teach Qur'an, hadith, and fiqh to a new generation of Turkish Muslims. Some people also believe that Muslim schools were supported as a bulwark against leftist nationalism. Since then, the Imam Hatip schools have expanded to provide a wide ranging curriculum in a seven-year, post-primary programme of study that includes Arabic language.

In the late 1980s, Turkish Muslim scholar and author Fethullah Gulen returned from external exile and established a charitable foundation. The Fethullah Gulen Hodja Foundation soon opened a series of private Islamic schools, universities, and student hostels which have attracted an increasing number of Muslim students away from the public school system. In recent years, graduates of Imam Hatip and Fethullah Gulen Hodja schools have become the top performing candidates for Turkish university degrees. Imam Hatip and Fethullah Gulen Hodja schools provide separate facilities for male and female students, and encourage female students to wear hijab. Both have generally provided a supportive Islamic environment in which to study, and offer relatively standardized curricula similar to those found in most Turkish public schools.

Fethullah Gulen Hodja (Imam) hostels also serve as meeting places for members of various jama'ats and tarikats (Islamıcs sects). In the hostels, students partake of informal and self-directed Islamic learning, especially studying the 20th century Turkish mujaddid, Bediuzzaman Said Nursi, whose works are either cautiously avoided in private schools, or outright prohibited in the case of official State schools.

There are also organizations of the segment that is called the Islamic capital. The business world organizations that are close to Prime Minister Recep Tayyip Erdoğan are organized under the umbrella of the Independent Industrialists and Businessmen's Association, abbreviated as MÜSİAD. Those segments that are close to the Fethullah Gülen community are organized under the Turkish Confederation of Businessmen and Industrialists (TUSKON). Besides these, there are several businessmen's associations at the regional and sectoral levels.

After 2003, while MÜSİAD and TUSKON that were close to the Justice and Development Party (AKP) government were in a rising trend, TÜSİAD fell into a more defensive position. The TOBB on the other hand, even though it has a more heterogeneous structure, holds a closer position to the AKP government, in a balancing mission to the TÜSİAD.

The growing success of Muslim students in the Turkish educational system is causing increasingly loud rumblings of distemper in the bowels of Kemalist secularism. Earlier this summer, the rectors of all major Turkish universities signed a pact vowing to ban any women in hijab from classes beginning with the Fall 1998 semester. Rectors who are not wholeheartedly in support of the proposed measures are summarily terminated from their positions.

The exclusion pact would have broadened an earlier policy, in place since the late 1980s, in which hijab was banned in Istanbul University and at Dijla University in Diyarbakir, Eastern Turkey.

Most students, sums up their situation: 'If they cover themselves, they won't let them go to school, and they will not be able to get a job.' Though these students study undergraduate or postgraduate studies Most of them were concerned. 'Even though though their academic numbers were high, they believe if they Do not continue to wear their scarf, they will not be able to continue their education,'. With the exception of the Imam Hatip schools, headscarves have always been forbidden for Turkish primary and secondary schoolgirls, but despite this many girls wear them during summer and winter recess, and on weekends but nowdays it is free to wear them at any level of schools after the new law came into force by AKP Government.

In a related measure also aimed at Muslim education, the government is working on a plan to monitor and regulate the Fethullah Gulen Hodja Foundation's network of educational institutions. Especially worrisome to the regime is the informal network of hostels, which have begun to provide sanctuary for students at government institutions like Istanbul University. Regulatory measures will be more controversial still, since the Fethullah Gulen Foundation and its affiliates are privately funded and administered under rules that govern many other private schools in Turkey. The various British, French, and American academies prosper here, many of which are quasi-missionary in form and character, and are responsible for converting some of their Turkish students to Christianity. It will be interesting to see if these 'freedom loving' westerners will extend their calls for freedom to the Muslim schools currently under attack in Turkey.

For now, Imam Hatip schools will likely suffer the most as a result of the new educational policies, which are set to begin countrywide in Fall 1998. Under one proposed new programme, instead of the usual five years of compulsory public primary schooling, after which students could opt to attend the seven-year secondary programme in Imam Hatip schools rather than attending public secondary schools, the government will now require eight years of compulsory primary schooling for all students in the Turkish public school system. Because the schools are government run, and their teachers and administrators officially appointed, Muslim parents and teachers who wish to provide Islamic education for their children will have little say in any restructuring.

The lengthened time frame for compulsory primary schooling means that Imam Hatip schools will have to reduce course offerings and limit their curriculum to three or four years, since few students will be able to study for seven years in secondary school after eight years of primary schooling. It will be virtually impossible for Imam Hatip schools to maintain their delicate balance between Islamic studies and other academic subjects in such a short period of time.

Remarks on the Old & the New educational system

Neo-liberal policies have been affecting in waves all public services in Turkey since 1980s. Following the military coup so we assume that most affected institutions in this process were education in general and the higher education institutions in particular. Turkish higher education system, and was actually the shaping of the process into flesh and bones which started in 1980s. Also, this process shows similarities with the countries where neo-liberal policies are implemented, and a common language is used in the destruction of the public space.

The difference between the old system and the new one is that the former consisted of the 5+3+4 system, in which the students could choose their fields later than the new one. The high school is of great importance insofar as it helps determine the future choice of studies at the university. Students already have to choose between different domains in high school (sciences, literature, languages etc...) As an example, if you major in sciences in high school and apply for the 'English Language and Literature' department at the university, your chances are much slimmer than if you had applied for 'Maths'.

This is very important for the students, since there is a lot of demand and only few places to get into a good university, and every point that you get from the university exam counts. The centralized exam for the university admissions happens once per year. So being sick on the test day postpones for one year the taking of the examination.

The pros and cons of the new system

First of all many people are concerned that the students will choose their fields too young, at an age where they cannot make well-thought-out decisions for their future. The system is also criticized insofar as it pushes students to attend vocational schools, being consequently less 'educated'. Another criticism is that this system will favour religious high school students, who will be free to apply for any department at the universities, whereas this was not possible before. This is a big concern for many people, since many of them accuse the AKP government of trying to bring 'Islamism' to the secular Turkey. One of the interesting criticitisms deals with the EU and the USA: people accuse the government of implementing this policy solely because of the 'funds' that come from the EU and the 'pressure' made by the USA. This means that some people blame the EU and USA for using their financial powers on Turkey, by telling them what to do in their education system, with the threat of pulling out their funding in case Turkey does not do what it is told.

Even though this is a one-party government, there are three other parties that have seats in Parliament in Turkey. Let's see at what is their overall approach about the new system.

The other two big parties CHP (Republican People's Party) and MHP (Nationalist People's Party) that have seats in Parliament do not publicly reject this proposal, but they unofficially do it. They argued a lot to 'put it on hold', so it could be 'thoroughly discussed and evaluated'. One MP from the MHP (Nationalistic Movement Party) said *'If we politicize this topic, we will put a bullet on our foot'*, meaning that the topic of education should never be politicized. However, an MP from the BDP (Peace and Democracy Party), which is a party that 'represents' the Kurdish minority in Turkey, said *'If you reject one of your main languages (Kurdish), one day you will not be able to find an MP like Kaplan* (his name)'

Many people that are pro the new education system blame the others for being antagonistic and for wanting to keep the '28 February Coup' laws: after the religious Prosperity Party (Refah Partisi) won the elections in 1997, the national security council had a meeting on 28 February, and ended up with the decision to over throw the Prosperity Party. This decision taken during this meeting was also named as the 'post-modern coup'. The previous education system was adopted after the meeting on 28 February 1997 and was highly against any Islamist movement or any system that could foster it.

Whether usefull or useless to some, there may be some substantive changes that the new system brings. The most remarkable one is that the period of compulsory education will be increased from 8 to 12 years.

Another change concerns the starting age for the children. With the new system, children can start primary school at the age of five. Even though this system is accused of being sexist (because of the increase of students in vocational schools, that generally male students prefer), by preventing female population from working, others say that this system will help the girls with 'headscarfs' to be more integrated at school and in the working life but l am sure the next step will be to create policies against co education at publisc schools in the country.

It is clear that the new system is favoured by the government and their supporters, and disliked by the opposition and their supporters. It is easy to find convincing arguments from both sides. What can be said for sure is that there is a clear difference between the previous system, and the new one. What is not sure, is how this system will work, whether this is a conspiracy to make Turkey more religious, or just a good-willed law to develop Turkey's education system where l believe it would make the country more conservative and of course, fundamentalist.!

Analysis of the transformation of educational policies in Turkey

Neo-liberal policies have certainly political affects on all public services in Turkey since 1980s where military coup took the power. One of the major affected institutions in this process were education on the whole l and the higher education institutions in particular.

One of the most important steps for the realization of the neo-liberal transformation in Turkey is the transformation of the overall educational system. This transformation might be important for several reasons. First, with Amin's words (1997:198), the "social reproduction" function the education, and the second is that the education being the largest part of the social services in terms of both social funding and the social workers employed. In other words, when the educational system is transformed institutionally and constitutionally, almost half of the public sector will be transformed. Discussions forming a basis for transformation at higher education level, and the emphasis that the higher education is a "semi-public" service which has a higher private return than societal return have been the justifications for the decline of public funding reserved for higher education. The higher education service perceived as a public service until 1980s was defined as a "semi-public" service with the Higher Education Law passed in 1981 (law number: 2547). In the background of this definition is the Economic Stabilization Package enacted in 24 January 1980 which could be called the Constitution of the neo-liberal transformation in Turkey. Starting from the related legal regulations the higher education students participated in certain percentages to the cost of education they received. This contribution, called contribution margin, has been increasing with years. It is seen from the examination of the income resources of the Turkish state universities that the student contribution was 2% in 1990, 4% in 2000, and 5% in 1995 and 2005 (YÖK, 2005:132). An interesting development was experienced in 2011 when the neo-conservative party –Justice and Development Party- made a change in the Article 46 of the Higher Education Law and brought the provision that the government was going to address the "current service One of the most important steps for the realization of the neo-liberal transformation in Turkey is the transformation of the educational system. This transformation is important for two reasons. First, with Amin's words (1997:198), the "social reproduction" function the education, and the

Second, The education appears to be the largest part of the social services in terms of both social funding and the social workers employed. In other words, when the educational system is transformed institutionally and constitutionally, almost half of the public sector will be transformed. The higher education service perceived as a public service until 1980s was defined as a "semi-public" service with the Higher Education Law passed in 1981 (law number: 2547). In the background of this definition is the Economic Stabilization Package enacted in 24 January 1980 which could be called the Constitution of the neo-liberal transformation in Turkey. Starting from the related legal regulations the higher education students participated in certain percentages to the cost of education they received. This contribution, called contribution margin, has been increasing with years. It is seen from the examination of the income resources of the Turkish state universities that the student contribution was 2% in 1990, 4% in 2000, and 5% in 1995 and 2005 (YÖK, 2005:132). An interesting development was experienced in 2011 when the neo-conservative party –Justice and Development Party- made a change in the Article 46 of the Higher Education Law and brought the provision that the government was going to address the "current service increased 3.7 times (27%) from 1 322 345 (MEB, 1999: 139) in 1997-1998 educational year to 4 936 591 (www.osym.gov.tr) in the 2012-2013 educational year.

The preference of the state related to education investments is one of the indications where we can see the effects of neo-liberal policies. It can be seen from the Table 1 that the MEB investment budgetvi decreased significantly between 1997 and 2012. While the rate of the MEB investment budget in the total education budget was 15.01% in 1997, it fell to 6.64% in 2012. Also, the rates of the MEB budget decreased significantly in the consolidated investment budget (28.35% in 2000; 8.09% in 2012) and in the GDP (0.40% in 2000; 0.18% in 2012). These data show that while the number of students increased, the State resigned slowly but significantly from education in general and higher education in particular.

Conclusion

Education in Turkey, which has a young population, is an important area of investment because of the high demand. For example, the number of students at all levels of the educational system was 22.171.043 in total in 2012-2013 educational year. In the same educational year, the number of students registered in elementary schools was 1.756.618, and 1.128.557 in secondary schools (MEB, 2013). The student placement at the higher education level is done through a central examination organized by the Student Selection and Placement Centre (OSYM). In the 2012-2013 educational year, 1.895.479 students applied to take the Student Selection and Placement Examination (OSYS). While 29% of those students were placed in the license and pre-license programs of the state universities, 4% were placed in the trust/private universities (http://osym.gov.tr). The number of students applying for the higher education every year changes between 1.5 million and 2 million

Various changes have been made in Turkey recently with the purpose of making national education system more qualified and catching up with the standards of developed countries. With "Primary Education Law no 6287" adopted on 30 March 2012, a radical decision is made in our education system and put into practice. This law, which is known by public as 4+4+4 and made a sudden change in Turkish education system, has brought along many discussions. In this study, it is aimed that the impacts of 4+4+4 education system, which is created with the purpose of increasing the period of compulsory education in Turkey to the average of EU and OECD countries and providing a more qualified education environment to the students, are analysed since the time it has come up for the first time. Literature review method is used in the research and the reviews covered in the media, texts published by universities, unions and various organisations and articles reflecting the opinions of the domain experts regarding the new education system are analysed. This data is evaluated and a critical perspective is developed about the effectiveness of the 4+4+4 system.

the results of some public examinations also show how bad the situation is in Turkish education. This year's Transition to Higher Education Examination (YGS), whose results were announced on the website of the Student Selection and Placement Center (ÖSYM) on March 29, was a shock for many as there were high numbers of zero-scorers in various sections of the exam. According to the exam results, the number of students who failed to correctly answer a single one of the 40 questions on the YGS mathematics section was about 420,000, while nearly 900,000 students scored zero on the science section of the YGS, which is the first round of exams for university applicants in Turkey.

The number of those zero-scorers tends to rise every passing year. The number of students who end up with a zero score on the YGS university entrance examination was 14,000 in 2010, while this figure rose to 38,269 in 2011 and to 50,805 in 2012, which marks an exact 362.8 percent rise in the number of students who did not get any scores

Considering huge budgets that have been allocated to the education system, primarily in the last few years, and successive educational reforms introduced by the government, I wonder what is really missing from the educational system in Turkey

Overcrowded classrooms, teacher shortages, the practice of having substitute teachers, unqualified teachers, inequality of opportunity between public schools and private colleges, lack of necessary facilities to provide a good education for their students and an exam-based education system are factors that emerge as the reasons behind the failure of Turkish education. All those factors may all be specific reasons due to infrastructural reasons.

Apart from those are infrastructural reasons, there are also some administerial mistakes made by top educational authorities in Turkey. The Education Ministry, which is the primary institution responsible for adopting educational policies in the country, turned the Turkish education system into a scratch pad with its rapidly adopted successive "educational reforms" in recent years. Undoubtedly, the most radical reform that has been adopted in the last few years was a 2012 education reform, formulated as the 4+4+4 education system, which increased the period of compulsory education from eight years to 12. With this law, compulsory education was separated into three four-year stages as primary, middle and high school education. With this reform, children who reach 66 months of age are obliged to register at a primary school. These changes were met by strong negative reactions from the public and educators, but the ministry never changed its mind and put this reform into effect without any pilot scheme or any satisfactory preparation period at the beginning of the 2012-2013 academic year.

However, such serious changes should be made after a long preparation and test period in order to not cause irreversible damages both in children, who can in no way been considered guinea pigs, and the education system in general. The ministry didn't even bother to consult educators and educational psychologists while introducing the 4+4+4 educational system.

I believe this problem stems from the fact that top educational authorities generally consist of state bureaucrats who have no direct experience in the field of education. For example, current Education Minister Nabi Avcı studied administrative science for his bachelor degree, and completed his master's and PhD in the field of communication. Former Education Minister Ömer Dinçer studied business economics at university. How can we expect educational policies that are effective both pedagogically and educationally from those ministers who are unqualified in the field of education? It is unfortunately very challenging to give a good answer to this dilemma.l Do not believe they have necessary organizational behaviour to organize the decision making policies at ministerial level for new methods and technology in education.

Okay, these all infrastructural and administerial reasons contribute to the failure of education system in Turkey to some degree. However, the reasons that are directly related to learning and teaching process cause more serious negative impacts on the Turkish education, but they are generally neglected.

Unfortunately, the learning process is still based on rote-learning at Turkish schools due to their conservative traditional values, at public schools in particular. The schools are perceived as the places where students are loaded with necessary amounts of information. Are schools the places where certain knowledge is transmitted via strict curriculas placed by the Education Ministry? Certainly not! The Turkish educational curricula for each stage of education are burdensome and include very unrealistic objectives due to various changes with their curriculums. The curricula are therefore not aimed at filling the students with as much as information as they can during an academic year. However, this doesn't work. Preparing a busy scheduled curricula doesn't mean to provide better qualied education to its nationals

in addition those complex curricula, the teaching methods and techniques are also very troublesome in the country. For instance Majority of Turkish teachers still use some traditional educational methods that have already become outdated in most developed countries long ago.

İnstead of The teacher-centered education system the prefered to replace it with a student-centered education system. In classrooms where traditional methods and techniques are used, students become passive recipients of knowledge. They will know and comprehend these ideas, concepts, principles or theories taught at the class, but will be unable to develop higher-level thinking skills such as analysis, synthesis, application and evaluation. As we provide the knowledge readily to students, they don't feel the necessity to search for knowledge, understand it or produce new informative knowledge at all.

Thus, Turkey needs to change its general perspective and vision about learning and teaching as in modern technology used by west. New educational opportunities in which students will be able to construct knowledge and produce new ideas in flexible and unconstrained educational environments should be provided. In this way, Turkey will be able to improve the general intellectual level of its citizens by teaching them how to produce knowledge, not how to memorize the existing knowledge. İn case they give up their dogma mottos in their national inheritence.

CHAPTER 11

E-Learning System Evaluation towards Improving Entrepreneurial Competencies Supported by Modern Automated Systems: Case Study of Balkan Countries

Prof. Dr. Mirjana Radović-Marković, FRSA,
FWAAS, EA, EMAAS, SKANU[1]
Akamai University

Lecturer Dušan Marković, Ms. C
Akamai University

Abstract

The environment for learning has changed rapidly through the applying of new technologies as well as expectations towards professional knowledge in the information age. Application of various technologies improves learning environment and provides preconditions to transform teaching into learning. The online learning environment is quite different from a traditional classroom, in which one had limited interaction and

---

[1] The paper is written as a part of the projects OI 179015 and II 47009, financed by Ministry of Science of the Republic of Serbia.

almost unlimited access to learning resources. The main objective of this paper is to explore the possibilities of improving entrepreneurial competencies through e-learning and new tools of studying. This paper also focuses on the application of an Agent-Based Intelligent System (ABIS) for enhancing e-learning in Serbia and Turkey in the field of entrepreneurship education. In this context, the authors conducted surveys of Turkish and Serbian college students and compared the results. The two countries were selected for the study because they belong to the Balkan region and therefore have certain characteristics that distinguish the region. Although there are some specific features of the region, the results showed significant differences between the two countries. Explanations can be found in the social, cultural, economic and other characteristics of Turkey and of Serbia.

Keywords: Intelligent agent, software development, e-Learning, entrepreneurial skills, individuality, entrepreneurial competencies, Serbia, Turkey.

Introduction

E-learning is recognized in many countries as a catalyst for national development. In line with this, the rapid development of e-learning and its modalities geared towards practical skills in business enterprises and entrepreneurship competencies is necessary for national self-reliance and development. Delivering learning content anytime, anywhere is a goal that underpins the e-learning paradigm. In addition, based on new technologies, e-learning can support creativity and assist students in developing their individual potentials. For this reason, emphasis should be focused on the individual needs of students and personalized training programs. Computer-based educational techniques have been considered as our best hope for individualization.[2] The different levels of interaction and collaboration characteristic of new technologies facilitate the personalisation of learning paths. The development and

---

2   Marvin Croy, "Distance Education, Individualization, and the Demise of the University," *Technology In Society,* no. 20 (1998): 320.

implementation of student-centric technology will bring shift to student-centered pedagogy and the ownership of learning by learners, a quality that is indispensable for fostering creativity. However, personalisation of learning content delivery requires system adaptivity supported by using a suite of collaborative intelligent agents. The agent's roles in e-learning is not only to personalize the learning programs but also to create real-life business situations used for the purposes of training. Some fields of software systems (e.g. the automation of business processes or information management) have already found their way into real-world applications.[3] For example, the goal of a business simulation is of particular importance for the development of competencies for existing or potential entrepreneurs. Besides, intelligent agents perform specific tasks on the behalf of instructors and other members of the educational community. Due to the vast possibilities of these applications, scientists are considering new modalities. Some of these options will be analyzed in this paper as well. We will try to implement them in the education system in Serbia, where the e-learning is in its infancy. Our proposals should help students to obtain knowledge faster, as well as fostering better interaction among them, professors, and the business environment.

Theoretical Background

In literature, online learning has been compared to face-to-face learning from different points of view. Thus, Hoben et al.[4] explored the effectiveness of online tools such as discussion boards and chat rooms, while Spatariu et al.[5] addressed evaluating effective online instruction.

---

3   Thomas Wagner, *Applying Agents for Engineering of Industrial Automation Systems* (Stuttgart: Universität Stuttgart, 2003), 13.

4   George Hoben et.al., *Assessment of Student Learning in an Educational Administration Online Program* (New Orleans: American Educational Research Association, 2002), 4.

5   Alexandru Spatariu, Kendall Hartley, Lisa Bendixen, "Defining and Measuring Quality in Online Discussions," *The Journal of Interactive Online Learning* 4, no. 2 (2004), 1-15.

Graham et al.[6] and McCombs[7] assessed the value of online courses in specific fields of study. In particular, the use of virtual worlds to reach remote online learners is creating new opportunities for face-to face engagement and motivation with difficult-to-reach groups. Draves[8] provides a list of reasons why he believes the Internet enhances learning, including such advantages as being able to learn at a peak time of the day, learning at your own speed, accessibility to much information, an ability to track personal progress, and the capability of testing personal learning efforts. In addition, e-learning students are ideally in an environment where professors respond to their needs on demand.[9] However, most learning environments neglect the learning services and pedagogical aspects of e-teaching. Hence, its development has lagged behind the massive investment in hardware and teacher training in using ICT.[10] According to some researchers, e-learning pedagogy should incorporate the learning pedagogy but go beyond it to include a deeper study into the incorporation of instructional strategies that

---

6   Charles Graham, Kursat Cagiltay, Byung-Ro Lim, Joni Craner, and Thomas M. Duffy, "Seven Principles of Effective Teaching: A Practical Lens for Evaluating Online Courses," *Technology Source* (Chapel Hill: University of North Carolina, 2001), accessed October 20, 2013, http://technologysource.org/article/seven principles of effective teaching/

7   Barbara L. McCombs, "Assessing the Role of Educational Technology in the Teaching and Learning
Process: A Learner-Centered Perspective," in *The Secretary's Conference on Educational Technology* (Denver: University of Denver Research Institute, 2000), accessed October 27, 2013.

8   William Draves. *Teaching online* (River Falls : LERN Books, 2002), p.10-15, accessed June 21, 2013.

9   Mirjana Radović-Marković, "Special Benefits of E-learning for Women: Sample of Program Entrepreneurship," edited by Priscilla Achakra. In *Gender and Informal Economy: Developing Developed and Transition Countries* (Lagos: ICEA and Prenticeconsult, 2007), 156-166.

10 Len Newton and Laurence Rogers, *Teaching Science with ICT* (London: Continuum, 2001), p.1-2. Accessed November 15, 2013.

take into account of real-time personalized learning content-to-learner adaptability.[11]

In addition, in Serbia, our research showed that conventional educational concepts do not provide educational curricula development in the field of entrepreneurship, which is meant to facilitate self-employment. There needs to be closer connections between educational institutions and manufacturing and other types of organizations, as well as with the business environment.[12] According to other recent research,[13] the introduction of virtual environments into higher education has the potential to bring a positive change in the learning experience. The online learning environment is quite different from a traditional classroom, especially since the appropriation of technological platforms requires new approaches to learning styles. An adequate e-learning theory should take into account four related dimensions[14]:

1. Learning theories
2. Psychological dimensions and demands of the learner
3. Technology (ICTs)
4. Content to be learned

Various online applications could be used to empower teachers to become innovative in their teaching, as well as helping students develop their creative skills and learn creatively. In the first place, online courses

---

11   Teo Chao Boon, Robert Gay, and Kheng Leng, "Pedagogy Considerations for E-learning," *International Journal of Instructional Technology and Distance Learning* 3, no. 5. (2006) : 3-26.

12   Mirjana Radović-Marković, "Impact of Globalization on Organizational Culture, Behaviour and Gender Role" (Charlotte: IAP, 2011), p.15-20.

13   Fotis Liarokapis, Anastasios Doulamis, Vassilios Vescoukis (Eds.), "Games and Virtual Worlds for Serious Applications," *Third International Conference on Games and Virtual Worlds for Serious Applications* (Athens: IEEE, 2011).

14   Mirjana Radović-Marković et al., "Fostering Entrepreneurship in Higher Education through E-learning: A Case Study of Serbia and Turkey," in *Employment, Education, Entrepreneurship,* ed. M. Radović Marković (Belgrade: Faculty of Business Economics and Entrepreneurship, 2012), p.10-27.

require participants to take on new, different teaching and learning behaviors. In addition, e-learning content differs from other educational materials, in that it can be disassembled as individual learning objects, tagged, and stored for re-use in a variety of different learning contexts. Further, in e-learning, the role of the teacher is not only to be a presenter of knowledge, and e-learning requires that teachers to adopt a new teaching style. The teachers are supported by the new ICTs, which offer new opportunities for teaching. Adding distance entrepreneurship courses to existing offerings will increase the number of alternatives from which students can choose. Certainly, students can individualize their own education through their choices.[15] If their alternatives can be expanded, then individualization can be increased. In addition, we can soon expect that the students will learn with software that is developed for their kind of intelligence and learning style.

Of a key importance are intelligent agents which can help students in learning. Intelligent agents are one of the most useful tools with various redundant in e-learning. Therefore, much research has been done focusing on the adoption of intelligent agents to integrate e-learning systems and support e-learning pedagogy. Intelligent agents have received considerable attention by scientists over the last decade due to their great potential for addressing the limitations of the current learning systems by supporting learning processes.

Hence, in literature we can find a great number of definitions of "intelligent agent." According to Bowen,[16] the definition of intelligent agent includes five characteristics and roles of an agent:

- Searches for information automatically
- Answers specific questions
- Informs student when an event (e.g., an article has been published, your favorite book is on sale, the road you travel is

---

[15] Marvin Croy, "Distance Education, Individualization, and the Demise of the University," *Technology In Society*, no.20 (1998): 318.

[16] Ed Bowen, "Intelligent Agents: What They Do and How They're Changing Online Learning," in *Proceedings of TELECOOP Conference* (Estes Park: TELECOOP, 2007), pp.1-31.

under construction, your name has been mentioned on the web) has occurred
- Provides custom news to student in a just-in-time format
- Provides intelligent tutoring.

In line with this, there is research in the areas of intelligent tutoring systems, virtual mentors, and adaptive hypermedia--the techniques and tools that can provide improved learning outcomes.[17] [18] They target and deliver just-in-time learning materials required by the individual learners.[19] According Gregg, software agents can be used to support instructors and domain experts with course design and delivery, as well as individual learners by personalizing course materials based on learning objectives. Pedagogical agents have positive effects on learning and have the following characteristics[20]:
- Adaptation: understand the student's needs and adapt the lesson plan.
- Motivation: offer encouragement to the students and give them feedback.
- Evolution: keep students current in a rapidly changing culture.

Modern Automated Systems

Making high-quality software for complex systems is a very difficult and comprehensive task. Development of software in areas such as

---

17 Peter Brusilovsky, "Adaptive Educational Hypermedia: From Generation to Generation," in *Proceedings of 4th Hellenic Conference on Information and Communication Technologies in Education* (Athens: University of Athens, 2004), pp. 19-33.

18 Steven Hanks and Gaylen Chandl, "Funder Competence, the Environment and Venture Performance," *Entrepreneurship Theory and Practice* 18, no. 3(1994): 77-80.

19 Dawn Gregg, "E-learning Agents," *The Learning Organization* 14, no. 4 (2007): 300-312.

20 Mirjana Radović-Marković, *Impact of Globalization on Organizational Culture, Behaviour and Gender Role* (Charlotte: IAP, 2011), p.25.

managing business processes in industry, and business processes in education are among the most complex project tasks. One goal of such software goal is the automation of processes. In that context, software engineering has created a broad spectrum of paradigms. Each successfully developed phase improves the performance of engineering processes and makes it easier to construct complex applications.

Modern automated systems are characterized by the following properties:

- **Automated systems are complex and distributed systems.**
- **Automated systems require different views of system operation**–Automated systems require different problem-solving approaches. Among the most important are the engineering approach, the approach of people from production processes and management, and so on. All of these different approaches offer different views of structure, data, and the functionality of automatic systems.
- **System automation requires flexible and adjustable software** –Software changes can relate to data, structure, or the working sequences of the system.

These characteristics can be compared to the general characteristics of complex and decentralized systems. Complex systems have a large number of parts among which many interactions exist. Because of their complexity, these systems often take the form of an organizational structure. Relations between systems are different and change over time.

Agent-oriented Software Systems

The agent-oriented approach is a modern way of systemic decomposition in software engineering. It consists of subsystems and their components. Interactions between a subsystem and its components are mapped in a cooperation, coordination, and negotiation mechanism, and "relations between them are mapped as an explicit mechanism for introduction of organizational relations."[21]

In agent-oriented software systems, manifold agents enable decentralized problem solving, control from different locations, viewing a problem from various perspectives, and so forth. In addition, through the highest level of interaction, system of agents provides mechanisms for creating flexible organizational structures. With these dynamic effects "from the bottom to the top," coordination is done, and there is a possibility that changing one area can lead to dynamic adjusting of software. Having in mind possibilities that it offers, it can be concluded that agent-oriented concepts are more suitable for fulfilling demands of modern automated systems than other software systems.

We have designed an architecture using web service based on intelligent agents providing students use of educational services in e-learning networks. This is an opportunity to empower and improve the learning skills and experience of individual learners, instructors or teachers, and the business environment through user-agent interactions.

The Use of Agent-Oriented System in E-Learning

There are five principles that could be used by an institution that wants to use the untraditional model of andraversity or televersity for e-learning and life-long improvement. These principles are as follows[22]:

1. Innovative structure and system, where industry/business and college can share academic goals and work together on strengthening teaching and learning, both inside and outside the campus, through digital and electronic learning methods.

---

21 Thomas Wagner, *Applying Agents for Engineering of Industrial Automation Systems* (Stuttgart: Universität Stuttgart, 2003), p.15.

22 Hon Cheung Lee, "The New Era of Televersity and Andraversity in the Campusless Society: The Virtual University and its Implications in Korea," in *Virtual University? Educational Environments of the Future*, ed. U. H. J. Molen (London: Portland Press), p.126.

2. Educationally opened system, which means flexibility of teaching plan and program, as well as various forms of education.
3. Decentralized system, where individual academic units that are formed on campus and in the private sector are equally responsible for the delivery of various educational programs in their domain of interests and competence, no matter their location and the areas of interest of their students.
4. Connection of models on the community level, where the part of technical/professional education at the university level has to include appreciation of detailed information and industry needs. That includes joint running of educational and research activities.
5. Formation of a telecommunication structure that uses different kinds of tele-electronic technologies for connecting industrial/business location to faculties with the aim of offering virtually-educational services.

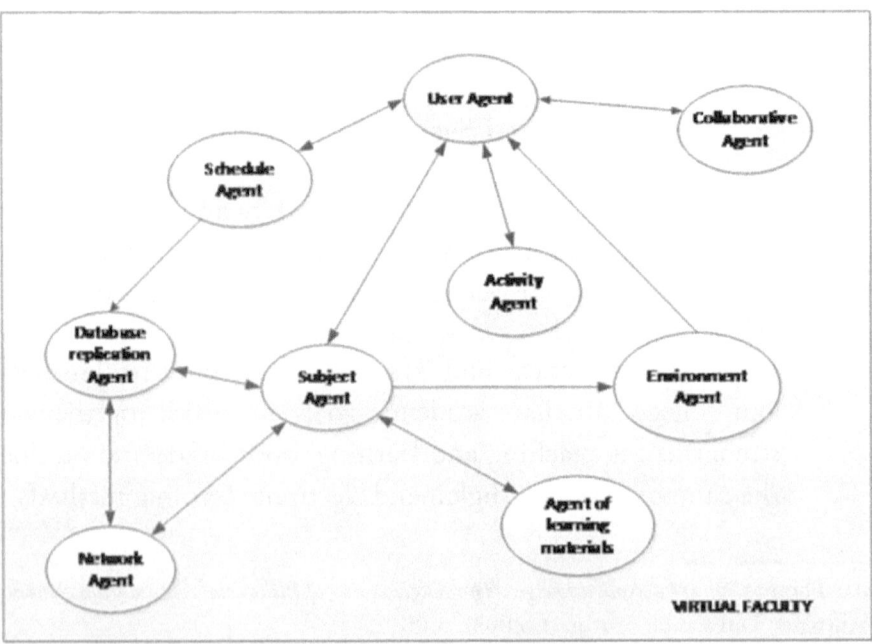

Fig. 1: Agent- oriented virtual education
Source: Authors

On the basis of the first three andraversity/televersity principles of education model, one realization of this model is given in Graph 1. One can observe a large number of agents, each with a role as explained below:

- **Schedule agent**--allows access to users and the specific educational programs in which users are interested. This agent directly manages the user agent and the database replication agent.
- **User agent**--is an agent whose main role is to identify the logging capabilities of the individual, his or her role in the system (whether a student or a teacher logged in), what his or her rights are, and what he or she has failed to complete since the last login--unless it is his or her first login. In that case, the agent also activates the activity agent.
- **Activity agent**--is an agent that records when users log in, when they log out, and how much time they spend in the system.
- **Subject agent**--has a role to know which facility and subjects that the user has chosen or needs to belong to. This agent is also in correspondence with the agent of learning materials (if the subject is at the current facility) which work together in the modification of user environment.
- **Agent of learning materials**--monitors what the currently selected subject is and makes appropriate materials for individual learning modules available.
- **Environment agent**--for each user who has selected the appropriate subject and teaching material, a learning environment is formed. This environment displays teaching materials as the student progresses in learning.
- **Database replication agent**--transfers the basic information about the user who has chosen the subject from another facility, and also shows the success that was achieved in that subject, thus completing the information on the students' progress.
- **Collaborative agent**--allows direct communication between the system users who are located in different virtual classrooms.

- **Network agent**--is used for connecting systems from the list of available addresses. If the negotiations between network agents are successfully implemented, faculty can access other faculty resources. The same agent is used in the database replication of students, whether the student has chosen a subject in some other facility or wants to join the teaching process.

Any user who wants to use the system can use it from the moment when schedule agent allows it and work in the appropriate study group, which is provided at that time. The intelligent agents can effectively support a user's learning and training process. When logging in to the system, the user agent is activated and identifies the user, what his or her role in the system is, as well as what his or her last activity was in the case it is not his or her first login. As soon as the user agent is activated, it sends a message to the activity agent to record all of his or her activities in the system, such as the date and time of the start of the login, as well as the end of it when logging out of the system.

If users are logged into the system for the first time, they choose the subjects among the ones in the curriculum which the subject agent stores into the database, as well as choosing which facility is the home facility for the appropriate subject. Each of these subjects has teaching material arranged through the modules and delivered by the agent of learning materials. If the student chooses a subject whose home facility is not the holder of the materials in that subject, at intervals the schedule agent activates the database replication agent whose role is to transmit basic information about the user of a selected subject, and after completing a certain course at different facility, to collect data on the results achieved. For all selected items in the scope of the home facility, a working environment is formed through the environment agent together with the curriculum, and this is shown as a student progresses. To exchange information about the student and his or her success at another facility, it is necessary to have a network agent, which establishes a connection with appropriate facility which is on the list of possible links. The same agent is used to share information or to connect students because of the access to the resources of another facility in order to learn appropriate subject.

Since facilities have their own complex structures, and since application software does not have to be exactly the same (they can be heterogeneous), in order to collaborate, each facility should be equipped with some of these agents. Firstly, it should have a network agent which enables connection, as well as a database replication agent and a user agent.

Developing Entrepreneurial Competencies through E-Learning

Research shows that there is a strong relationship between education level and entrepreneurship.[23] Entrepreneurship education means many different things to educators from primary schools to the university. At each level of education, it is reasonable to expect different outcomes, but the overall purpose remains to develop expertise as an entrepreneur. Higher education is of especially key importance for entrepreneurs. Education, on one hand, encourages entrepreneurship and sets the substructure of entrepreneurship culture; on the other hand, it develops competencies of entrepreneur will need when he sets up a company.

Researchers define entrepreneurial competency as the ability to interact with the business environment effectively. Competencies consist of knowledge, skills, attitudes, behaviors, and abilities necessary to do a job successfully. They are easily identified and measured. Competencies can be improved through experience, education, and training. That is to say, while entrepreneurs often learn and gain experience through practice and from their role models in business, without education they will not be able to test their ideas, and education will help them turn those ideas into reality more easily. Besides, education develops the creativity and skills that are important for rapid decision-making in a business environment that is constantly changing. Hence, the

---

23 Mirjana Radović-Marković, "Female Entrepreneurship: Theoretical Background," *Journal of Women's Entrepreneurship and Education* 4, no.1-2 (2013): 1-9.

entrepreneurship education programs can be of relevance to develop entrepreneurship competencies.

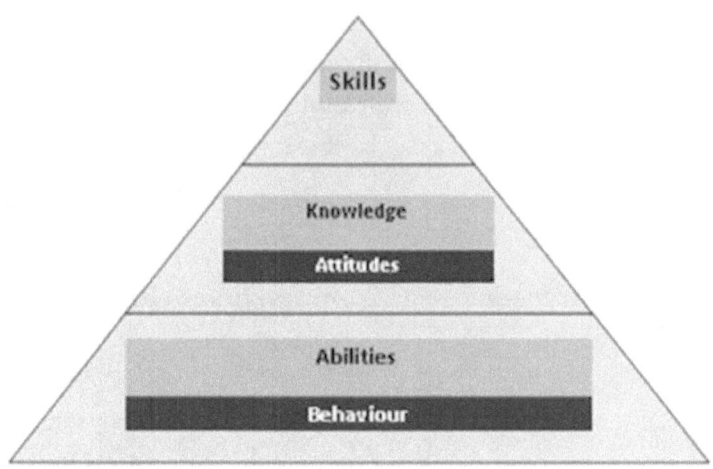

Fig. 2. Entrepreneurial competencies
Source: Authors

Entrepreneurship E-Learning Programs Supported by Intelligent Agents

E-learning is a current technological solution to the problem of finding the best match between the needs of a given set of learners and a given content, using a given set of learning tools or the delivery of education through various electronic media. It can be best understood in the broad context of using technology to meet needs for learning. According to our research,[24] the most important aspects of e-learning are learning objects and the various software tools that aid in their development, storage, use in teaching, and administration. E-learning

---

24 Mirjana Radović-Marković, et al., "Freedom, Individuality and Women's Entrepreneurship Education," in *Entrepreneurship Education--A Priority for the Higher Education Institutions*, eds. Catalin Martin and Elena Druica (Bologna: Medimond, 2012), 426.

is often delivered using specialized intelligent agents that assist teachers in creating their courses, the student in performing coursework, and administrator in making previously developed coursework available for re-use. An agent, intelligent agent, or agent-based system is a software-based computer system that has many properties, such as autonomy, social ability, reactivity, goal-directedness, mobility, and collaboration.

Recently, there has been much research on agent-oriented programming because the intelligent agent technique has developed rapidly. According to Tsai et al.,[25] intelligent agents have the following three characteristics:

(1.) Autonomous: an agent can control its inner states and act based on its experience.
(2.) Interactive: an agent can communicate with its environment and other agents to complete missions given by users.
(3.) Adaptive: an agent can respond to its environment and other agents, thereby determining its actions based on its experience.

Through the online entrepreneurship programs, learners can complete projects whether at work, home, or selected locations. On many occasions, busy executives, managers, or entrepreneurs may not be able to leave the office, and yet assignments, term papers and even research projects have to be completed somehow; finishing assignments may only be made possible through the online mode. Where programs are completely in the online mode, all class lectures, assignments, tests and instructions are delivered through the Internet. Some programs have voice and/or video assisted delivery, and may also include PowerPoint and iPod presentations. That is the main reason that an Internet service provider, a browser, and a computer with plenty of random access memory (RAM) are needed prior to an online course commencing in order that students may receive lectures from anywhere and anytime.

---

25 Hua-Lin Tsai, Chi-Jen Lee, Wen-Hsi Lydia Hsu, Yu-Hsin Chang. *An Adaptive E-Learning System Based on Intelligent Agents in Recent Researches in Applied Computers and Computational Science* (Rovaniemi: WSEAS Press, 2012), p.139.

Methodology

Distance Education has been actually applied in Turkey since 1982.[26] Thousands of students today earn university diplomas studying at a distance. On the other hand, Serbia does not have extensive experience deploying online studies and virtual faculties.

The questionnaire was designed to investigate the concepts of "e-learning"/ "distance learning" and "entrepreneurship," from the standpoint of view of students in this field. This questionnaire was given to Anadolu University, Faculty of Economics, Turkey,[27] and Belgrade Business School, Serbia.[28] The sample of students who participated in the survey is approximately the same for both countries (205 respondents were from Turkey and 200 respondents from Serbia).

The gender ratio of the respondents in Turkey is 65:35 (female and men respectively), but in Serbia, it is 72:20 (female and men respectively). The highest percentage of women (71%) in Turkey consists of those between 21-23 years old, whereas the highest percentage of women (65%) in Serbia consists of those between 19 to 22 years old.

Our research included nine questions as follows [29]:

1. Do you intend to run your private business as soon as you graduate?
A) Yes
B) No

---

26 Nursel Ruzgar, "Distance Education in Turkey, Turkish Online Journal of Distance Education," *Turkish Online Journal of Distance Education* 5, No 2.(2004), 22-32. Accessed 16 May 2006, http://tojde.anadolu.edu.tr/tojde14/articles/ruzgar.htm.

27 Conducted by professors Ugur Demiray and Emine Demiray in 2012.

28 Conducted by professor Mirjana Radović-Marković and Dušan Marković in 2012.

29 Mirjana Radovic-Markovic et al., "Fostering Entrepreneurship in Higher Education through E-learning: A Case Study of Serbia and Turkey," in *Employment, Education, Entrepreneurship*, ed. M. Radović-Marković (Belgrade:Faculty of Business economics and Entrepreneurship, 2012), p.10-27.

2. Why do you want to be an entrepreneur?
A) This is the only way to get a job
B) I can earn more than working for someone
C) I have a good business idea which I want to realize

3. Do you have any role models among successful entrepreneurs?
A) Yes
B) No

4. Is formal education necessary for entrepreneurship?
A) Yes
B) No

5. Do you believe that distance learning would be a good solution for future young entrepreneurs?
A) Yes
B) No

6. Would you like to attend one of these distance learning programs?
A) Yes
B) No

7. What would be the most important in selecting such a program, and ways of learning?
A) Acquisition of knowledge
B) Faster and easier way to graduate
C) Flexibility in studying

8. What do you think is crucial to be successful in an entrepreneurial career?
  A) To be highly motivated to succeed
  B) To have the ability to innovate and original business ideas
  C) To have good business contacts

9. Do you believe that application of an Agent Based Intelligent System (ABIS) can enhance e-learning in Serbia in the field of entrepreneurship education?
  A) Yes
  B) No
  C) I do not know

Research Findings

29% of respondents from Turkey answered "Yes" to the first question, and 71% said "No." Only a third of responders intend to start up a business after graduation. Although young people in Serbia generally prefer to seek employment in state institutions rather than starting their own businesses, this study showed different results. About 90% of the Serbian respondents are ready to launch their own businesses as soon as they graduate (Figure 3). The explanation lies in the fact that the respondents attend a business school. Certainly, the results would be different if the same question were asked to students attending a technical university or college.

For the second question, the third option was rated the most important by 50% of the responders from Turkey ("I have a good business idea which I want to realize"). However, this opinion is not shared by respondents from Serbia. For them, it is of key importance to earn more if they work for themselves (45%)(Figure 4).

66% of all respondents from Turkey are answered "Yes" to the third question. It can be concluded that the most responders from Turkey have a role model among that country's many successful entrepreneurs. But the responses from Serbia were quite different: the majority of respondents (50%) answered "No," and 42 % respondents said "Yes."(Figure 5).

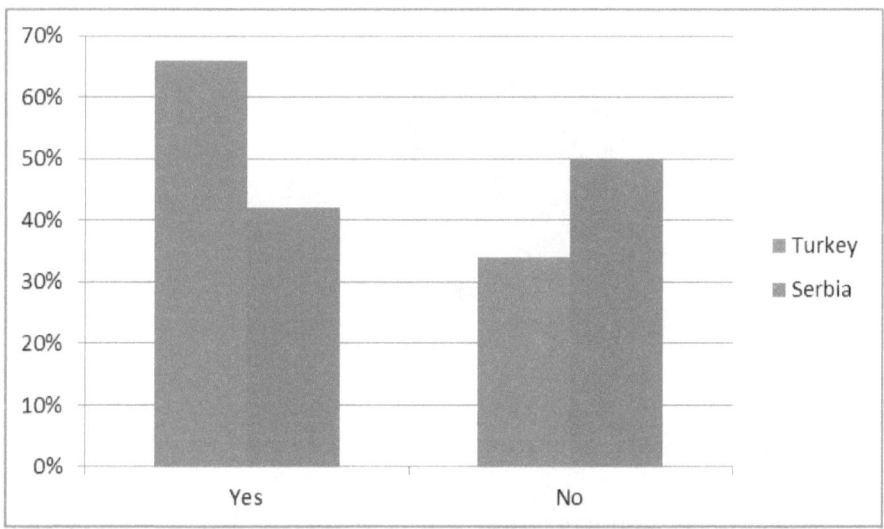

Fig. 5. Do you have any role models among successful entrepreneurs?

The reason that young people in Serbia do not have role models (or to a lesser extent than students in Turkey) can be explained by the fact that private businesses have a shorter tradition here. Moreover, there is a much smaller number of true role models given the high level of corruption enabling successful yet unethical businesses.

57% of all respondents from Turkey answered "Yes" to the question four and 50% from Serbia. This shows that, in this case, there are no major differences between the two countries (Figure 6).

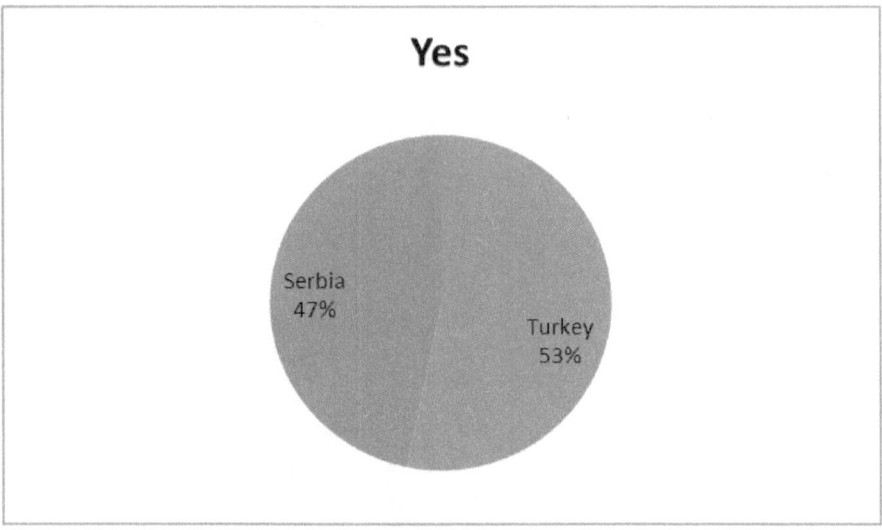

Fig. 6. Is formal education necessary for entrepreneurship?

44% of the respondents from Turkey answered "Yes" to the question five, while 26% percent of responders from Serbia said "Yes." (Figure 7).The majority of women did not believe that distance learning would be a good solution for future young entrepreneurs. They share the same opinion equally with men.

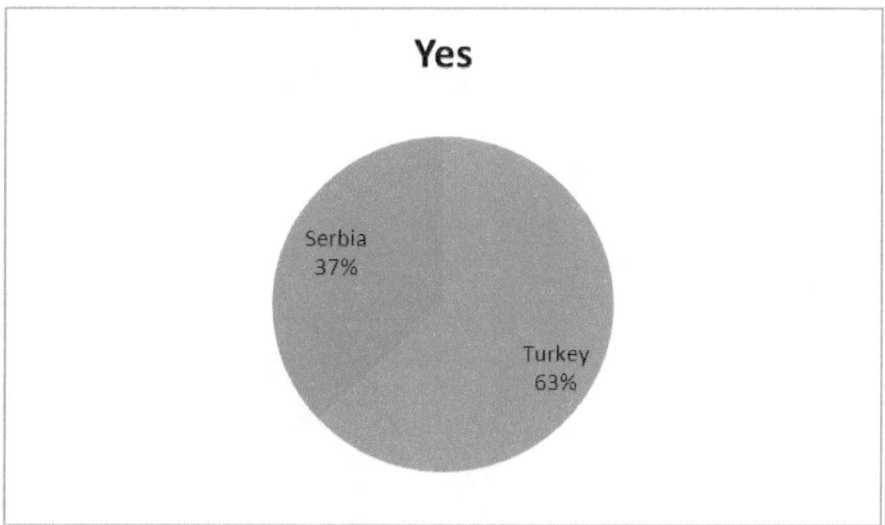

Fig. 7. Do you believe that distance learning would be a good solution for future young entrepreneurs?

31% of the total number of respondents from Turkey answered "Yes" to the question six, while 69% respondents answered "No." On the other hand, almost all respondents from Serbia said "Yes." Probably, the reason for such a large number of respondents who gave a positive answer can be found in the fact that the students would like to see how e-learning works in practice because it is still not very much applied in Serbia (Figure 8).

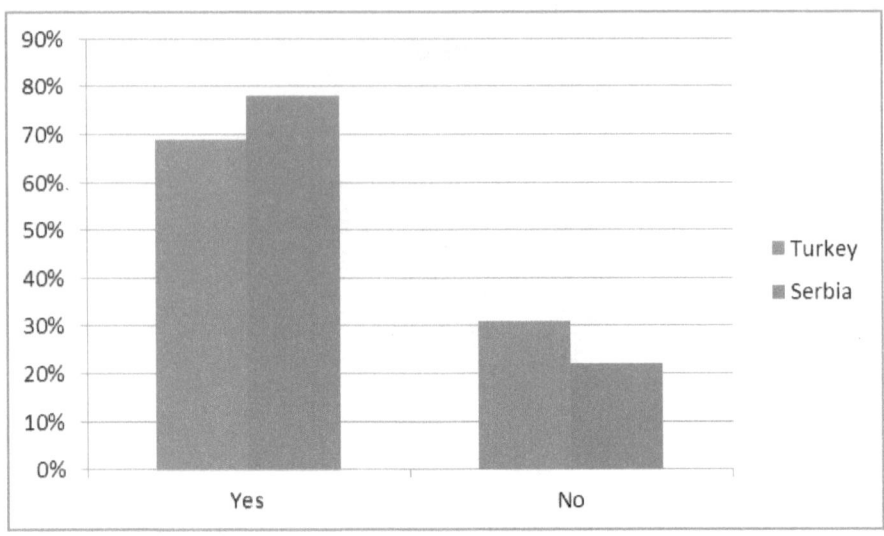

Fig. 8. Would you like to attend one of these distance learning programs?

Regarding question seven, 44% from Turkey and 25% from Serbia said that "Acquisition of knowledge" was the most important thing to consider when selecting an e-learning program. The second option, "The faster and easier way to graduate," was chosen by 29% from Turkey and 27% from Serbia. The third option, "Flexibility in studying," was chosen by 27% from Turkey and 48% from Serbia (Figure 9). There are no significant differences between respondents divided by gender for this question for the both countries. It should be noted that the top priority for respondents from Serbia in selecting an e-learning program was "flexibility in studying," while for those from Turkey, "acquisition of knowledge" was chosen as most important.[30]

---

30 Mirjana Radović-Marković, "Female Entrepreneurship: Theoretical Background," *Journal of Women's Entrepreneurship and Education* 4, no.1-2 (2013):1-9.

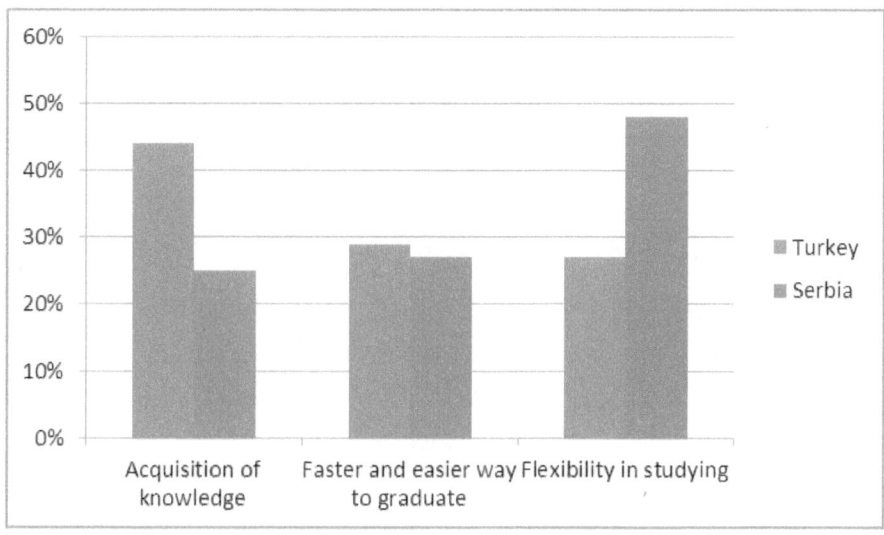

Fig.9. What would be the most important in selecting such a program, and ways of learning?

For question 8, "What do you think is crucial to be successful in the entrepreneurial career?," the first option "Have the ability to innovate and original business ideas" was selected by 58% from Turkey and 22% from Serbia. The second option, "Having good business contacts," was selected by 26% from Turkey and 70% from Serbia. The third option, "To be highly motivated to succeed," was selected by 16% from Turkey and 6% from Serbia (Figure 10).

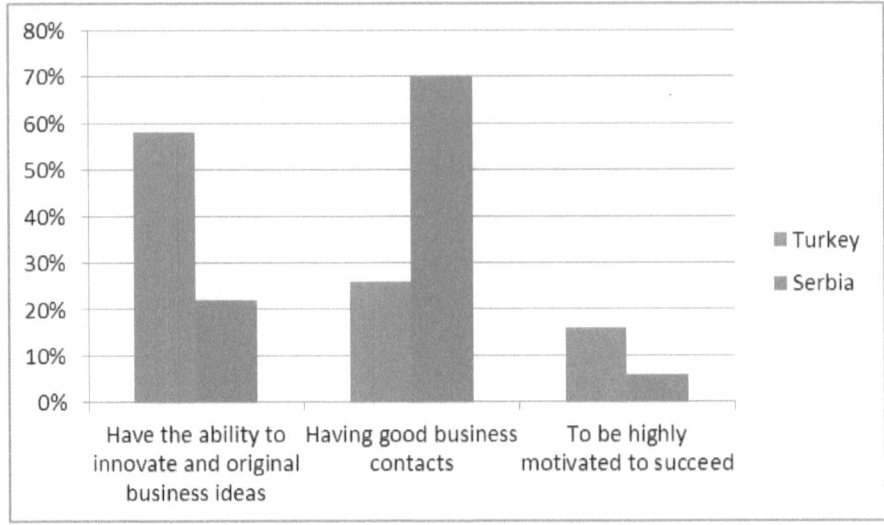

Fig. 10. What do you think is crucial to be successful in an entrepreneurial career?

Figure 8. What do you think is crucial to be successful in an entrepreneurial career?

As many as 90% of respondents from Serbia believe that the distance learning would be a good solution for future young entrepreneurs. The majority of women and men believed that distance learning would be a good solution for future young entrepreneurs.

Regarding question 9, "Do you believe that application of an Agent Based Intelligent System (ABIS) can enhance e-learning in Serbia in the field of entrepreneurship education?," our respondents in the both countries gave a common answer: 45% from Serbia and 49% from Turkey selected "I do not know." This can be explained by their lack of knowledge of the application of intelligent agents in education (Figure 11).

The findings on students' perception regarding the most appropriate direction for the educational strategies to be developed in order to reach the above mentioned goal, i.e. to encourage the creativity and entrepreneurial abilities of students, show that the new educational strategies should encourage creative abilities and original thinking, individuality, and freedom of learning. It is showed by the following regression:

$y = 2,4167x^3 - 10,5x^2 + 10,083x + 5$

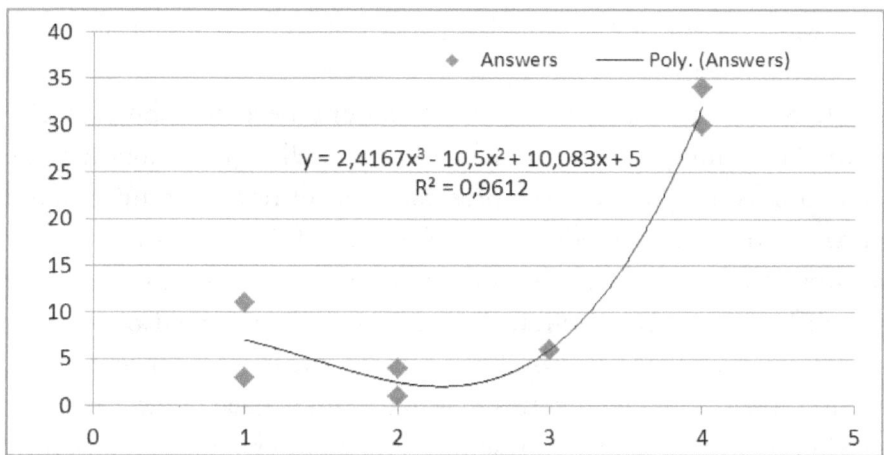

Fig. 11: In what direction the educational strategies should be developed?

Source: Radović-Marković[31]

Our research shows that education based on freedom in both learning and teaching helps to foster creativity. Accordingly, the existing education system should be redefined as well as educational programs for entrepreneurship.[32]

If Serbians or citizens of other nations become more familiar with the techniques, potential learners as well as educators may be able to effectively discern the pros and cons of how e-learning would enhance and improve education.[33] One hopeful sign is that recently a number of studies have been done in Serbia in order to investigate the different aspects of e-learning, especially in the field of business and entrepreneurship.[34][35] Building a more inclusive distance learning environment in Serbia involves making technological choices built on flexibility and an ability to respond quickly to changes in constantly evolving technology and informational resources. Collaboration, involving teachers, mentors, and instructional designers who truly represent the hard-to-reach learners, and a willingness to invest monies

---

31 Mirjana Radović-Marković., et al., "Freedom, Individuality and Women's Entrepreneurship Education," in *Entrepreneurship Education--A Priority for the Higher Education Institutions*, eds. Catalin Martin and Elena Druica (Bologna: Medimond, 2012), 426.

32 Mirjana Radovic-Markovic, "Female Entrepreneurship: Theoretical Background," *Journal of Women's Entrepreneurship and Education*, 4, no. 1-2 (2013):1-9.

33 Mirjana Radović-Marković & Spariosu-Bodroski, Biljana, "Education in Serbia: Inclusive and E-learning Opportunities," *Serbian Journal of Management* 5, no. 2 (2010), 271-281.

34 Mirjana Radović-Marković, *Impact of Globalization on Organizational Culture, Behaviour and Gender Role* (Charlotte: IAP, 2011), p.15-20.

35 Mirjana Radović-Marković & Spariosu-Bodroski, Biljana, "Education in Serbia: Inclusive and E-learning Opportunities," *Serbian Journal of Management* 5, no. 2 (2010), 271-281.

in developing a cyber-infrastructure that reaches all learners regardless of where they live will be crucial.[36]

Conclusion

E-learning is now an essential component of education in many countries. It has changed the face of education, training, and vocational learning forever. The online learning environment is quite different from a traditional classroom, in which one had limited interaction and almost unlimited access to learning resources. In other words, online courses require participants to take on new and different teaching and learning behaviors, which are quite different from the old ones. New technologies also can improve communication between students and teachers. They allow each student greater diversity for learning, enhance interactivity between individual students and individual teachers, provide a space for personalized, flexible learning beyond the classroom walls, and allow students to live locally whilst learning globally through the use of external resources accessed via the world wide web. In addition, the use of different learning materials and resources allows students with various principle learning styles to understand information in the most effective way. Also, the use of intelligent agents as a support to online studies intended for entrepreneurs would provide significant resource savings. On one hand, it would allow students an easier access to information and literature, as well as testing their knowledge and ideas. On the other hand, it would reduce teachers' administrative duties, which would be performed by intelligent agents, thus giving them more time to devote to each student individually and develop their potential entrepreneurial ideas, talents, and skills.

In addition, the Internet enhances learning, including such advantages as being able to learn at a peak time of the day, learning at

---

36 Mirjana Radovic-Markovic, et al., "Freedom, Individuality and Women's Entrepreneurship Education," in *Entrepreneurship Education--A Priority for the Higher education Institutions*, eds. Catalin Martin and Elena Druica (Bologna: Medimond, 2012).

one's own speed, accessibility to much information, the ability to track personal progress, and the capability to test personal learning efforts. The online education also fosters self-motivated education, giving precedence to the autonomy of the learner. This improves access by increasing the number of available courses and thus number of students served.

Although there are differences between the results obtained for Serbia and Turkey, educators in both countries should apply more effective learning strategies. Furthermore, it is necessary to explore how to make e-learning more popular and more accessible for students and to identify their needs and tailor a program to meet them. Nearly everywhere in the world, the existing education system is being redefined, and educational programs that closely relate to entrepreneurship are being improved. If Serbs and Turks become more familiar with ICTs and their implementation in learning and teaching entrepreneurship in high education, potential learners as well as educators can expect the benefits from them.[37] In line with this, it can be concluded that an agent based recommendation system should help students in getting knowledge faster as well as enabling better interaction among students, professors and the business environment. Besides, in Serbia, there is no synergy among scientific institutions, educational institutions, and the business environment. There is a similar situation in Turkey. In other words, communication between universities and public and private sectors must flourish. Therefore, the modern business environment should be accompanied by a change in the educational environment. Consequently, it is necessary that permanent adjustments between these two environments should be made.[38] Thus, it can be concluded

---

37 Mirjana Radović-Marković et al., "Fostering Entrepreneurship in Higher Education through E-learning: A Case Study of Serbia and Turkey," in *Employment, Education, Entrepreneurship*, ed. M. Radović-Marković (Belgrade: Faculty of Business Economics and Entrepreneurship, 2012).

38 Mirjana Radović-Marković et al., "Fostering Entrepreneurship in Higher Education through E-learning: A Case Study of Serbia and Turkey," in *Employment, Education, Entrepreneurship*, ed.M. Radović-Marković (Belgrade: Faculty of Business Economics and Entrepreneurship, 2012).

that an agent-based education system should help students in getting knowledge faster as well as ensuring better interaction among students, professors, and the business environment.

Finally, with new technologies in hand, the process of learning in the classroom can become significantly richer as students have access to new and different types of information and can combine face-to-face learning with e-learning opportunities. This combination provides them many opportunities to learn more new things in a quite different environment. Unfortunately, according to our key findings, these opportunities are not exploited enough in Serbia.

References

Bowen, Ed. "Intelligent Agents: What They Do and How They're Changing Online Learning." In

Proceedings of TELECOOP Conference, 1-31. Estes Park: TELECOOP, 2007.

Brusilovsky, Peter. *Adaptive Educational Hypermedia: From Generation to Generation*. Athens: University of Athens, 2004.

Croy, Marvin "Distance Education, Individualization, and the Demise of the University." *Technology In Society*, no.20 (1998): 317–326.

Charles Graham, Kursat Cagiltay, Byung-Ro Lim, Joni Craner, and Thomas M. Duffy. "Seven Principles of Effective Teaching: A Practical Lens for Evaluating Online Courses." In *Technology Source*. Chapel Hill: University of North Carolina, 2001. Accessed October 20, 2013.

Draves, William. *Teaching Online*. River Falls: LERN Books, 2002. Accessed June 21, 2013.

Gregg, Dawn. "E-learning Agents." *The Learning Organization*14, no. 4 (2007): 300-312.

Hanks, Steven and Gaylen Chandler. "Funder Competence, the Environment and Venture Performance." *Entrepreneurship Theory and Practice* 18, no.3 (1994): 77-89.

Hua-Lin Tsai, Chi-Jen Lee, Wen-Hsi Lydia Hsu, Yu-Hsin Chang. *An Adaptive E-Learning System Based on Intelligent Agents in Recent Researches in Applied Computers and Computational Science.* Rovaniemi: WSEAS Press, 2012.

Hoben, George, et.al. *Assessment of Student Learning in an Educational Administration Online Program.* New Orleans: American Educational Research Association, 2002.

Lee, Hon Cheung. "The New Era of Televersity and Andraversity in the Campusless Society: The Virtual University and Its Implications in Korea." In *Virtual University? Educational Environments of the Future*, edited by U. H. J. Molen, 117-31. London: Portland Press.

Liarokapis, Fotis, Anastasios Doulamis, Vassilios Vescoukis (Eds.). *Games and Virtual Worlds for Serious Applications.* Athens: IEEE, 2011.

McCombs, Barbara L. "Assessing the Role of Educational Technology in the Teaching and Learning

Process: A Learner-Centered Perspective." In *The Secretary's Conference on Educational Technology.* Denver: University of Denver Research Institute, 2000. Accessed October 27, 2013.

Newton, Len and Laurence Rogers. *Teaching Science with ICT.* London: Continuum, 2001. Accessed November 15, 2013.

Radović-Marković, Mirjana. "Female Entrepreneurship: Theoretical Background." *Journal of Women's Entrepreneurship and Education* 4, no.1-2 (2013): 1-9.

---, et al. "Fostering Entrepreneurship in Higher Education through E-learning: A Case Study of Serbia and Turkey." In *Conference Proceedings, Employment, Education, Entrepreneurship*, edited by Mirjana Radović-Marković. Belgrade: Faculty of Business Economics and Entrepreneurship, 2012.

---, et al. "Freedom, Individuality and Women's Entrepreneurship Education." In *Entrepreneurship Education--a Priority for the Higher Education Institutions*, edited by Catalin Martin and Elena Druica. Bologna: Medimond, 2012.

---. & Biljana Spariosu-Bodroski. "Education in Serbia: Inclusive and E-learning Opportunities." *Serbian Journal of Management* 5, no. 2 (2010), 271-281.

---. *Impact of Globalization on Organizational Culture, Behaviour and Gender Role*. Charlotte: IAP, 2011.

---. "Special Benefits of E-learning for Women: Sample of Program Entrepreneurship." In *Gender and Informal Economy: Developing Developed and Transition Countries*, edited by Priscilla Achakra, 156-166. Lagos: ICEA and Prenticeconsult, 2007.

Ruzgar, Nursel. "Distance Education in Turkey." *Turkish Online Journal of Distance Education* 5, No 2 (2004), 22-32. Accessed on 16 May 2006. http://tojde.anadolu.edu.tr/tojde14/articles/ruzgar.htm.

Spatariu, Alexandru, Kendall Hartley, and Lisa Bendixen. "Defining and Measuring Quality in Online Discussions." *The Journal of Interactive Online Learning* 2, no. 4 (2004). Available online: http://www.ncolr.org/jiol/archives/2004/spring/02/.

Teo, Chao Boon, Robert Gay, and Kheng Leng. "Pedagogy Considerations for E-learning." *International Journal of Instructional Technology and Distance Learning* 3, no. 5. (2006): 3-26.

Wagner, Thomas. *Applying Agents for Engineering of Industrial Automation Systems*. Stuttgart: Universität Stuttgart, 2003.

CHAPTER 12

The Debates between Quantitative and Qualitative Method: An Ontology and Epistemology of Qualitative Method- The Pedagogical Development

Medani P. Bhandari[39]
Akamai University

Introduction

The debates between quantitative and qualitative method are essentially for and against positivism and interpretive perspectives of social inquiry. Methods associated with positivism are grounded in the work of Comte, Mill and Durkheim in social sciences, who believed that the social world can be viewed in the same way as natural sciences. In contrast, philosophers like Dilthey, Rickert and Weber who followed the Kantian tradition challenged the positivist philosophy and developed the interpretive approach (Smith 1983). The positivist tradition of

---

[39] Dr. Bhandari is Faculty and Deputy Program Director Sustainability Studies, Akamai University and International Program Director at the Atlantic State Legal Foundation, Syracuse NY. Dr. Bhandari also serves as Managing Director of Human Survival Foundation, Glasgow, UK. He can be reached medani.bhandari@gmail.com

social inquiry has been followed by the quantitative scholars and the interpretive path by the qualitative scholars. In my literature search I find engagement in debates from both the quantitative and qualitative scholars. However as a qualitative sociologist, I also did not focus very much on what quantitative scholars say; therefore most of the authors I have cited in this essay are from qualitative disciplines. In this essay firstly, I will explore why there is debate, and what are the fundamental differences between qualitative and quantitative methods in sociology. To understand this I will explain the major theoretical ground of debates between qualitative and quantitative methodologies in terms of their origin from major classical sociological authors Durkheim and Weber. I think to understand the root cause of debate, it is essential to understand its historical root, its ontological and epistemological position, as well as its paradigms and methodological approaches. I found that there is a debate between quantitative and qualitative scholars from the epistemological level. However, there are no debates on the objectives of research because both methods have been trying to capture the social reality and investigate the causes of social problems. To explore this situation, I will discuss the ontological, epistemological and theoretical grounds and paradigms of qualitative method. Quantitative scholars follow the positivist approach and qualitative scholars follow the constructivist and interpretive approaches. At the epistemological level debates are about the application of knowledge. Quantitative scholars follow the established notion (deductive) to explore the social reality and qualitative scholars construct the knowledge doing inductive research. In the second section I will briefly reexamine the development of interpretive philosophy in social science and note three best exemplary works of qualitative sociologists, followed by how researchers apply qualitative method in their research in the third section of this essay.

Section one
Debates quantitative versus qualitative historical perspective

There has been a long debate between qualitative and quantitative sociologists. These debates in social sciences are linked directly to the assumptions about ontology, epistemology and human nature (Morgan and Smircich 1986). Rudra and Peter J. Katzenstein (2005) state that the most scholars think of the theoretical universe as divided between different schools of thought. What most consistently divide these schools are not their substantive claims but the metatheoretical *cognitive structures* within which such claims are formulated. These structures shape what phenomena are considered important and explainable, how research questions about such phenomena are posed, what concepts and methods are most suited for investigating these questions, whether the objectives of the investigation are to confirm axiomatic laws or engender an interpretive understanding of contexts, and what standards are reasonable for evaluating specific research products. The necessarily abstract responses these questions elicit reflect enduring ontological and epistemological, that is metatheoretical, assumptions shared by members of some research communities but not others. Social scientific disciplines and subfields are often characterized by the emergence of, competition between, and evolution or degeneration of discrete traditions of scholarly research. These traditions distinguish themselves on the basis of programmatic understandings that provide the foundation for the construction, communication and evaluation of various forms of models or narratives (Sil and Katzenstein 2005, page 4). I totally agree with the Sil and Katzenstein arguments. The debates between quantitative and qualitative are embedded from the origin of the practice of the social investigation, which first assumes that social reality can be quantified and second assumes that social reality cannot be explained with the application of mathematics but can be interpreted in the words.

There is a fundamental distinction between qualitative and quantitative studies. Both have different epistemological positions. Quantitative methodology is associated with positivist epistemology and qualitative method with interpretive epistemology. Quantitative method refers to the collection of numerical data and analysis through using statistical tools, with the emphasis on facts and figures. On the other hand, qualitative methodologies refer to the forms of field data collection with emphasis on meanings and rely on understanding (Marshall (1998). Quantitative and qualitative methods have different assumptions, purposes and approaches and researchers' roles. For example, quantitative researchers assume that social facts have an objective reality and can be separated in variables. Those identified variables can be measured with fixed methods and observed from outside (Lincoln and Guba 1985). In contrast, qualitative researchers assume that social reality is socially constructed, and that variables can be complex, interwoven and difficult to measure. They assume that to understand social reality the researcher needs to be in the field physically, mentally and emotionally (Goffman 1959). Quantitative method is embedded through positivist paradigms and qualitative method is grounded on interpretive paradigms. Qualitative research tends to start with 'what, how and why' type of inquiry and quantitative tends to investigate how much or how many (Draper 2004). Further Draper (2004) notes that "qualitative research can thus be broadly described as interpretive and naturalistic, in that it seeks to understand and explain belief and behaviors within the context that they occur" (page 642). Qualitative researchers contextualize the problem from the root; they interpret the situation with personal involvement. They are flexible and believe that researchers should have the freedom to acquire information in their own way, which ultimately provides the way-out to generate new epistemology.

On the other hand, quantitative methodology is based on the positivist approach, which has as a fundamental limit the extent to which the methods and procedures of the natural sciences could be applied to the social world (Devers 1999). There has been a canonical tradition of positivist approaches to investigate social facts. In sociology this approach was developed and used by Emile Durkheim (1858-1917), who examined social behavior as social facts. The primary task of sociology was the description and observation of social facts.

According to Durkheim, the study of social facts is the first step in the program of scientific sociology because they: (1) indentify collective phenomena separate from individuals (2) they are not part of individual psychological motivations (3) they are the subject matter of observation (4) they are diffused throughout the society and (5) they exist in their own right independent of the individual (Durkheim 1938:2, 10, 13, as cited by Morrison 1995:334). Durkheim advocated that social facts should be considered as things. To do so Durkheim provided the three characteristics of social facts (1) they are 'general throughout society and 'diffused within the group' (2) they are 'external to individuals' and exist independently of their will and (3) they exercise external constraint over individuals which is recognized by the power of external coercion, by the existence of some sanction or by the resistance offered against individual efforts to violate them (Durkheim 1938: 55-56 as cited by Morission 1995: 334). According to this approach, social realities are different from ideas, and ideas should be considered as things. For Durkheim idea has no reality. He distinguished sociology from philosophy and other social sciences disciplines. Durkheim's sociology is empirical and investigates causes. Sociological method is objective; social facts are things and studied as such; and sociological method is unique to sociology because social facts are social (Morrison 1995). Durkheim was trying to relate the sociological phenomena with the natural sciences where facts and figures remain unchanged in a specified time period and can be replicated in other environments. His major objective was to establish the compatibility of sociological events with the natural sciences. The positivist social scientists still follow the same traditions.

On the basis of the Durkheimean notion, quantitative sociologists claim that qualitative method produces a scientific result which can be tested and validated with the application of statistical tools. They state that quantitative method can be replicable and generalized in a broader arena. They criticize qualitative method and question the representation, reliability and validation of the research outcome. Further they argue that qualitative method is impressionistic, piecemeal and idiosyncratic and this method cannot be replicable, comparable and cannot capture the notion of social problems in the holistic approach (Bryman 1984). Another criticism they pose with regard to qualitative method is the researcher's relationships with the population and the possibility of human bias because of the close relationships. These claims of quantitative sociologists about the qualitative method are rooted in positivism, based on the social situation as natural environment and concern for research criteria such as internal and external validity, reliability and objectivity. In this perspective their focus is how to define and measure concepts. They believe that concepts must be made observable because, if the concept cannot be observed and measured, it does not exist (Lin 1998). Such prescriptions of making science have been challenged and methodological pluralism has been developed through multiple and diverse research procedures (Jessor 1996). This notion was first challenged by Max Weber (1864-1920), who developed the interpretive approach to investigate the social events and social environment.

The ontological assumptions of the qualitative sociologist differ from positivist arguments because the social world is seen as more dynamic, contextual, complex and socially constructed. Qualitative sociologists do not agree that society can be examined as natural environment. This notion was primarily explained by Max Weber, who stated that there are fundamental differences between natural and social sciences such as (1) the subject matter of natural sciences and social sciences are different, where physical science studies natural events and social science studies social events (2) each seeks to obtain different kinds of knowledge i.e. in natural sciences, knowledge is of the external world which can be explained in terms of valid laws. In the social science, knowledge must be 'internal' or 'subjective' in the sense that human beings have an inner nature that must be understood in order to explain outward events and (3) in natural sciences it is sufficient to observe events in the natural world and to report relationships between things observed. On the contrary, in social sciences investigations must go beyond observation to look how individuals act on their understanding, and how this 'understanding' may be related to their social action (Weber 1978 Economy and Society: 3-26, as noted by Morrison 1995:

274). Weber focused on social action and the role of individual actors. He did not provide rules for social inquiry (as Durkheim had established rules to investigate social facts) but focused on how social action can be understood (VERSTEHEN).

Weber focused on social action which involves four central concepts: the concept of understanding or *verstehen*; the concept of interpretive understanding; the concept of subjective meaning; and the concept of social action (Morrison 1995). Weber looked at sociology as an interpretive science. In his own words "Sociology is a science which attempts the interpretive understanding of social action in order to arrive at causal explanation of its course and effects. In action is included all human behavior when and insofar as the acting individual attaches a subjective meaning to it. Action in this sense may be either overt or purely inward or subjective; it may consist of positive intervention in a situation or of deliberately refraining from such intervention or passively acquiescing in the situation. Action is social insofar as, by virtue of the subjective meaning attached to it by the acting individual, it takes account of the behavior of others and is thereby oriented in its course" (Weber 1978:4, as cited by Morrison 1995: 274). Actually this definition provides a ground to argue that social events can only be understood with the application of interpretive paradigms, because social events are not fixed and cannot be explained as things (which was proposed by Durkheim and other positivist theorists). The social environment is complex, changeable and human actors act meaningfully. To reveal the social reality, the investigator needs to understand the meaning of social action. *Verstehen* is seen as a concept and a method central to a rejection of positivistic social science. It refers to understanding the meaning of social action from the actor's point of view.

Weber's notion accepts that human beings think, have feelings, communicate through language, attribute meaning to their environment and have different beliefs and characters. Because of this reality social science theories are unlikely to apply across time and place. They cannot be the sole source of hypotheses, or cannot be judged only through a deductive approach. Therefore to reveal the social truth qualitative inquiry (inductive approach) has been widely used in the social sciences.

The notion of qualitative method is to find out the social truth through in depth inquiry. In other words, qualitative research is a broad umbrella term for research that describes and explains persons' experiences, behaviors, interaction and social context (Fossey et al. 2002) through inductive inquiry.

My objective in this paper is to examine the debates of quantitative and qualitative method historically. Qualitative method was developed as a counter of the positivist approach, therefore it is important to know how qualitative methods were developed and who were the major figures to bring in the current situation. Many institutions have contributed to the development of qualitative method in the United States such as Columbia University, Harvard University, Michigan University and so on, however the Chicago School is consider the original institution for sociological knowledge production, particularly qualitative method.

I think there is a major contribution of Max Weber in the development of qualitative method; however; the documents do not illustrate his direct influence. I tried to trace the date when *verstehen* was written and how it was adopted in the sociological research. I did not find any illustration of Max Weber in the historical documents. Supporting the opposite viewpoint Jennifer Platt (1985) has provided evidence stating that there was no Max Weber's *verstehen* influence in the early American sociology. According to her "interviews and documentary sources show that he was not influential in the American sociology generally or in qualitative research before First World War" (448). She gives an outline of the historical account of qualitative method development in United States and highly acknowledges the contribution of the Chicago School. "Crucial steps in the emergence of qualitative research methods are generally agreed to have taken place at the University of Chicago in the 1920 and 1930, and then more specifically in the elaboration of participant observation as a distinct method in the decade following World War II and classic exemplars were produced there; the argument will, therefore, focus mainly on that body work, and on the extent to which Weber's Verstehede soziologie was known to those producing it, drawn on by them in their thinking about it, and was necessary to produce the research outcomes" (449).

However, the development of qualitative research method was not solely the production of American sociologists. Even in the United States the scholars were from Germany who applied the qualitative method in the United States. However, there is no traceable record whether they were influenced by Max Weber or not. Most importantly Platt (1985) states that even Parson [who is Parson – have you mentioned him above?] was not aware about Max Weber when he went to Heidelberg in 1925. If so then it raises more interesting point about Weber. His influence came late but became dominant in a very short period of time. Emerson (2001), who provides an outline of qualitative method history, cites Platt (1985) to show the importance of the Chicago School but does not illustrate about her argument about Max Weber. However, one cannot deny that the University of Chicago sociology department was the first to challenge the positivism tradition of research design and significantly contributed to the development and diffusion of the qualitative method. The Chicago tradition was diffused to Western Europe and Western European influence was similarly diffused to the United States.

Transmission of knowledge has been occurring throughout the history of civilization; however this process was more accelerated since the "tracing back to the societas civilis in Aristotelian tradition" (Kocka 2004). Particularly in Europe it has a long association with politics and society. Kocka (2004) states that the modern interpretation of society began in 17th and 18th century largely through the writers of enlightenment such as John Locke, Adam Ferguson, Montesquieu, the Encyclopedists, and Immanuel Kant etc. I think sociological research has a positive connotation with the Enlightenment process. Sociological Research History is essential to understand the production and circulation of knowledge. History gives the idea to categorize contemporary thoughts, to make judgments about the process of knowledge production throughout. Further historical accounts provide the experiences faced by the authors, explains their relationship to contemporary society, explores their research method and analysis and also provides information about the debates and explanation within their context as well as with the previous authors, predecessors, allies, and rival connections (Jean-Michel Chapoulie 2004).

As supportive argument about the historical challenges to the positivist research paradigms, Robert Emerson (2001) provides extensive evidence of empirical research conducted by the British anthropologists. He takes the example of Bronislaw Malinowski's extensive field work as a "model of field work as a means for direct observation requiring intensive, prolonged stay in the midst of the daily life of those studied, proclaimed and promoted by publication of Argonauts of the Western Pacific 1922" (Emerson 2001: 6). Actually Malinowski provides the importance of being in the field. Malinowski's description provides two aspects of extensive field method, the first is how important it is to be in the field, and the second is the historical value of participant observation, which equally implies in the current context a major challenge for the quantitative research design.

In sociology according to Emerson (2001) "the roots of sociological fieldwork extended back in late 19th century social reform movements, in which observers sought to describe the life conditions of the urban poor in order to change and better them. Particularly significant for later sociological fieldwork was the social survey movement. Charles Booth's Life and Labor of the People in London (1902) remains the best known of these massive surveys, one more systematic form of the "social exploration" (Keating 1976:11ff) following the dramatic changes produced by rapid industrialization and urbanization" (9). This survey carried out by Booth and others (Life and other) was applied by DuBois in study of the Philadelphia Negro (1899). In the United States the classic Chicago school sociology department dominated the academic research during first century of the 20th century.

Jean-Michel Chapoulie (2004) notes that Chicago sociology was paramount to diffuse the western modality of research sequences, particularly the ethnic relation to white, protestant Anglo-Saxons. Nigel Fielding (2005) states that "with the quantitative approach growing alongside the general march of positivism and the budding discipline of statistics, the Chicago School is usually seen as the champion of qualitative method during sociology's childhood (Fine 1995, Platt 1995, 1996, Abbott 1990, Becker 1999). We know the School for its declaration that the city offered a vast natural laboratory for exploring social phenomena, using ethnographic methods. This was the stance of the first Chicago School, then regarded as the top US sociology department and associated with the empirical approach of figures like W.I. Thomas (appointed in 1895) and Robert Park. But in 1927 William Ogburn was appointed to bring in a "scientific" sociology based on statistics and by the 1940s, with Parsons' rise at Harvard and Columbia's growing dominance in survey research and opinion polling, US sociology had shifted to a quantitative paradigm. In the 1950s a group of quantitative sociologists came to Chicago from Columbia and Everett Hughes stood virtually alone as representative of the earlier tradition (Fielding 2005).

The leadership of Robert E. Park who join Chicago University in 1913, helped to explore the city area's problems associated with the anonymous rooming dwellers, occupational institutions forms and development change (Emerson 2001). Park emphasized the value of the fieldwork, its importance and application. Emerson quotes McKinney (1966:71) to illustrate Park's focus on fieldwork is much more relevant in this context; "you have been told to go grubbing in the library, thereby accumulating a mass of notes and a liberal coating of grime. You have been told to choose a problem wherever you can find musty stakes of routine records based on trivial schedules prepared by tired bureaucrats and filled out by reluctant applicants for aid or fuzzy do-gooders or indifferent clerks. This is called "getting your hands dirty in real research". Those who counsel you are wise and honorable, the reasons they offer are of great value. But one more thing is needful; firsthand observation. Go and sit on the luxury hotels and on the doorsteps of the flophouses; sit on Gold Coast settees and on the slum shakedowns; sit in Orchestra Hall and in the Star and Garter Burlesque. In short, gentleman, go get the seat of your pants dirty in real research" (11). Park provides the insights of the real settings which cannot be achieved without 'being in the real field". Park with Burgess developed the multi-method approach. Emerson (2001) notes the contribution of Thomas and Znaniecki through a monograph on the Polish immigrants (The Polish Peasant in Europe and America 1917).

This was based on diary, life history written by the ordinary people. These combinations of field research methods show that case study, life history, participant observation, interviews and autobiography analysis were considered as multi-method approach. Case study was based on direct observation and informal interviews. Observation method was used by Nels Anderson "the Hobo 1923, Paul G. Cressey "the taxi dance hall 1932" and Fredric Thrasher's "Gang 1927. These researches were done without formal information to the "subject, the research population" (Emerson 2001). In the early Chicago School research case study was not achieved by the investigator's systematic participation role (Platt 1996). Emerson (2001), notes that in the early time of the Chicago School research "the case study had tended to separate observation on the one hand, understanding the point of view of those studied through personal documents on the other, participant observation displaced this dichotomy, transforming the prior heavily naturalistic conception of observation into a more experiential one emphasizing empathetic involvement as a means for grasping local and subjective meaning" (13). Anderson, Cressey and Thrasher used the observation method but did not describe it as participant observation (Emerson 2001). I think it clearly shows that the Chicago School was the pioneer in developing (qualitative) observation method in the United States, which later on diffused back to Europe (first it was initiated in Europe then diffused to USA) and diffused to the rest of the world.

Likewise, the Chicago School also was pioneer for the development of field interview techniques in the United States. Interview tool is a major data collection technique in contemporary sociological research. However, up to the second decade of 20th century in depth interview method was not developed in sociological research. There was 'verbatim interview' where researchers were carrying out unstructured interviews which often relied on the mood of the interviewee. Cavan, 1929: 107 states that "It represented instead an attempt to obtain as nearly as possible a 'report of the interview, in anecdotal form, including gestures, facial expressions, questions, and remarks of the interviewer' (recited from Lee 2004). According to Lee (2004) "In much of the writing associated with the Chicago School the term 'interview' is scarcely differentiated from the term 'life history.'

The life history was a form of autobiography usually written by a research subject. Like more modern versions of the unstructured interview, it involved a degree of sustained interaction between the researcher and research participant, was relatively unstructured in form, and focused largely on subjective elements of the interviewee's life. This last aspect reflected the importance to early writers in the Chicago tradition of the concept of 'personality' (something overshadowed by the attention later writers have paid to the work of George Herbert Mead)" (4). However, the historical account of Chicago school in academic debate is not fully out of criticism. David Nock's article "The myth about "myths of the Chicago School": Evidence from Floyd Nelson house" in The American Sociologist, Volume 35, Number 1 / March, 2004 raises the questions on reliability authorship of the Chicago School in the qualitative method development: "Some important work (Bulmer, Harvey) in the history of sociology questions whether the Chicago School should be identified with qualitative as opposed to more quantitative, statistical, and correlation methods. This paper will examine whether *this* characterization is a "myth" or whether there was some real basis for this association of Chicago sociology with qualitative research and a broader epistemological stance critical of radical neo-positivism" (from the abstract). Although I do not think it makes any different whether Chicago School was the pioneer or not, its contribution to the qualitative method knowledge production cannot be avoided.

The above paragraph provides the general overview of how qualitative method was developed. In this context, one can state that basically qualitative methods were originated in anthropology and diffused to sociological research. The historical context of qualitative method was not a planned phenomenon but methodological knowledge was developed by learning by doing. Emerson (2001) Contemporary Field Research, Perspective and formulations, provides a nice explanation of this development trend. Likewise other authors such as Denzin, Norman K. and Lincoln, Yvonna S. (2000) also provide the historical account of qualitative research method development and the Chicago School's contribution. According to them the history of qualitative research in the human disciplines consists of seven moments, which are the traditional (1900–1950); the modernist or golden age (1950–1970); blurred genres (1970–1986); the crisis of representation (1986–1990); the postmodern, a period of experimental and new ethnographies (1990–1995); post experimental inquiry (1995–2000); and the future (2000–) (re-cited from Alasuutari, Pertti 2004: 565). This notion shows that there is a shift in the use of qualitative method since 1960, because of the new technology development (use of tape recorder, shorthand writing etc.). Raymond M. Lee (2004) provides a historical account of recording technologies and the interview in sociology, from 1920 to 2000, which is very significant in terms of method development to track the debates between qualitative and quantitative methods.

The above historical account presents qualitative method development particularly in United States, and British, German and French scholars influence to United States or United States or vice versa. The literature is silent about the rest of the world's contribution to sociological knowledge formation. This seems a field of new research. Whatever is the case qualitative method has a long history of applicability in researching society in both the action and the academic field, which challenges the positivist approaches of research? Why qualitative research? Why ethnographic theory? Richard A. Shweder (1996) has the following answer "ethnographic theories will tell us what it means to be differently situated—what it is like to have different preferences (values, goals, tastes, desires, ideals of personal well-being and of developmental competence) and/or what it is like to live with different constraints (information, causal beliefs, abilities, dispositions, resources, technology, systems of domination or control). Its methods make use of the things people say and do to each other in everyday life, as well as the things they strategically and deliberately say and do to us on special "scientific" occasions (for example, when we ask them to answer questions in an interview or to narrate a life history), to construct a plausible and intelligible account about what it is like to be someone else. Yet true ethnography also aims to deepen our understanding of "otherness" and to move us beyond the cover stories, idealized self-representations, well-rehearsed verbal modes of public image management, and strategic manipulations of those whose lives we seek to understand" (17-18). Qualitative method covers many methods such as participant-observation, ethnography, photography, ethno-methodology, dramaturgical interviewing, sociometry, natural experiment, case study, unobtrusive measures, content analysis, historiography and secondary analysis of data and other. The application of qualitative method is global phenomena. Alasuutari, Pertti (2004) and many others have explained qualitative method and its relevance in the modern neo-liberal globalized world as a counter of quantitative (positivist) research design.

Related to the historical connection of quantitative and qualitative debates, there is also strong argument in favor of qualitative method from feminist scholars (Oakley 1998). They argue that traditional social science ignores or marginalizes women, that all the major social theories explain the public world of labor but not the private world of work and the home and the areas of social life. Traditional social science research based on the quantitative method often implicitly supports sexist values; female subjects are excluded or marginalized; relations between researcher and researched are intrinsically exploitative; the resulting data are superficial and over generalized; and quantitative research is generally not used to overcome social problems (Jayaratne and Stewart 1991, Jayaratne 1983). Oakley (1998) adds more points on this notion. She states that there are three major problems of quantitative method such as three Ps i.e. positivism (objectivity is male subjectivity), power (hierarchy, valid/invalid through male judgment) and p added value (quantitative method is ideologically linked with men's desire to dominate, to exert power over people as well as nature, in other words it is a veritable 'exercise in masculinity' (709-11).

The qualitative inquiry accepts the notion of social variation. Qualitative inquiry searches the causal effects of social problems from individual to group level. Qualitative methodologists believe that each individual can reveal the social environment differently as they have perceived it; therefore, basically there are no hard and fast rules and regulations in qualitative method (Sofaer 1999). Qualitative sociologists prefer open perspectives in social inquiry and therefore they believe that predesigned structure in an investigation may not be able to capture the complexity and dynamism of social questions. To capture the social complexity qualitative sociologists have developed various epistemologies.

Qualitative ontology and epistemology:

The sociological ontological question searches the answer of what is the form and nature of reality and therefore, what is there that can be known about it (Guba and Lincoln 1994: 108). Snape, D. and Spencer, L. (2003), note that "Within social research key ontological questions concern: whether or not social reality exists independently of human conceptions and interpretations; whether there is a common, shared, social reality or just multiple context-specific realities; and whether or not social behavior is governed by `laws' that can be seen as immutable or generalizable" (Snape & Spencer, 2003: 20). There are three positions on whether there is a captive social reality and how this reality is constructed: they are realism, materialism and idealism (Anneline 2003), where realism accepts the notion that there is external reality which is independent to people's perspective, materialism accepts that there is a real world but holds only material features and idealism differs with these two and asserts that reality can be understood through human interpretation and through socially constructed meanings. Only idealism can fit with the qualitative epistemology.

Social sciences have various epistemologies to understand the social world. These epistemologies attempt to specify how we can learn about social reality and which form of knowledge is appropriate to investigate the social problems. The major problem of qualitative epistemology is the way of exploring the relationship between researchers and researched (population) (Taylor and Bogdan 1998). In quantitative research researchers are supposedly independent from the phenomena being studied, therefore, quantitative scholars argue that they can produce value free research outcomes. However, qualitative scholars do not agree with this notion, because in the social world, the research process itself affects the people. According to qualitative epistemological understanding, the relationship between researchers and social phenomena is an interactive process. The qualitative scholars believe that social environments cannot be fully understood without this interactive process between researchers and population. Howard Baker (1996) states that epistemology has characteristically concerned itself with 'oughts' rather than 'is's' and settles its questions by reasoning from first principles rather than by empirical investigation. In explaining qualitative epistemology, Becker (1996) with the illustration of exemplary works of Erving Goffman, Clifford Greertz and William Foote White (and others) notes that the epistemology of qualitative research is 'being there', 'taking the point of view of the other' and 'think description'. There are few studies available which discuss directly the epistemology of qualitative sociology (Bryman 1984, Denzin 1994 Chin Lin 1998, Sofaer 1999, Michelle, et al. 2000). Denzin (1994) states that the epistemological question is "What is the nature of the relationship between the knower or would-be knower and what can be known? The answer that can be given to this question is constrained by the answer already given to the ontological question; that is, not just any relationship can now be postulated" (Denzin 1994: 108).

Qualitative researchers try to gain the knowledge of social reality, with their own interpretation and with their own deep understanding of the social context embedded in it. Taylor and Bogdan (1998) in the introduction of their book 'Introduction to Qualitative Methods' provide several examples of qualitative knowledge. They note "As qualitative researchers, we develop social constructions of social constructions (and sometimes others come along and deconstruct our social constructions)" (Taylor and Bogdan 1998: 19). This account gives a sense that through qualitative methods we discover our own knowledge while doing fieldwork. Taylor and Bogdan (1998) make clearer the nature of qualitative knowledge with the citation of Laurel Richardson (1990b). "Sociological discovery, generally, happens through finding out about people's lives from the people themselves - listening to how people experience their lives and frame their worlds, working inductively, rather than deductively. Quantitative researchers, generally, learn about other people through interaction in specified roles, such as participant observer/informant, interviewee/ interviewer, and so on. As a result, their knowledge of people's lives is always historically and temporally grounded. Most ethnographers are keenly aware that knowledge of the world they enter is partial, situated and subjective knowledge" (Richardson 1990b, cited by Taylor and Bogdan 1998: 19). This thesis shows that qualitative knowledge formation occurs with the interaction of the researched population. As qualitative researchers, we need an established epistemology to produce new knowledge. I agree with Taylor and Bogdan (1998) who state that 'qualitative research is a craft that can only be learned and appreciated through experience. It requires skills and a devotion that must be developed and nurtured in the real world' (Taylor and Bogdan 1998: 259).

I think research skills can be learned through reading and practicing, however, devotion can be generated only when the researcher fully embraces and enjoys the fieldwork. Qualitative inquiry assumes that reality is socially constructed by every unique individual from within their own unique contextual interpretation (Joniak 2003:5), therefore, the knowledge formation differs according to the social context of researcher and researched. This situation is nicely summarized by James A. Holstein (2000). He notes that "If we are to study lives, including selves in social interaction, we must study them from within the social contexts they unfold, not separate from them. ... Human beings don't settle their affairs with meaning once and for all. Rather, they continually engage the interpretive process, including the interpretation of what they mean to themselves....The methodological directive here is to document the articulation and emergence of meaning in rich detail as it unfolds, not in lifeless analytic categories and statistical tables" (Holstein 2000: 33). Therefore qualitative epistemology development occurs through the in-depth investigation of social context. It requires both the application of researcher skills to investigate the social reality and the interpretation of learned knowledge from the social phenomena (Bhandari 2010, 2011, 2012, 2014).

Relating to the debate on qualitative and quantitative method there is not much argument, because both inquiries are 'to explore the social reality and truth'. "Qualitative and quantitative research are not merely different ways of doing research, but different ways of thinking" (Joniak 2003:3). When the debate is about exploring social reality both methods can be valid for specific purposes. There may be disagreement on whether these methods of qualitative research hold different epistemology or not. Denzin (1997) with the debates with Huber, states that there is a clear debate. He states that the research field is divided into two camps, the nonpositivists and the positivists. This division creates another, those who believe in science and who also hold to a conception of a disciplinary core consisting of demography, social organization, and stratification (Denzin 1997: 1418). This explanation clearly shows that the positivist line totally differs not only at the methodological level but is rooted in the ontological and epistemological level. In my opinion, each of these methods has a certain epistemology and can be the subject matter of further investigations (Bhandari 2010, 2011, 2012, 2014). The qualitative inquiry examines social reality with inductive reasoning which involves various processes. There are diverse ontological and epistemological perspectives within qualitative traditions.

The paradigms of qualitative methods:

Following the inductive inquiry process in knowledge building, qualitative method has various paradigms. Denzin (1994) notes that "paradigm may be viewed as a set of basic beliefs (or metaphysics) that deals with ultimate or first principles. It represents a worldview that defines, for its holder, the nature of the "world," the individual's place in it, and the range of possible relationships to that world and its parts, as, for example, cosmologies and theologies do. The beliefs are basic in the sense that they must be accepted simply on faith (however well argued); there is no way to establish their ultimate truthfulness. If there were, the philosophical debates reflected in these pages would have been resolved millennia ago" (Denzin 1994:107). Denzin's explanation gives an overview of what paradigms are and why there is no end of theoretical debates in social science. Sociologists need to be knowledgeable about the multiple paradigms and perspectives to understand the social actors' activities in the society and to understand the social problems (Ellie Fossey, Harvey, McDermott, and Davidson 2002). They also need to know the interactive pattern of social behavior to understand social conflicts, social dynamism and social inequality, which is the major subject to be addressed by the social scientists. By nature human beings are sensitive to their niche as well as familiar with its phenomena. Many scholars have tried to address sensitive issues through qualitative methods (Riley and Love 2000, Lincoln and Guba 1985 Schwartz and Ogilvy 1979). To address sensitive issues raised in qualitative inquiry is not that simple. Because of the complexity of the social environment, fixed rules or knowledge may not explicitly address social problems; therefore new paradigms have been developing to address the problems.

These frameworks or paradigms are not static. Paradigms are shifting (Guba 1990, Danzin and Lincoln 1994) and alternative paradigms have been developed in terms of ontology and epistemology in qualitative methodology. Guba and Lincoln (1994) examine paradigms in four major categories such as positivism, postpositivism, critical theory et al. and constructivism. They explain these categories in three major questions i.e. ontological, epistemological and methodological, which help to explore the root cause of debates between qualitative and quantitative sociology. Gareth Morgan and Linda Smircich (1980) suggest that this ontological and epistemological difference is crucial. They devised a spectrum from subjectivist to objectivist which embodies ontological stances of reality as a project of human imagination/socially constructed to reality as a concrete process or structure; and the epistemic stances of knowledge for the purpose of revelation and for understanding of social construction to knowledge for construction of a positivist science (Bhandari 2010, 2011, 2012, 2014). The manifestation of these two sets of assumptions is the relation between the knowing subject and the studied object.

Norman K. Denzin (2008) explains why paradigms are related to debates between quantitative and qualitative sociology. In his paper presented at the (QSE/QR/1,01; 12-6, 7, 10, 11, 17, 18/07;

2-11-08—Israeli conference) in the heading of The New Paradigm Dialogs and Qualitative Inquiry; he cites Amos Hatch (2006) to illustrate that the paradigms war is not over. According to Hatch "Let us engage in the paradigm wars. Let us defend ourselves against those who would impose their modern notions of science on us by exposing the flaws in what they call scientifically-based research. Let us mount a strong offense by generating qualitative studies that are so powerful they cannot be dismissed' (Hatch, 2006: 407). Hatch's and Denzin's argument is true, because debates between qualitative and quantitative are in the same position as they were in the 1980's. As Hatch (2006) notes "let us open up the publishing possibilities for qualitative researchers working within a variety of qualitative paradigms. If we do not fight back, qualitative research in education could become self-absorbed, fragmented and ineffectual. And the neo-conservative dream of a return to scientific modernity will have come true" (407). This notion equally applies to research in sociology. The strength of qualitative paradigms can only be established with the application of qualitative method as broadly as possible.

Theories and approaches of qualitative method:

Qualitative method searches the answers of questions unanswered by pure (hardliner) scientific research, with development of new theory. "Theory is about starting points. Research usually relies on theory to justify starting with pre-commitments to independent variables, background factors, or structural conditions that will explain historically and geographically varying phenomena, which are treated as dependent, fungible, superficial upshots, or otherwise secondary and essentially inferior. I propose that we start by trying to describe the phenomena to be explained as they exist for the people living them. For this, we need theory of another sort, a theory of social ontology that indicates the lines of inquiry required to produce a complete description. If we start research by describing the nature of social phenomena as they are experienced, it will make a difference in structuring data gathering; in developing a research craft capable of seeing practice, interaction manouvers, and tacit embodiment; in shaping a research agenda; and, ultimately, in where we end substantively" Katz 2002 : 255). In this connection Jack Katz (2002) provides an answer to what theory is, why theoretical approaches are needed and how theory can be constructed. More concisely Meleis (1997) explains "Theory is defined as `a symbolic depiction of aspects of reality that are discovered or invented for describing, explaining, predicting, or prescribing responses, events, situations, conditions, or relationships' "(Meleis 1997, p. 12). The following approaches of qualitative methods fulfill the objectives of the theory postulated by Katz and Meleis.

There are several theories /approaches in qualitative research. The methodological frameworks (paradigms) help to address the ontological question: to find the nature of social reality and the way to discover knowledge through which the emerging social problems can be tackled. The epistemological inquiry arouses debates in qualitative research because the relationship between researchers and their subject matter (population) cannot fix the problem. It is also difficult to answer how much knowledge is sufficient to resolve such issues or what is the saturation stage of information. The major qualitative approaches are interviewing (open-ended, semi-structured, narrative), single-case study, action research, conversation analysis, discourse analysis, narrative analysis, protocol analysis, interpersonal process (recall), interpretative analysis, IPA, hermeneutic, biographical methods, q methodology, feminist research, cooperative inquiry, participative inquiry, human inquiry groups, focus groups, grounded theory, phenomenological inquiry, heuristic inquiry, diary, diary-in-group, ethnomethodology, naturalistic/ field study, lived inquiry, integral inquiry, intuitive inquiry, organic inquiry, transpersonal- phenomenological inquiry, exceptional experience etc. In the following paragraphs I will only very briefly discuss phenomenology, ethnography, grounded theory, ethnomethodology, symbolic interaction, hermeneutical phenomenology which uses most of the tools of qualitative data collection. These approaches are fundamentally different with qualitative techniques of data collection.

Phenomenology views human behavior, examines how people say and act and how people define their world. In other words it studies how people construct their realities (Taylor and Bodgan 1998). Social phenomena are complex and associated with multilayered events so are not easy to understand. Qualitative inquiry searches the meaning of individual events and texts and helps us to understand the underlying situation within the social environment. In other words, qualitative method provides a basis for "thick description" (Ryle 1971, Geertz 1973, Bogdan & Biklen, 2003; Creswell, 1998; Denzin, 1989; Denzin & Lincoln, 2005; Lincoln & Guba, 1985; Marshall & Rossman, 1999; Patton, 1990), which is not possible in quantitative research method. I think as phenomenology, ethno-methodology, symbolic interactions are common concepts in qualitative method, "thick description" adds new strength to the qualitative epistemology. The term 'thick description' was first coined by Ryne (1971) to explain about golfing, (Geertz 1973) which was used to interpret culture. Clifford Geertz interpreted 'thick description' as a philosophical term to describe the work of ethnography. He states "From one point of view, that of the textbook, doing ethnography is establishing rapport, selecting informants, transcribing texts, taking genealogies, mapping fields, keeping a diary, and so on. But it is not these things, techniques and received procedures that define the enterprise. What defines it is the kind of intellectual effort it is: an elaborate venture in, to borrow a notion from Gilbert Ryle, "thick description" (Geertz 1973:6, as cited by Ponterotto 2006: 539). This notion enables authors to interpret the contextual situation of how and under which conditions data were collected.

This strength of qualitative method is nicely explained by Norman K. Denzin. He states "A thick description ... does more than record what a person is doing. It goes beyond mere fact and surface appearances. It presents detail, context, emotion, and the webs of social relationships that join persons to one another. Thick description evokes emotionality and self-feelings. It inserts history into experience. It establishes the significance of an experience, or the sequence of events, for the person or persons in question. In thick description, the voices, feelings, actions, and meanings of interacting individuals are heard" (Denzin, 1989: 83 as cited by Ponterotto 2006: 540). Quantitative method has no provision for investigators to describe the situation nor do they provide the interpretations of the situation. In other words "think description' articulates or helps to interpret the "insider" or "native" perspectives through external eyes (to describe the perspective of those experiencing the phenomena under investigation: emic perspectives). On the contrary a *'thin description"* simply reports facts, independent of intentions or the circumstances that surround an action (Denzin, 1989), what normally qualitative researchers do (etic observation).

Other widely used qualitative methods are ethnography and grounded theory, which also invite major criticisms from non-qualitative scholars (bias, time consuming, chances to be native etc.). However, these are the major approaches qualitative scholars use. According to Katz "the ethnographic method is distinctively committed to displaying social realities as they are lived" (Katz 361). According to Duneier and Back (2006) "I think that ethnography is one of the sub-set of cases where those kinds of transcendent connections and recognitions of the humanity of others are possible, where it is possible to gain access to the humanity of 'others' despite the normal barriers that are there" (Voices from the sidewalk 548-549). This argument is not different from what Kathy Charmaz (2000) has stated in explaining grounded theory. She states that the grounded theorist's analysis tells a story about people, social processes, and situations. The researcher composes the story; it does not simply unfold before the eyes of an objective viewer. The story reflects the viewer as well as the viewed. Furthermore she states that in grounded theory research might limit understanding because grounded theorists aim for analysis rather that the portrayal of the subject's experience in its fullness ... fracturing the data imply that grounded theory methods lead to separating the experience from the experiencing subject, the meaning from the story, and the viewer from the viewed. Grounded theory limits entry into the subjects' worlds and thus reduces understanding of their experience" (: 335 in Emerson edited Book 2001). I think ethnography opens a totality of circumstances and produces accounts of everyone who is involved during the study process. Katz focuses on the stand and warrant of ethnography. He asks "Assuming your argument is empirically sound, so what?" Ethnographers are especially vulnerable to this question because their warrants are commonly diffused throughout their texts, because they aim to describe what is obvious to their subjects, and because such rude questions usually are raised only silently. Perhaps the most common warrant for ethnography is a claim that social forces have created a moralized ignorance that separates research subjects and the research audience" (Katz 1997: 391). The warrant concept in ethnographic research is complicated. The basic problem is to link "warrant" with empirical illumination. How it can be publicly visible and generalizable? How can qualitative research warrant the research outcome?

I think my problem of understanding is more basic, such as how to link the research with the accessible methods and theory development? I am having a hard time understanding how a particular social setting can be claimed to be sound or unquestionable. Social circumstances change according to the time and spatiality. Most probably qualitative information represents the particular time and mood of researcher and respondent. However, the information which the researcher gets presents the truth of that time and spatiality and also the social setting. As Goffman (1989) suggested "Embodied presence in the daily lives of those who host the research" (: 157 in Emerson edited Book), the ethnographer reveals the observed and unseen reality of particular social settings. I think, the research outcomes of ethnographic research is not only as Katz states "projections of readers of the researcher's imagination" (Katz 1997: 361). Doing ethnographic research is not an easy task, as most of the qualitative research methodologists acknowledge that (Ibarra, DeVault and McCoy, Emersion, Goffman, Katz, Kathy Charmas, Dorothy Smith etc.). However, the richness and thickness of qualitative research and success of research depends on the understandings of the audience. "What is obvious to the subjects has been kept systematically beyond the cognitive reach of the ethnographer's audience because of the moral character of the social life under investigation." (Katz 361), in this respect I think, there will be differences in understanding between audiences too. The in-situ audiences may find the narratives shallow yet the same narratives can be very thick and rich to the ex-situ audiences.

Another important approach that the qualitative methodologist uses is hermeneutical phenomenology, developed by Wilhelm Dilthey (1833-1911), with the influence of Emmanuel Kant's ideas. Qualitative method ... tries to be attentive to both terms of its methodology: it is a descriptive (phenomenological) methodology because it wants to be attentive to how things appear, it wants to let things speak for themselves; it is an interpretive (hermeneutic) methodology because it claims that there are no such things as un-interpreted phenomena (Van Manen 1991: 180). Likewise the Ethnomethodology approach developed by Harold Garfinkel (1960) states that "Ethnomethodological studies analyze everyday activities as members' methods for making those same activities visibly-rational-and reportable-for-all-practical-purposes, i.e., "accountable," as organizations of commonplace everyday activities. The reflexivity of that phenomenon is a singular feature of practical actions, of practical circumstances, of common sense knowledge of social structures, and of practical sociological reasoning. By permitting us to locate and examine their occurrence the reflexivity of that phenomenon establishes their study" (vii). Garfinkel (1960) focuses on commonplace activities and practical action as a key element of ethnomethodology.

Similarly, another important approach is Symbolic Interaction Perspectives in qualitative method developed by Herbert Blumer (1900-1987), for which there is a remote influence from Weber and close influence from George Herbert Mead of the Chicago school. According to Blumer "The term "symbolic interaction" refers, of course, to the peculiar and distinctive character of interaction as it takes place between human beings. The peculiarity consists in the fact that human beings interpret or "define" each other's actions instead of merely reacting to each other's actions. Their "response" is not made directly to the actions of one another but instead is based on the meaning which they attach to such actions. Thus, human interaction is mediated by the use of symbols, by interpretation, or by ascertaining the meaning of one another's actions. This mediation is equivalent to inserting a process of interpretation between stimulus and response in the case of human behavior" (Blumer 1963, p. 180). Blumer focuses on (in symbolic interaction) human interaction, interpretation or definition rather than mere reaction, response based on meaning, use of symbols and interpretation between stimulus and response. His approach is based on human beings acting toward things on the basis of the meanings that things have for them, while the meaning of things arises out of the social interaction one has with one's fellows and the meanings of things that are handled in and modified through an interpretive process used by the person in dealing with things he encounters (Wallace, Ruth A. and Alison Wolf 1995). I think there is close association of pragmatic thought and ethnomethodology, particularly practicality of qualitative method application. Having clear influence from George Hebert Mead, qualitative methodologists such as William Foote Whyte, Herbert Blumer, Harold Garfinkel and Erving Goffman have focused on the notion of being in the field "in reality" to show the practicality of the field. The pragmatic approach asserts that if there is a problem then there is a practical way to figure out that problem.

So far I have explained the major theoretical ground of debates between qualitative and quantitative in terms of their origin from major sociological canons of Durkheim and Weber. Further I discussed the ontological, epistemological and theoretical grounds of qualitative method. Quantitative scholars follow the positivist approach and qualitative scholars follow the constructivist and interpretive approaches. In the epistemological level debate is about the application of knowledge. Quantitative scholars follow the established notion (deductive) to explore the social reality and qualitative scholars construct the knowledge doing inductive research (Bhandari 2010, 2011, 2012, 2014). However at the objective level, there are no debates because both try to reach better understanding of social reality. "Considering the facts, it is argued that each approach should be evaluated in terms of its particular merits and limitations, in the light of the particular research question under study (Duffy 1987). However this implies that there are only technical differences between the two: those of research strategies and data collection procedures (Bryman 1988)' (as cited by Carr L.T. 1994: 720). There is also similarity in applications of research tools. For example both quantitative and qualitative researchers heavily use the interview method, through which they first convert acquired information in numbers and use statistical tools to analyze the data. On the other hand qualitative scholars interpret the information in language. For the qualitative scholars the social environment, respondents' situation, the way respondents respond, what their body language tells and their other gestures, all of which have a greater meaning than exactly what they are saying, but for the quantitative researcher, there is no such room in their analysis.

There is also a tendency for researchers to bridge the gap between the two methods such as the application of both methods simultaneously (mixed method) or application of statistical tools to analyze qualitative data through coding with new software programming etc. This is particularly relevant to environmental and sustainability research in which people's social conditioning and behavior, studied using qualitative methods, are likely to have an effect on environmental or socioeconomic outcomes that are measurable and hence investigated by quantitative methods. However, at the paradigms level the distance between qualitative and quantitative is increasing (J. Amos Hatch 2006, Denzin 2008). As Hatch (2006) argues and Denzin (2008) supports, ("*I agree with Amos Hatch. Let us re-engage the paradigm disputes of the 1980s (Gage, 1989). But after Guba (1990a, b), I call for a paradigm dialog, not a new war" Denzin*) there is a need of more quality research and publications to win the paradigms war with quantitative paradigms (positivism).

In the beginning of this section I also noted that quantitative method is by nature superficial in many ways because quantitative scholars commonly do research with preset questionnaires and there is usually little room for the researcher to include any interpretation about the social settings. Normally such data cannot be applicable in statistical testing for sociological interpretation. In other words, the quantitative researcher goes out with a half filled pot or preoccupied mind so they can fill in a little more in the field but the qualitative researcher goes to the field mostly with the open bag and open mind, therefore, they generate new epistemology through learning by doing. The quantitative method has no such options to allow the researcher to interpret the field situation and to investigate the unseen social environment. More strongly, Pauly (1991) explains the beauty of the qualitative method: "The 'something' that qualitative research understands is not some set of truisms about communication but the awful difficulties groups face in mapping reality. The qualitative researcher is an explorer, not a tourist. Rather than speeding down the interstate, the qualitative researcher ambles along the circuitous back roads of public discourse and social practice. In reporting on that journey the researcher may conclude that some of those paths were, in fact, wider and more footworn than others, that some branched off in myriad directions, some narrowed along the way, some rambled endlessly while others ran straight and long, and some ended at the precipice, in the brambles, or back at their origin" (Pauly 1991: 7). This explanation illustrates the major strength of qualitative method. In other words, there is no such option (of learning by doing) in deductive research paradigms which purport to reveal the grounded social reality.

I also note that outsiders' (positivist / quantitative methodologists') major criticisms of qualitative methods are about the nature of data collection techniques (i.e. open ended questions, participant observation, content analysis, subjectivity and time and space). Quantitative sociologists assume that reality is single, tangible, that investigator and social population are independent, and that social facts can be time and context free. They claim that such inquiry goes beyond the context or objective of research (which excludes the meaning and purpose) (Fossey et al. 2002). This criticism is valid to those who believe that social issues can only be understood through quantitative measurement (positivist). In contrast Qualitative sociologists oppose this thesis and argue that realities are multiple, constructed and holistic, and that researcher and research population are interactive. Further, qualitative sociologists argue that human social systems are complex, socially constructed and dynamic; therefore, to reveal the social facts in- depth knowledge is essential, which cannot be captured through a positivist approach. In addition to debates between qualitative and quantitative methods, there are also debates within the methods of qualitative sociologists (Merriam 1988, Creswell 1994).

These debates particularly concern procedures relating to researcher identity issues and research population. However qualitative method has various approaches and there is no universal standard of data collection. Therefore, even within teams of colleagues there is debate on qualitative method. These debates are mostly on the interpretation of meaning of subject matter (conflict, problems), and the problem of generalization, because every individual case can be different from other individual cases. These debates are particularly related to the paradigms and nature of qualitative inquiry. Furthermore, such debates relate to the identity of the researcher and the research populations. In another words, insiders' debates are basically about the identity of researcher and research populations in terms of sex/gender, race/ ethnicity, insider/ outsider, black and white, Northern and Southern etc (DeVault 1990, Lois. 2005, Fine, Michelle, et al. 2000, Bryman 1984, Devers 1999, Sanday 1979). However, debates are helpful for knowledge building and to frame new ways to examine social issues. In the following section I will briefly reexamine the development of interpretive philosophy in social science and note three best exemplary works of qualitative sociologists.

Section two
Features of successful qualitative-based work by discussing three exemplary texts

In the first section of this essay I briefly illustrated the major debates, ontology, epistemology and paradigms and approaches of the qualitative method. In this section, I will briefly illustrate the works of William Foote Whyte, Erving Goffman, and Robert J. Thomas, who have successfully applied the qualitative method in their research.

Three Successful Examples of Qualitative Research

1. William Foote Whyte

For the development of qualitative method the publication of Street Corner Society,' written by William Foote Whyte in 1943 was a milestone in sociology. It provided the way of application of participant observation, and also helped to popularize ethnographic fieldwork in sociological research. I think Street Corner Society is one of the best examples of development of qualitative epistemology. Whyte in the appendix notes that "when I began my work, I had had no training in sociology or anthropology. I thought of myself as an economist and naturally looked first toward the matters that we had taken up in economics courses, such as economics of slum housing" (Whyte 1943: 288). This account of Whyte's experience shows that if there is wish and devotion the researcher can learn the way to conduct research. Being in the field Whyte invented his own interpretive style and own way of participant observation, which is not admissible in the positivist approach to social research. Whyte was for the creation of one's own knowledge and he insisted that society should create its own knowledge to resolve its social problems. He notes "I emphasize the autonomous creation of social invention to suggest that human beings have enormous resources of creativity that permit them to devise their own social inventions, without waiting for an outsider to intervene and invent what the community or organization needs" (Whyte 1982: 1). Whyte's following statement provides the conditionality of being a real participant observer. "I also had to learn that the field worker cannot afford to think only of learning to live with others in the field. He has to continue living with himself. If the participant observer finds himself engaging in behavior that he has learned to think of as immoral, then he is likely to begin to wonder what sort of person he is after all, Unless the field worker can carry with him a reasonably consistent picture of himself, he is likely to run into difficulties" (Whyte 1943: 317). This account gives the idea of how much the qualitative researcher needs to be sensitive about the field situation. However, quantitative scholars criticize ethnographic field studies as very time consuming and sometimes the researcher may not be able to generate the desired outcome in the time available. Whyte accepts this. He states "In describing Cornerville study, I have often said I was eighteen months in the field before I knew where my research was going. In a sense, this is literally true" (Whyte 1943: 321) - eighteen months in the fieldwork but no idea about what a researcher is doing can be really frustrating. However, it also indicates that qualitative research, ethnographic fieldwork and interpretation are not easy, piecemeal or story writing as quantitative scholars suggest.

In addition to "Street Corner Society", William Foote Whyte (June 27, 1914–July 16, 2000) authored or co-authored 22 books and hundreds of journal articles, ranging from the study of slums to multinational corporations such as oil companies in Oklahoma and Venezuela, restaurants in Chicago, worker cooperatives in Spain, factories in New York State, and villages in Peru. I consider Whyte to be one of the pioneer qualitative sociologists who applied participant observation and in-depth interview methods to the study of formal organizations.

Another exemplary work of William Foote Whyte that I would like to illustrate here is his research article "Social Inventions for Solving Human Problems" published in (1982) in *American Sociological Review*, Vol. 47, No. 1. In this article, Whyte states that a social invention can be: - a new element in organizational structure, or interorganizational relations, - new sets of procedures for shaping human interactions and activities and the relations of humans to the natural and social environment, - a new policy in action (that is, not just on paper), or - a new role or a new set of roles" (1). This approach is relevant to the conduct of research in organizational sociology. He explores *the legal and financial structure* of the Mondragon firm, *Caja Laboral Popular (*cooperative bank), and coordination and cooperation between agriculture firms. He points out how research in agriculture was not coping with the contemporary social setting. He examines Research and Development systems in agricultural research with an example from Peru and notes that there was no coordination among researchers. In addition to an interpretation of field outcomes, Whyte also provides an outline of what fieldwork actually is and how the researcher should conduct the research. He states "In the research strategy required for the study of social inventions, you do not start out with a pre-established research design. Of course, you don't start out with a blank mind either. You consult the research literature, but you refuse to be bound by it. In the first place you assume that the published literature is likely to be a decade behind the most interesting things happening in the field. Furthermore, while the literature may illuminate a problem, it may also impose intellectual blinders that guide you along traditional pathways. In many cases it is less important to gather new data than to develop a new way of organizing and interpreting data. For example, few problems in sociology have received more research attention that the diffusion of innovation, yet, as I have pointed out, researchers on changes in agriculture in developing countries have generally followed a conceptual scheme based on a misdiagnosis of the problem and have therefore provided findings that are worse than useless" (Whyte 1982: 10). This account clearly shows that Whyte was not in favor of the positivist research paradigms and approaches for which some of the contemporary qualitative scholars have blamed him (such as Denzin, Taylor and Bogdan etc).

Whyte was much interested in multidisciplinary approaches and did not ignore the quantitative form of research. The following passage reveals how much he enjoyed working in a multidisciplinary team. Whyte states "For each day in the field, the members of this joint team went out in pairs, a social scientist with a plant scientist, and each evening the team got together to discuss results and to raise questions for further checking. Each day also the composition of the pairs was changed so that each social scientist gained experience with each plant scientist, and vice versa. This strategy gave each team member a broad range of interdisciplinary and inter-personal experience. As the new methodology came into widespread use, we found plant scientists increasingly basing their experimental strategies upon information provided by the field farming system surveys" (Whyte 1982: 7-8). For his holistic approach to research design, he faced several criticisms from authors like Norman Denzin and others (Taylor and Bogdan 1998). His record of excellent work in the multidisciplinary team offers a basic guideline for new scholars of qualitative methods. He extensively utilizes teamwork to conduct open ended interviews, participant observations and to collect the secondary information needed to examine cooperative forms of organization. I favor the multidisciplinary approach for large scale research. I have extensively used his approach as one of the GURU MANTRA in my research.

2. Erving Goffman

A prominent scholar of qualitative method Erving Goffman in On Fieldwork (1989) asks us to internalize the field situation, observe each and every aspect of ongoing processes during field work and asks us to reveal the underlying facts during the observation. According to him the overall phenomena to be described needs to incorporate all these aspects during the field observation. Goffman asks the researcher to internalize the field situation, capture untold or unanswered questions and visualize in such a way that research can reveal the reality.

The contribution of Erving Goffman is nicely summarized in the Book titled "Erving Goffman" (edited by Gary Alan Fine and Gregory W. H. Smith, in four volumes published by SAGE in 2000). They state that "Goffman fundamentally revised how we think of social life. After him, the study of social encounters, behavior in public, the construction and deconstruction of the self, stigma and forms of everyday communication, were never the same again. Without being obviously attached to any discrete research tradition, Goffman drew from the best thought on social interaction, applied it in his fieldwork, and produced a richly satisfying and extraordinarily influential approach to making sense of social life. He was a sociological virtuoso, producing unmatched insights into how life with others is sustained and why forms of interaction break down or cause personal damage" (from the back cover page of the Book). I totally agree with Fine and Smith (2000). Goffman particularly concentrated and developed two major concepts in sociological theory, i.e. the dramaturgical approach and symbolic interactionist perspective. In developing the idea of the dramaturgical approach Goffman thinks that the most meaningful individual behavior occurs in the chance, intimate encounters of each day. These encounters include greeting people, appearing in public, and reacting to the physical appearance of others (Goffman 1959). For me all works of Goffman are exemplary. His epistemology of "be in the field physically, emotionally and mentally" is the key factor of qualitative method, especially for those who want to apply the participant observation approach in their fieldwork.

Asylums was published in 1961, as a collection of four essays. The book explores the mental patients' condition, their behaviors, and perceptions of selves, dramatic actions, and interactions with the hospital staff and with other people who visit them. Mental hospitals are prison for mental patients, where mental asylums seek for transformation from their prison-like situation into the socially accepted condition. Goffman sees mental hospitals as institutions, where patients and staff interact according to their own positions. His research describes the experience of the inmates and staff within the institution and he explains the institutional system as a problematic situation for the mental patients. His central focus is the study of society, and in his opinion the relationship between society and individual is like a voluntary agreement, which is permanent and cannot be discarded. He states that mental illness is a byproduct of the lack of individual capacity to cope with the individual as well as a societal problem. He sees society as a bond. Most importantly, he examines organizational interaction as social or individual interaction and applies his "face to face" method to analyze the social organization. His perspective of study of organization is "observation of participants". He gives the example of a musician tuning as prescribe activities before beginning of the music. This account also values the ethical and moral obligations of other participants in the organization and accepts that the individual is not free in managing the self.

In the chapter '*The underlife of a public institution: A study of ways of making out in a mental hospital*' he explores how mental patients deal with the under control situation of the mental hospital. He examines free spaces behavior of inmates, under observation behavior and coping strategy of inmates and hospital staff. The most valuable aspect of this research for me is his minute study of the inmates' behavior. Goffman not only examines the inmates' condition but also analyzes the institutional condition and strategy within the institution. He finds several drawbacks within the institution which were not favorable to the mental patients. The most important aspect of the book is his theorizing of institution: "the total Institution". He deals with five types of such institutions (1) homes for the aged, blind, orphans, or poor (2) mental asylums, TB sanitariums, leprosy camps (3) jails, prisons, POW camps, concentration camps (4) army barracks, ships, military bases, boarding schools and (5) abbeys, monasteries, convents, retreats. This notion of total institution provides not only the institutional functions, the institution's role and its structure, but also gives a general idea of societal interaction with institutions.

Goffman further clarifies how total institutions are related to modern organizational form and explores the in-depth situation of individual and society. In Asylums he has provided two frames. The first is the theory of the institution and the second is the application of qualitative method to study the organization. Goffman explains bureaucracy within the institution, power dynamism and social interactions. I found that Goffman has built an institutional theory, but has been largely ignored by the main stream organizational theorists. My examination of an institution explores similar notions in terms of power dynamism and interaction with the individual and group, not in a similar situation to that which Goffman is talking about, but in a national or international context. Goffman's research and approach have considerable relevance in my study.

His work has also helped in finding a new way of analyzing social problems, although there are some complications in application. I prefer to choose Goffman's approach which I think leaves sufficient room to examine the organization's connectedness. My approach and focus in my research will be more open and flexible towards Goffman's and Whyte's findings on the open nature of fieldwork and learning by doing. These two authors are both qualitative theorists and researchers whose works are considered as forerunners in the application of qualitative method. There are several other authors and researchers who have been following Goffman and Whyte's approach in organizational study. In the following paragraph I will note how Robert J. Thomas studies various industries with the application of qualitative method.

3. Robert J. Thomas

Generally each and every industry or manufacturing company tries to improve their machinery and make a plan for advancement. In other words, manufacturing companies try to adopt "automatic forms of machinery" to boost their production cycle. However, Robert J. Thomas' book "Machines Can't Do (Politics and Technology in the Industrial Enterprise)" reveals that advancing machinery was not only the ground of industrial revival.

His research is based on organizational sociological theory. He states "Organizations are composed of social and technical systems; that these systems are interdependent; and that changes in one usually occasion adaptation in the order" (1). In elaboration of the power process perspectives, he argues that power affects the process, as well as the outcomes of technological change (10). He says that history is very important for industrial advancement due to different reasons. "Most important, the choice of temporal context has serious implications for how we define "process" and therefore, for how attentive we are to the variety of activities associated with technological change in organizations" (11). He highlights the chain of relationships in the organization which he finds most important for industrial advancement.

He uses case study methods, in-depth interview techniques and observation approaches. He focuses on information from individuals although he also compiles case studies, observes groups and managers, officials and worker communities. His emphasis is on individual information. To get in-depth information on the relation of production organization and worker he used in depth interviews. He was able to get detailed information from industry personnel, because he had established very good relationships with both high level officials and workers.

Another most important technique Thomas has used to draw samples was the investigation of official records through company library research. He states that his reputation as a faculty member at MIT helped him to get into the companies and access the official documents. Through the official records he was able to figure out what is happening inside the organization and this allowed him to investigate influencing events inside the organization. He states that this helped him to understand current events rather than intervening to change future events. He also recorded individual accounts. He states that recording of individual accounts aimed to give power to people and influence strategy in the course of making them more noticeable. In this book he attempts to integrate qualitative research for human empowerment and strategy advancement for humanity. This leads him to conclude what machines can't do but humans can do.

Thomas focuses on a holistic approach, where he tries to clarify industrial enhancement or development. He has evaluated development as an interconnected process with two different dimensions in terms of high-tech and worker inter-relationships. Using a holistic approach, Thomas investigates different dimensions separating the economic and social impacts of technology implementation in the factories. He tries to recognize the inter linkages and tensions between the owners and workers. Thomas evaluates the complexity in an aircraft company, a computer company, an aluminum company, and the auto industry, and he tries to figure out the interrelationship between politics and technology. Through this evaluation he gets an accurate reflection of reality based on recognition of multiple realities where realism is seen as essentially subjective. He uses his own expert knowledge to differentiate stakeholders attitude (owners, managers, workers), and usually finds different perceptions of power relations within organizations. Thomas is flexible, open in many ways and has nicely used the qualitative methods. Thomas identifies the power struggles between owners, managers, workers and the ultimate effects of the political environment. He treats these complexities and differences both hierarchically as well as parallel to draw the conclusion that human empowerment is more important than implementing higher technology. This conclusion is not without criticism; however, the narrative presentation of the situation is well structured.

Thomas offers a comprehensive discussion of the guidelines, strong points and dissimilarities in fundamental linkages between organizational patterns and technologies employed in private sector organizations. He recognizes that upper-management control cannot be assumed, for "choices of technology could be influenced as much by efforts to alter structure and power relations as they could by efforts to reinforce or reproduce existing relations" (229). He further elaborates on the point (in chapter three) that computer information technology does not always have the outcomes intended by its designers or implementers. This is a central finding of the community of researchers focused on social issues of computing over the past thirty to forty years. This finding has been stable across all time periods, every sort of information technology, and in many social contexts. He recommends that this should be taken into consideration, not only the possibility, but the likelihood, that there will be many and various unintended consequences in our individual and collective actions (253-254). The author provides in-depth information about technological innovation and shows the relationships between workers' work and workers' life. He explains more about the integration, reflection, openly or perfectly achieved combination and effect of management judgments about hi-tech implementation on industries. This account shows how workers respond to managerial decisions. The author describes challenged scenarios which are more than the operation of tools. This has a tendency to focus on managerial interests in competence and control. He emphasizes the importance of managerial statements regarding what expertise can and should do, predominantly with respect to enhancing outputs.

These three illustrated works show how qualitative method can explore the organizational problem. Without application of qualitative methods such in-depth investigation was impossible. In other words, there is no way in quantitative method which can provide such vivid interpretation in the living environment. I do not think that the complexities that Whyte, Goffman and Thomas have explored through qualitative inquiry could be as effectively investigated with the application of quantitative method. There are critics of the Whyte approach of research method (for example, no women's participation in the entire research: Denzin 1992). However in Goffman's case he is well accepted. There is very limited citation of Thomas' work, however in my case, Thomas' work is more appropriate because he directly addresses the organizational problems on the basis of organizational theory. In the following section I will explain why and how I have been applying the qualitative method in my research.

Section three
Application of qualitative method

In the first two parts of this essay I noted that methodological paradigms are shifting as challenges emerge, because the notion of qualitative method is to accept the changing social environment and induce appropriate skills to reveal the social reality. In the second part I illustrated the development scenario of qualitative method and its application in organizational research from three prominent authors i.e. Whyte, Goffman and Thomas. These accounts clearly show that qualitative method has its own strengths.

The debates between quantitative and qualitative method are basically about the epistemology. Knowledge can be acquired with prescribed methodology, measurements and mind set, however there is a limitation. I think predesigned measurable procedures, which are the major ground of positivist paradigms, cannot be perfect to investigate complex, dynamic and socially constructed social facts. Therefore, interpretive open and knowledge driven investigation is necessary to investigate the social reality. In this position, I think qualitative method is more appropriate to reveal the social reality.

I do not mean that qualitative method is perfect. This method has room for error. It can be very time consuming, confusing, and sometimes overly subjective. It needs an inner capacity of the researcher to recognize record and interpret the interplay between the observed and the observer. Sometimes, what I hear and see and feel may not be true of the individuals or groups I am researching. All research is value laden, and my observations and conclusions may reflect own background and influences. Qualitative research sometimes faces questions of reliability, validity, generalizability, and applicability because normally it is not based on the situation of controlled or semi-controlled data-gathering, which normally is possible in quantitative research.

Furthermore some researchers raise the questions of credibility - internal validity, transferability -external validity, dependability-reliability and conformability–objectivity (LeCompte and Schensul 1999). These can be valid criticisms; however, we can pose similar types of questions to both qualitative and quantitative methods. The most important point is that each method has its limitations and strengths. The choice and application of methods basically depends on the purpose of the study.

Both qualitative and quantitative paths need equal energy to travel, and the main difference is that the qualitative way allows travelers to change the way during their journey as they feel appropriate, but the quantitative route does not to the same extent. Qualitative pilgrims have the right to change their faith and can test the existence of a superpower in any incarnated form of deity, but the quantitative devotee has only one god, which may not be omnipresent. Therefore, qualitative is flexible, open, and appropriate to investigate human behavior which always changes direction and never remains in a motionless situation.

Conclusion

Why qualitative method?

Qualitative method has a long history of applicability in sociological research in both action and academic fields. Why qualitative research? Why ethnographic theory? Many qualitative sociologists (Shweder 1996, Devers 1999, Fossey et al 2002, Emerson 2001, Denzin and Yvonna S. 2000, Marcus 1998, Taylor and Bogdan 1998 and many more to note) and the exemplary authors I noted in the second section of this essay (Whyte, Goffman and Thomas) have provided answers. The qualitative method produces the descriptive data, people's own written or spoken words and observable behavior (Taylor and Bogdan 1998). Taylor and Bogdan (1998) note that qualitative researchers (1) are concerned with the meanings people attach to things in their lives (2) use an inductive approach (3) look at settings and people holistically (4) examine how people think and act in their everyday life (5) consider all perspectives are worthy of study: the goal of qualitative research is to examine how things look from different vantage points (6) emphasize the meaningfulness of research (7) believe that there is something to be learned in all settings and groups (8) trust that qualitative research is a craft (c.f. from Taylor and Bogdan 1998 : 7-10). Furthermore, qualitative methods help us (1) to understand what is happening in my case in a large international organization.

The qualitative method, helps to make the selection of criteria and indicators for how organizations are functioning, what are the limitations or complexities with the application of interviews and observation method. Qualitative method is appropriate to investigate complex and sensitive impact of how the organization is functioning at headquarters and regional and national level, which is not possible to quantify. (2) This method contributes to the understanding of who is affected and in which ways. In my case how bureaucracy is structured, how executive officials treat the program level staff and how the bureaucratic culture is diffused to the field level offices. Qualitative method helps to investigate who are the most advantaged and most disadvantaged groups of people through observations, which is impossible to quantify. (3) Qualitative method can only able to capture why a particular impact is occurring in certain phenomena. This method will help me to investigate the context and development process through interaction with the executive officers to the field level staff. Through a series of interactions it will allow me to understand the interactions between the contexts, strategies and institutional intervention at global to national level. (4) And finally this method will enable me to investigate the ongoing policy (through archival review) and its impact at global as well as national level, which will further enable me to make recommendations for the policy improvement which will be one of the major contributions of my research. I think that these are the mantras of qualitative method. In other words this is the main reason why scholars use qualitative method. Qualitative method allows us to use expert knowledge and is appropriate to develop our own epistemology through learning by doing.

Acknowledgement: I acknowledge the input of Mrs. Prajita Bhandari, for creating a peaceful environment to complete this chapter and insightful comments and language editing. I would also like to thank the reviewer panel for their input and comments.

References:

Abbott, Andrew (1990) A Primer on Sequence Methods, *Organization Science*, Vol. 1, No. 4, 375-392

Anderson, Nels (1923) *The Hobo: The Sociology of the Homeless Man.* University Of Chicago Press, Chicago (reprinted in 1961, 1965 and 1967).

Alasuutari, Pertti (2004) The Globalization of Qualitative Research. In: Clive Seale et al.: Qualitative Research Practice, London: Sage 2004, 595-608.

Atkinson, Paul (1992) Understanding ethnographic texts. Newbury Park, CA: Sage.

Becker, Howard S. (1996) "The Epistemology of Qualitative Research," in Richard Jessor, Anne Colby, and Richard Schweder, edit., Essays on Ethnography and Human Development (Chicago: University of Chicago Press, 53-71.

Becker Howard S. (1999) The Chicago School, So-Called, *Qualitative Sociology*, Vol. 22, No. 1.

Bhandari, Medani P. (2002) Interview Techniques in Field Research, APEC-Nepal.

---- (2012) Environmental Performance and Vulnerability to Climate Change: A Case Study of India, Nepal, Bangladesh, and Pakistan, "Climate Change and Disaster Risk Management" Series: Climate

Change Management, Springer, New York / Heidelberg, ISBN 978-3-642-31109-3

---- (2012) Centre for Integrated Mountain Development (ICIMOD) [for conservation and management of the Hindu Kush-Himalayas – Afghanistan, Bangladesh, Bhutan, China, India, Myanmar, Nepal, and Pakistan Environment], in Ritzer, George (Ed.) Blackwell Encyclopedia of Globalization, Wiley-Blackwell Publication Volume 3, 1076-1078.

---- (2012) International Union for Conservation of Nature (IUCN) [Implication of the global conservation policies and its contribution for the biodiversity conservation in the developing world], in Ritzer, George (Ed.) Blackwell Encyclopedia of Globalization, Wiley-Blackwell Publication Volume 3, 1086-1088.

---- (2012) The Intergovernmental Panel on Climate Change (IPCC) [The forth assessment reports on climate change: a factual truth of contemporary world], in Ritzer, George (Ed.) Blackwell Encyclopedia of Globalization, Wiley-Blackwell Publication Volume 3, 1063-1067.

---- (2012) South Asian Association for Regional Cooperation (SAARC) [Problems and opportunities in improving the livelihood of its member countries: Sri Lanka, India, Pakistan, Afghanistan, Bhutan, Maldives, Bangladesh and Nepal], in Ritzer, George (Ed.) Blackwell Encyclopedia of Globalization, Wiley-Blackwell Publication, Volume 4, 1891-1898.

---- (2011) "Viewpoints: What do you think should be the two or three highest priority political outcomes of the United Nations Conference on Sustainable Development (Rio+20), scheduled for Rio de Janeiro in June 2012? Natural Resources Forum 36, 251-252 (Wiley-Blackwell)

---- (2011) The conceptual problems of Green Economy and Sustainable Development and the Theoretical Route of Green Economy Initiatives, Applicability and the Future, Compilation Document - Rio+20 - United Nations Conference on Sustainable Development, United Nations, New York, (Major groups), 141-153
http://www.uncsd2012.org/rio20/content/documents/compilationdocument/MajorGroups.pdf
http://www.uncsd2012.org/rio20/index.php?page=view&type=510&nr=138&menu=20
http://www.uncsd2012.org/rio20/content/documents/138apec.pdf

Brechin, Steven R. and Bhandari, Medani P. (2011) Perceptions of climate change worldwide, *WIREs Climate Change* 2011, Volume 2:871–885.

Mathiason, John and Bhandari, Medani P. (2010) Getting the Facts Right: The Intergovernmental Panel on Climate Change and the New Climate Regime, Journal of International Organization Studies, Volume 1, Number 1, (September 2010) 58-71 http://www.journal-iostudies.org/sites/journal-iostudies.org/files/JIOS1014.pdf

Mathiason, John and Bhandari, Medani P. (2010) Governance of Climate Change Science: The Intergovernmental Panel on Climate Change and the New Climate Change Management Regime, the UNITAR-Yale, Geneva, USA, 2nd Issue.

Bhandari, Medani P. (2004) An Assessment of Environmental Education Programs in Nepal, Environmental Awareness, *International journal of Society of Naturalist, Vol.27, No.1. (ISSN 0254-8798)*

Blumer, H. (1963) "Society as Symbolic Interaction," in Arnold Rose, editor, Human Behavior and Social Processes: An Interactionist Approach, Boston, Houghton Mifflin, 179-192.

Boas, Franz (2007) In Encyclopedia Britannica. Retrieved October 4, 2007, from Encyclopedia Britannica Online: http://www.britannica.com/eb/article-9015808

Boelen, W.A.M. (1992): Street corner society: Cornerville revisited. Journal of Contemporary Ethnography, 21, 1, 11-51

Bogdan, R. & Biklen, S. (2003). Qualitative research in education: An introduction to theory and methods. Needam, MA: Allyn and Bacon.

Bruce, L. Berg. (1995) Qualitative Research Methods for the Social Sciences, 2nd edition. Allyn and Bacon Boston, MA.

Bryman, A. (1984) The Debate about Quantitative and Qualitative Research: A Question of Method or Epistemology? The British Journal of Sociology, Vol. 35, No. 1.

Bryman, A. (1988) Quality and Quantity in Social Research, London: Unwin Hyman.

Campbell, Marie (2008) Dorothy Smith and knowing the world we live in" Journal of Sociology and Social Welfare. March 2003. FindArticles.com. 15 May. 2008.

Carr, Linda T. (1994) The strengths and weaknesses of quantitative and qualitative research: what method for nursing? *Journal of Advanced Nursing,* 1994, 20, 716-721.

Charmaz, K. (2000). Grounded theory: Objectivist and constructivist methods. In Denzin, N.K. & Lincoln, Y.S. (Eds.), Handbook of qualitative research (2nd ed., 509-35), Thousand Oaks, CA

Charmaz, K. (2001) Grounded Theory. In Contemporary Field Research: Perspectives and Formulations, Edited by Robert M. Emerson, Prospect Heights: Waveland Press. 335-352.

Charmaz K. (2004) Premises, Principles, and Practices in Qualitative Research: Revisiting the Foundations Keynote Address: Fifth International Advances in Qualitative Methods Conference, Qualitative Health Research, Vol. 14 No. 7, Sage Publications.

Chase, Susan (2003) Taking Narrative Seriously: Consequences for Method and Theory in Interview Studies, in Turning Points in Qualitative Research: tying knots in a handkerchief (edited by Yvonna S. Lincoln, Norman K. Denzin) 2003 Rowman Altamira publisher.

Chapoulie, Jean-Michel (2004) Being here and Being there, Field Work Encounters and Ethnographic Discourses, The Annals of the American Academy of Political and Social Sciences, Vol. 595, 2004.

Clifford, James (1997) "Traveling Cultures," in Routes. Travel and Translation in the Late Twentieth Century (Cambridge/London: Harvard University Press, 1997): 25.

Cook, Judith A., (1991 Editor), Beyond methodology: Feminist scholarship as lived research, Indiana University Press, Bloomington, IN (1991), 85–106.

Cockburn J. (2004) Interviewing as a Research Method, The Research and Development, Vol. 2: 3

Cockburn, J. (1984) The Use of Interviewing in Social Science Research. Unpublished PhD Thesis. Centre for Applied Research in Education, University of East Anglia.

Coser, Lewis A. (1977) Masters of Sociological Thought: Ideas in historical and social context (second edition), Harcourt Brace Jovanovich, Inc.

Cressey, Paul G. (1932) *The Taxi-Dance Hall: A Sociological Study in Commercialized Recreation and City Life.* Chicago, IL: University of Chicago Press.

Creswell, J. (1994) Research design: Qualitative and quantitative approaches. Thousand Oaks: Sage.

Du Bois W. E. B. (1899) The Philadelphia Negro a Social Study, Introduction by Elijah Anderson (paper edition publication on 1995), University of Pennsylvania Press,

Devers, K.J. (1999) "How Will We Know "Good" Qualitative Research When We See It? Health Services Research, December 1999, v.34, no. 5, Part II, S1153-1188

Denzin, N. (1994) The Qualitative Paradigm: An Overview of some basic Concepts, Assumptions, and Theories of Qualitative Research. [Available On-Line] http:// http://www.unf.edu/dept/cirt/workshops/joniak/qual_par.pdf (17/4/2008, 5.00AM)

Denzin, N. (2008) The New Paradigm Dialogs and Qualitative Inquiry, paper presented at the (QSE/QR/1, 01; 12-6, 7, 10, 11, 17, 18/07; 2-11-08—Israeli conference)

Denzin, Norman K. and Lincoln, Yvonna S. (2000) 'Introduction: the discipline and practice of qualitative research', in Norman K. Denzin and Yvonna S. Lincoln (eds), Handbook of Qualitative Research (2nd ed.). Thousand Oaks, CA: Sage 1–28.

Denzin N. (1997) Interpretive Anthropology: Ethnographic Practices for the 21st Century. Norman K. Denzin. Thousand Oaks, CA: Sage.

Denzin N. (1997) Whose Sociology is it? Comment on Huber Author(s): The American Journal of Sociology, Vol. 102, No. 5, (Mar., 1997), 1416-1423

DeVault, Marjorie (2004) What is Description? (One Ethnographer's View), Perspectives (ASA Theory Section Newsletter), 27 (#1): 4, January, 2004.

DeVault, Marjorie (1996) Talking Back to Sociology: Distinctive Contributions of Feminist Methodology. Annual Review of Sociology 22: 29-50.

DeVault, Marjorie, (1999) Liberating Method: Feminism and Social Research, Philadelphia: Temple University Press.

DeVault, Marjorie, and Liza McCoy, (2002) Institutional Ethnography: Using Interviews to Investigate Ruling Relations, 751-776, Handbook of Interview Research: Context and Method, J. Gubrium and J. Holstein (eds.), Thousand Oaks, CA: Sage Publications.

Draper, Alizon K. (2004) The principles and application of qualitative research, Proceedings of the Nutrition Society 63:641-646 Cambridge University Press

Duffy M. (1987) Methodological triangulation: a vehicle for merging qualitative & quantitative research methods. IMAGE:Journal of Nursing Scholarship 19(3), 130-133.

Duneier, Mitchell (1999) Sidewalk, New York: Farrar, Straus and Giroux.

Duneier Mitchell in conversation with Les Back (photographs by Ovie Carter) (2006) Voices from the sidewalk: Ethnography and writing race, Ethnic and Racial Studies Vol. 29 No. 3 May 2006 pp. 543_ /565

Durkheim, Emile (1997) Division of Labor in Society, by, (Introduction by Lewis Coser), (Translator W.D.Halls), publisher Simon & Schuster.

Durkheim, Emile (1979) Suicide: A Study in Sociology, Simon & Schuster

Durkheim, Emile (1982) Rules of Sociological Method, Simon & Schuster

Elwell, Frank, 1996, The Sociology of Max Weber, Retrieved June 1, 1999 (retrieved on May 21, 2008), http://www.faculty.rsu.edu/~felwell/Theorists/Weber/Whome.htm

Emerson, M Robert (2001) Contemporary Field Research, Perspective and formulations (second Addition) Waveland Press Inc. IL.

Emerson, Robert, Rachel Fretz, and Linda Shaw (1995) Writing Ethnographic Field Notes. Chicago: University of Chicago Press.

Fielding, Nigel (2005). The Resurgence, Legitimization and Institutionalization of Qualitative Methods Forum Qualitative Sozialforschung / Forum: Qualitative Social Research [On-line Journal], 6(2), Art. 32. Available at: http://www.qualitative-research.net/fqs-texte/2-05/05-2-32-e.htm [Date of Access: 04/04/2008)

Fine, Michelle, et al. 2000. "For Whom? Qualitative Research, Representations, and Social Responsibilities." 107-132 in Norman K. Denzin and Yvonna Lincoln (Eds.), Handbook of Qualitative Research (2nd ed). Thousand Oaks: Sage.

Fine, Gary and Greg Smith (Editors). 2000. Erving Goffman. V.1-4. London: Sage Publications.

Fossey, Ellie, Carol Harvey, Fiona McDermott, Larry Davidson. (2002) Understanding and evaluating qualitative research, Australian and New Zealand Journal of Psychiatry 36:6, 717–732

Gage, N. L. 1989. "The Paradigm Wars and Their Aftermath: A 'Historical' Sketch of Research and Teaching since 1989." Educational Researcher, 18, 7: 4-10.

Garfinkel, Harold (1984) Studies in Ethnomethodology. Malden MA: Polity Press/Blackwell Publishing. (ISBN 0-7456-0005-0) (First published in 1967).

Geertz, Clifford (1988) Works and Lives: the anthropologist as author, Stanford, Stanford University Press.

Geertz, Clifford (1973) "Thick Description: Toward an Interpretive Theory of Culture". In The Interpretation of Cultures: Selected Essays. (New York: Basic Books, 3-30.

Gerth, Hans and C. Wright Mills (1946 [1958] (translators and editors). *From Max Weber: Essays in Sociology.* New York: Galaxy Books.

Gobo, Giampietro (2005, September). The Renaissance of Qualitative Methods [22 paragraphs]. *Forum Qualitative Sozialforschung / Forum: Qualitative Social Research* [On-line Journal], 6(3), Art. 42. Available at: http://www.qualitative-research.net/fqs-texte/3-05/05-3-42-e.htm [Date of Access: 05/17/2008].

Goffman Erving (1959) The Presentation of Self in Everyday Life, University of Edinburgh Social Sciences Research Centre.

Goffman, Erving (1961) Asylums: Essays on the Social Situation of Mental Patients and Other Inmates. New York, Doubleday.

Goffman, Erving (1963) Behavior in Public Places: Notes on the Social Organization of Gatherings, New York, Free Press

Goffman, Erving (1961) Encounters: two Studies in the Sociology of Interaction, Indianapolis, Bobbs-Merrill, HM291 G58

Goffman, Erving (1967) Interaction Ritual, Chicago, Aldine, HM 291 G59

Goffman, Erving (1969) Strategic Interaction, Philadelphia, University of Pennsylvania,

Goffman, Erving (1989) On field work. Journal of Contemporary Ethnography 18:123-32.

Gobo, Giampietro (2005) the Renaissance of Qualitative Methods, Qualitative Social Research (ISSN 1438-5627) Volume 6, No. 3, Art. 42

Guba, E.G. & Lincoln, Y.S. (1994) Competing paradigms in qualitative research. Chapter 6 in N.K. Denzin & Y.S. Lincoln (Eds) Handbook of Qualitative Research. Sage.

Guba, Egon G. & Yvonna S. Lincoln. (2005). Paradigmatic controversies, contradictions, and emerging confluences. In Denzin & Lincoln (2005), 191–215. The Sage Book of Qualitative Research. 3rd ed. Thousand Oaks, Calif: Sage.

Hatch, Amos. 2006. "Qualitative Studies in the Era of Scientifically-based Research: Musings of a Former QSE Editor." International Journal of Qualitative Studies in Education, 19, 4 (July-August): 403-409.

Holstein, James (2000) The Self We Live By. (with J. Gubrium). 2000. Oxford University Press.

Holstein, James (2000) "An Interpretive Analytics for Social Problems." (with J. Gubrium), Japanese Journal of Sociological Criminology 25:29-48.

Holstein, James (2000) "Analyzing Interpretive Practice." (with J. Gubrium). 487-508 in Handbook of Qualitative Research, 2nd Edition, edited by N. Denzin and Y. Lincoln. Newbury Park, CA: Sage.

Ibarra, P.R. and J.I. Kitsuse (2003), "Claims-making discourse and vernacular resources." Constructionist Challenges, edited by James

A. Holstein and Gale Miller, 17-50. Hawthorne, NY: Aldine de Gruyter.

Ibarra, P.R. and M. Kusenbach (2001), "Feeling the field: Tracking shifts in ethnographic research." Studies in Symbolic Interaction 24: 193-219.

Platt, Jennifer (1996). A History of Sociological Research Methods in America 1920-1960. Cambridge: Cambridge University Press.

Platt, Jennifer (1995). Research Methods and the Second Chicago School. In Gary Fine (Ed.), A Second Chicago School? (82-107). Chicago: University of Chicago Press.

Platt Jennifer (1985) Weber's Verstehen and the History of Qualitative Research: The Missing Link, The British Journal of Sociology, Vol. 36, No. 3 -448-466

Jayaratne, Toby Epstein and Abigail Stewart (1991), Quantitative and qualitative methods in the social sciences: Current feminist issues and practical strategies. In: Mary Margaret Fonow and

Jayaratne, T. E. 1983. 'The Value of Quantitative Methodology for Feminist Research', 140–61 in Bowles and Duelli Klein (eds.).

Jessor, R. (1996) Ethnographic methods in contemporary perspective. In R. Jessor, R., Colby, A., and Shweder, R.A. (eds.). Ethnography and Human Development: Context and Meaning in Social Inquiry. Chicago, Illinois: University of Chicago Press.

Jessor, Richard., Anne Colby, and Richard A. Shweder (1996) Ethnography and Human Development: Context and Meaning in Social Inquiry. Richard Jessor, Anne Colby, and Richard A. Shweder, eds. Chicago: University of Chicago Press

Joniak, E. (2003) "How Staff Create, Sustain, and Escalate Conflict at a Drop-in Center for Street Kids." Annual Meetings of the American Sociological Association, Atlanta, GA.

Johnson, Sherrill (2001) "Strengthening the Generational Chain: Engaging the Next Generation of Social and Civic Leaders in Canada." Paper produced for the Canadian Centre for Social Entrepreneurship (10).

Johnson, Sherrill (2002) "Social Entrepreneurship Literature Review." Paper produced for the Canadian Centre for Social Entrepreneurship (18)

Johnson, Sherrill (2003) Young Social Entrepreneurs in Canada, Project Paper of Canadian Centre for Social Entrepreneurship School of Business, University of Alberta.

Kahn, Joel S (2001) "Anthropology and Modernity", Current Anthropology 42. 5: 651–664.

Katz, Jack (1983) A theory of Qualitative methodology, Social System and Analytical field work, In Contemporary Field Research. Robert Emerson, ed. (Boston: Little-Brown). 127-148.

Katz, Jack (1997) Ethnography's Warrants, Sociological Methods & Research, 25 (4, May): 391-423.

Keating, P. (1976) Into Unknown England 1866–1951: Reflections from the Social Explorers. Glasgow: Fontana/Collins.

Kocka, Jurgen (2004), Civil Society from a historical perspective, European Review, Vol 12, no.1.

Kusenbach, Margarethe (2005). Across the Atlantic: Current Issues and Debates in US Ethnography. Forum Qualitative Sozialforschung / Forum: Qualitative Social Research [On-line Journal], 6(3), Art.

47. Available at: http://www.qualitative-research.net/fqs-texte/3-05/05-3-47-e.htm [Date of Access: 09/22/07].

Lee, Allen S. (1991) Integrating Positivist and Interpretive Approaches to Organizational Research, Organization Science, Vol. 2, No. 4. 342-365.

Lee, Raymond M. (2004) Recording Technologies and the Interview in Sociology, 1920–2000, Sociology, Volume 38(5): 869–889, SAGE Publications

LeCompte, Margaret and Jean Schensul (1999) Designing and Conducting Ethnographic Research, Roman & Littlefield Publisher, USA

Lemert, Charles and Ann Branaman (1997) The Goffman Reader, Oxford, Blackwell Publishers, 1997.

Lincoln, Y., & Guba, E. (1985) Naturalistic inquiry, New York: Sage.

Lincoln, Yvonna S.; Guba, Egon G (1985) Naturalistic inquiry, Sage Publishing, Thousand Oaks

Lincoln, Y.S. (Ed.) (1985) Organizational theory and inquiry: The paradigm revolution. Beverly Hills, CA: Sage.

Lin, Ann Chin (1998) Bridging positivist and interpretivist approaches to qualitative methods, Policy study journal, vol 26, No 1.

McKinney, John C (1966) Constructive typology of social theory, Appleton Century Crofts, New York.

Marshall, C. and Rossman, G.B. (1999) Designing qualitative research (3rd ed.), Thousand Oaks: Sage Publications.

Malinowski, Bronislaw (1967) A diary in the strict sense of the term. London: Routledge & Kegan Paul.

Marcus, George E. (1998) Ethnography through Thick and Thin, Princeton: Princeton University Press.

Marcus, George E. (1995) Ethnography In/Of the World System: the Emergence of Multi-sited Ethnography, "Annual Review of Anthropology 24: 95.

Mariampolski, H.Y. (2006) Ethnography for Marketers: A Guide to Consumer Immersion, 2006 Sage Publications Inc.

McCoy, Norma L. (1998) Methodological problems in the study of sexuality and the menopause. Maturitas, 29(1), 51-60.

Meleis, A. I. (1997) Theoretical nursing: development and progress (3rd ed.). Philadelphia, PA: Lippincott-Raven.

Morgan, Gareth and Linda Smircich (1980) The Case for Qualitative Research, The Academy of Management Review, Vol. 5, No. 4. 491-500

Merriam, S. B. (1998). Qualitative research and case study applications in education. San Francisco: Jossey-Bass. Stage, F. (Ed.).

Morrison, Ken (1995) Marx, Durkheim, Weber: Formations of Modern Social Thought, London: Sage, 1995.

Northcutt, N. And D.McCoy (2004) Interactive Qualitative Analysis: A Systems Method for Qualitative Research, Thousand Oaks, CA: Sage

Nock, David (2004) The Myth about "Myths of the Chicago School ". Evidence from Floyd Nelson House, The American Sociologist / Spring

Oakley, Ann (1998) Gender, Methodology and People's Ways of Knowing: Some Problems with Feminism and the Paradigm Debate in Social Science, Sociology 32: 707-731

Oakley, Ann (1997a) 'The Gendering of Methodology: An Experiment in Knowing', Paper given at the Swedish Collegium for Advanced Study in the Social Sciences,

Patton, M. Q. (1990). Qualitative evaluation and research methods (2nd ed.). Newbury Park, CA: Sage.

Pauly, John J. (1991) 'A Beginner's Guide to Doing Qualitative Research in Mass Communication', Journalism Monographs 125 (February). Columbia, SC: Association for Education in Journalism and Mass Communication.

Pauly, John J. (1999) 'Journalism and the Sociology of Public Life', in Theodore L. Glasser (ed.) The Idea of Public Journalism. New York: Guilford.

Platt, Jennifer (1996). A History of Sociological Research Methods in America 1920-1960. Cambridge: Cambridge University Press.

Platt, Jennifer (1995). Research Methods and the Second Chicago School. In Gary Fine (Ed.), A Second Chicago School? (82-107). Chicago: University of Chicago Press.

Ponterotto, Joseph G. (2006) Brief Note on the Origins, Evolution, and Meaning of the Qualitative Research Concept "Thick Description" The Qualitative Report Volume 11 Number 3 538-549

Polkinghorne, D.E. (1982) What makes research humanistic? Journal of Humanistic Psychology 47-54.

Polkinghorne, D.E. (1983) Methodology for the Human Sciences: Systems of inquiry. SUNY.

Reetley, Anneline (2003), A literature review on grounded theory, Master thesis, Rand Afrikaans University, Suth Africa.

Richardson, L. (1990a) 'Narrative and sociology', Journal of Contemporary Ethnography, 19:116-35.

Richardson, L. (1990b) Writing Strategies: reaching diverse audiences, Newbury Park, Sage.

Richardson, L. (1992) 'Trash on the Corner: ethics and technography', Journal of Contemporary Ethnography, 21, 1, 103-119.

Ritzer, George (1996) Sociological theory (fourth edition), McGraw-Hill

Ryle, G. (1971) Collected papers. Volume II collected essays, 1929-1968. London: Hutchinson.

Sanday, Peggy Reeves (1979), "The ethnographic paradigm(s)", *Administrative Science Quarterly*, Vol. 24 No.4, 527-38.

Schwartz P, Ogilvy J. (1979) The Emergent Paradigm: Changing Patterns of Thought and Belief.Values and Lifestyles Program. VALS Report 7. Menlo Park, CA: SRI International.

Sharrock, Wes (1989) Ethnomethodology, The British Journal of Sociology, Vol. 40, No. 4. 657-677.

Sil, Rudra and Peter J. Katzenstein (2005) What is Analytic Eclecticism and Why Do We Need it? A Pragmatist Perspective on Problems and Mechanisms in the Study of World Politics, Paper presented on the Annual Meeting of the American Political Science Association,

Smith, J.K. (1983). Quantitative Versus Qualitative Research: An Attempt to Clarify the Issue. Educational Researcher, 12(3), 6-13.

Smith, Dorothy E., (1977) Feminism and Marxism: A Place to Begin, A Way to Go, Vancouver: New Star Books.

Smith, Dorothy E, (1984) The Renaissance of Women Knowledge Reconsidered: A Feminist Overview, Ursula Franklin, et al. (eds.),

Ottawa: Canadian Research Institute for the Advancement of Women, 3-14.

Smith, Dorothy E, (1987) The Everyday World as Problematic: A Feminist Sociology, Toronto: University of Toronto Press.

Smith, Dorothy E. (2005) Institutional ethnography: A sociology for people, Rowman Altamira Publisher.

Snape, D. and Spencer, L. (2003), 'The foundations of qualitative research', in J. Ritchie and J. Lewis (eds), Qualitative Research Practice, London: Sage, 1–23.

Sofaer, S. (1999) Qualitative Methods: What Are They and Why Use Them? Health Services Research3 4(5): 1102-18.

Sofaer, S, and R.C. Myrtle (1991) Interorganizational Theory and Research: Implications for Health Care Management, Policy, and Re-search. Medical Care Review 48(4):371-409.

Taylor, Steven & Robert Bogdan (1984), Introduction to Qualitative Research Methods: The Search for Meanings. Second Edition. New York: John Wiley and Sons.

Thomas, Robert J. (1994) What Machines Can't Do: Politics and Technology in the Industrial Enterprise, University of California Press

Thrasher, Frederic M. (1927) The *Gang: A Study of 1,313 Gangs in Chicago,* University of Chicago Press.

Turner, Jonathan H. (1991) The Structure of Sociological Theory, fifth edition, Belmont, CA Wadsworth.

Van Maanen (1979) The Fact of Fiction in Organizational Ethnography, Administrative Science Quarterly, Vol. 24, No. 4, Qualitative Methodology. 539-550.

Van Maanen (1979) Reclaiming Qualitative Methods for Organizational Research: A Preface, Administrative Science Quarterly, Vol. 24, No. 4, Qualitative Methodology.520-526

Van Maanen, J. (1983) The moral fix: On the ethics of field work. In Contemporary field research: A collection of readings, edited by R.M. Emerson. Boston: Little, Brown

Van Manen, M. (1990) Researching Lived Experience: Human Science for an Action Sensitive Pedagogy. Albany, New York: State University of New York Press.

Van Manen (1991). The tact of teaching: The meaning of pedagogical thoughtfulness, Albany, New York: State University of New York Press.

Wallace, Ruth A. and Alison Wolf (1995) Contemporary Sociological Theory: Continuing the Classical Tradition, fourth edition, Englewood Cliffs, New Jersey, Prentice Hall.

Welz, Gisela (2002) "Sitting Ethnography, Some observations on a Cypriot highland village," in Shifting Grounds. Experiments in Doing Ethnography. eds. Ina-Maria Greverus, Sharon Macdonald, Regina Römhild, Gisela Welz and Helena Wulff. Anthropological Journal on European Cultures 11 137–158.

Weber, Max (2002) The Protestant Ethic and the 'Spirit' of Capitalism and Other Writings, Edited by Peter R. Baehr, Gordon C. Wells, Penguin USA

Weber, Max 1903-1917 (1949) The Methodology of the Social Sciences. Edward Shils and Henry Finch (eds.). New York: Free Press.

Weber, Max (1962) Basic Concepts in Sociology by Max Weber. Translated & with an introduction by H.P. Secher. New York: The Citadel Press.

Weber, Max. (1904/1930) The Protestant Ethic and the Spirit of Capitalism, Translated by Talcott Parson, New York: Charles Scribner's Sons.

Weber, Max. (1946/1958) From Max Weber. Translated and edited by H. H. Gerth and C. Wright Mills. New York: Galaxy.

Whyte, William Foote, (1943) Street Corner Society: The Social Structure of an Italian Slum University of Chicago Press.

Whyte, William Foote (1982), "Social Inventions for Solving Human Problems," 1981 Presidential Address, American Sociological Association], American Sociological Review, 47:1-13.

Whyte, William Foote, Davydd Greenwood, and Peter Lazes (1989), "Participatory Action Research: Through Practice to Science in Social-Research," American Behavioral Scientist, 32:5, 513-551.

Whyte, William Foote, and Kathleen King Whyte (1988, 1991), Making Mondragon: The Growth and Dynamics of the Worker Cooperative Complex, Ithaca, New York: Cornell University Press,

Whyte, William Foote (1994), Participant Observer: An Autobiography, Cornell University Press.

BIOGRAPHIES OF AUTHORS

The authors of this textbook are all active members of the faculty team at Akamai University.

To be admitted to the faculty at Akamai University, faculty members must meet rigorous professional and academic standards. Most have earned doctorates at recognized and accredited institutions and have extensive experience in their areas of concentration. Certain outstanding individuals who are recognized experts in their professional field are accepted to the faculty with less than a recognized doctoral degree. Under very special circumstances, exceptionally qualified graduates of Akamai University are also admitted to the faculty.

Akamai University faculty members approach their positions in a cooperative and creative manner and encourage these traits in their students. They entertain dialogue and strive to build unity among the faculty. They participate in the governance of the institution and advocate for outstanding educational programs. Akamai University faculty members exhibit understanding and sensitivity to the diverse academic, socioeconomic, cultural, national, religious, ethnic, and geographic backgrounds of our students. They strive to instill in their students a sense of responsibility and citizenship within a diverse global community.

Akamai University faculty members uphold the highest standards of teaching, scholarship and research and maintain current knowledge of their discipline. They foster high aspirations in their students and communicate effectively and intelligently concerning the subject matter.

Faculty members promote autonomous learning, establish participatory education environments, identify high quality learning resources and guide students in developing broad networks of professional colleagues and advisors.

Dr. Douglass Capogrossi

Dr. Capogrossi earned his Ph.D. in Adult and Continuing Education from Cornell University, where he completed an extensive dissertation investigating the effectiveness of the American education system. He also holds a Master's in Curriculum and Instruction, and Bachelor's in Business Management from Cornell University. Dr. Capogrossi has directed a variety of successful formal and non-formal education programs including trade apprenticeships, work experience projects and on-the-job training within industry and the human services, and adult job training through center-based programs. He has served as President at other distance learning institutions and has provided leadership in achieving recognized institutional accreditation. Dr. Capogrossi facilitated development of the New York State Rural Literacy Initiative, a state-wide community- based project initiating adult literacy and community development ventures in the poorest counties, funded by the Community and Rural Development Institute at Cornell University. He holds permanent teaching credentials in commerce and social studies with special certification to teach the emotionally disturbed. Dr. Capogrossi has held leadership roles with two major federal pilot studies identifying effective models for educating at risk youth outside the traditional school environment. He has coordinated innovative community-based education projects for troubled youths through the Board of Cooperative Educational Services in New York State. He also served as Instructor with the Office of Continuing Education at Cornell University, where he developed and instructed distance-learning courses in basic and corporate accounting for career track employees. Dr. Capogrossi is an experienced human service administrator, having worked as Executive Director of South Valley

Collective, The League, and the United Minority Coalition, Assistant Director of Tompkins County Economic Opportunity Corporation and Director of Planning with the Community Service Organization in San Jose, California. Dr. Capogrossi has held top management positions in industry, serving as General Manager of Micrographic Systems, a medical camera-manufacturing firm in Santa Clara, California. For a number of years, he operated America Builders, a successful licensed general contracting firm in California. Dr. Capogrossi has extensive community volunteer experience emphasizing implementation and development of nonprofit organizations, preparing founding documents and serving as an officer of the Board of Directors. He was instrumental in developing an international professional membership organization dedicated to the amelioration of major world problems, a community legal center serving moderate-income communities, a human service coalition, an emergency service corporation, and an athletic league. Dr. Capogrossi has authored papers and textbook chapters with focus upon assurance of academic quality and meaningfulness or missions in higher education. He has taught programs in parenting effectiveness, anger management, transition to the community, job readiness training and basic education for many years within correctional facilities in East Hawaii. Most recently, Dr. Capogrossi has collaborated with leadership in the local Cristian Community to structure a dynamic Christian Parenting Program.

Dr. Anthony Maranto

Dr. Maranto currently serves as a senior environmental consultant and program manager for numerous clients at the National Oceanic and Atmospheric Administration where he supports a wide range of projects across the National Geodetic Survey, the Coast Survey Development Laboratory, the Office of Ocean and Coastal Resource Management, and the Office of Sustainable Fisheries, among others. Prior to his work with NOAA, Dr. Maranto provided scientific and program support to numerous organizations across the Department of Defense and the U.S. Army. In his twelve years of consulting for DoD, he oversaw research, management, and policy projects related to Chemical, Biological, Radiological, and Nuclear (CBRN) defense; environmental compliance and health; natural and cultural resource management; land use management; and pollution prevention technologies. Dr. Maranto received his BA in Biochemistry and Molecular Biology from the University of Maryland, Baltimore County; his MA in Environmental Science from Goddard College; and his Ph.D. in Environmental Science from the Union Institute. As a researcher and educator, Dr. Maranto has a wide range of experiences and interests. He was formerly the Director of the Maryland Department of Natural Resources' Radioecology Laboratory. Additionally, he has held posts in the Department of Chemistry and Biochemistry at the University of Maryland, Baltimore County and in the Department of Biology at Essex Community College in Baltimore. He currently serves as a member of the Planning Advisory Committee at Morgan State University and sits on the board of directors for two non-profit organizations; Kupenda for the Children (a charity that supports physically and mentally handicapped children in the developing work) and LEEK Mountain Preserve (an organization which provides conservation support and outdoor recreation opportunities to wounded US service members). Dr. Maranto is the founder and Chief Editor of the Pacific Journal of Science and Technology, presently in its tenth year of publication. He has authored or co-authored over 50 publications and presentations on numerous topics including carcinogenic risk assessment, environmental management, radioecology, health physics, data quality control, and neurological receptor modeling.

Dr. Michael J. Cohen

Recipient of the 1994 Distinguished World Citizen Award, Applied Ecopsychologist Michael J. Cohen, Ph.D., is a Program Director of the Institute of Global Education where he coordinates its Integrated Ecology Department and Project NatureConnect. He also serves on the faculty of Portland State University and the Akamai University Institute of Applied Ecopsychology whose program he initiated and has directed since 1990. In 1965, Dr. Cohen discovered that Planet Earth acted like a living organism and from this he founded sensory, Gaia based, degree granting Environmental and Expedition Education outdoor programs independently and for the National Audubon Society and Lesley University. He conceived the 1985 National Audubon International Symposium "Is the Earth a Living Organism," at the University of Massachusetts and established the sensory sciences of Organic Psychology and Natural Attraction Ecology in 2008. He is the Editor of the "Journal of Organic Psychology and Natural Attraction Ecology" and an award winning author of ten books dealing with Applied Ecopsychology including "Educating, Counseling and Healing With Nature" "The Web Of Life Imperative" and "Reconnecting With Nature." Dr. Cohen is also an accomplished folk song artist and contra dancer who presents traditional music programs accompanied by guitar, banjo and accordion for the U.S. National Park Service and Skagit Valley College Elder hostel on San Juan Island, Washington.

Dr. Niranjan Ray

Dr. Niranjan Ray is the Vice President, Dean, School of Engineering & Technology, and Deputy Program Director for the Akamai University Business Administration Program. He was the president of Roswell 83, LLC, and was a member of the board of directors of 101 Crescent, Inc. In the past, he was a consultant for Quality and Design Assurance of Saint Jude Medical, Siemens Healthcare Diagnostics and Beckman Coulter in Medical Device Division, and a consultant of Johnson & Johnson (Medical Device) Company. He has been business partner of many companies. Dr. Ray received his BSEE (Honors), MSEE and Ph.D. (Engineering) from Jadavpur University, Kolkata, India. He taught at several universities including Jadavpur University in India, Engineering University in Bangladesh, and International Institute of Management Science, Kolkata, India. He served as the Faculty Head of Computer Division of the Indian Institute of Material Management in Kolkata, India. He was an adjunct faculty of University of Redlands, California, and Greenwich University, Norfolk Island. In addition, he served as chair for Ph.D. research programs of Akamai University, and guided many international students in Ph.D research programs for the award of doctoral degree. He served as the Principal Adviser of EDSA Micro Corporation, USA. As a corporate trainer he taught managers and engineers of Parsons Corporation, USA in Relational Database Management System (DBMS). He also provided training on courses of Computer and DBMS to managers and engineers of State Electricity Board in Kolkata, India. He trained IAS (Indian Administrative Service) officers at Administrative Training Institute, Kolkata, India. In terms of professional organizations, he was a Competent Toast Master (CTM) of Toast Master of International, USA and a Senior member of IEEE, USA. He has a number of published papers to his credit. This includes Application of Computers in Homeopathic Medicine, Published in Computer Age Magazine, May 1985, Vol 3, no.8. His primary interests are in teaching and research in the fields of Computer Science and Engineering, Economics, Management Information Systems, Computer Applications in Business Administration including Project Management, Software, Hardware, Systems Analysis and Design, and Entrepreneurship.

Dr. Sandra L.M. Kolbl (Koelbl) Holman

Dr. Sandra Kolbl-Holman offers diverse, highly conceptualized international contexts in relation to her approach to sustainable landscapes, educational development, executive solutions and professional career interests, both for herself and those who work along side her. Kolbl-Holman has been educated in Canada, Germany and the United States. She received her undergraduate degree honors with distinction from Saint Thomas University in New Brunswick, Canada. Her nursing program was part of the fast track joint University of Lethbridge, and Lethbridge Community College RN degree program.

Her graduate scholarly training followed through Carlton University, the University of Lethbridge, and with Akamai University conferring her doctorate with high honors along with norming a new intelligence measure for Dr. Robert Sternberg during his tenure at Yale University. She additionally holds a post graduate diploma in Sustainability Studies. During Kolbl-Holman's academic career, she has received graduate teaching assistantships for undergraduate counseling and theories, full tuition scholarships at the graduate level, graduate scholarships for academic excellence, graduate awards for women in higher education, a national award in program evaluation for program logic model development, graduate and undergraduate research assistantships, two undergraduate teaching assistantships, presented at academic conferences and is academically published and recognized. Kolbl-Holman's passion for Art History and Fine Art studies began in Europe as a small child, evolved in the cobblestone streets of Germany as a teenager, and continues through her graduate studies at the Academy of Art in San Francisco. Kolbl-Holman's professional career history demonstrates her successes while serving in politics, working as a political journalist, coordinator of volunteer programs in criminal justice environments, developing treatment, cross-cultural and community programs, psychologist, a qualified past life regression therapist, shaman, CEO of her business consulting firm in Canada, entrepreneur/inventor with seven patents worldwide, preparing needs assessment studies, becoming familiar with various judicial systems as a probation officer, and as a lead researcher for the S.O.A.C Justice Committee that brought about new sexual offender laws, environmental supporter, author, and former Chief Advisor for Project Nature Connect. Kolbl-Holman received the Canadian Achievement Award for Small Business presented by Petro Canada in recognition of outstanding business practices and marketing in national and international forums. In the meantime, Kolbl-Holman holds several key positions including Director of the Akamai University Sustainability Studies Program, Dean of the Akamai University Think Tank for Global Betterment and Academic Council Chair, as well as a Senior Faculty member. She is working on a book project that researches, explores and gives hope for outlier complementary options titled "I Slept with the Bears". Her hope is to build a peace oriented, humanitarian- sustainability focused center with the mission goal of creating global human sustainability, that starts with the historical intersections of human life and moves to a gestalt that reaches out in all directions from the ground level of every village and every city block in the form of art, complementary medical research and practice, and sustainability. Kolbl- Holman states: *Knowledge makes a powerful statement. All knowledge is infinity itself, and is our unlimited resource. That right to knowledge can never be taken away from us.*

Dr. Khoo Voon Ching

Khoo Voon Ching holds two Master's degrees, namely, the M.Sc. by Research from Asia eUniversity and a Master of Business Administration degree from Akamai University, USA. Voon Ching obtained his professional qualifications as an incorporated engineer from the Engineering Council, UK, and as a certified planning engineer from the American Academy of Project Management, USA. He also studied in the University Technology of Malaysia to obtain his diploma in Mechanical Engineering and in Institute First Robotics Industrial Science to acquire an advanced diploma in Robotics and Automation Engineering. Voon Ching is also obtained the PhD in Management degree. Voon Ching has many years of industry experience, specializing in automation and semiconductor testing. He first worked for ASM Assembly Equipment as a service engineer before he moved to Semiconductor Testing Automation. As a sales manager with COHU, Inc., he was involved in multi-site test handler sales and service activities. He implemented multi-site testing handlers in many MNCs involved in semiconductor testing, which primarily aimed to reduce testing costs. His research interests include technology management, cost reduction through technology, and the efficiency of technology to improve human condition. Mr. Khoo is a member of the Institution of Mechanical Engineers and the International Associations of Engineers. He is a fellow of the American Academy of Project Management.

Dr. Lee Karling

Dr. Karling obtained her PhD from USM in early 2008. Her area of specialization is in Human Resource Management (HRM) with an emphasis on human resource development and learning. Her interest is also in industrial psychology and human behaviors at work. She has been involved in continuous research in linking personalities with job function and performance and hopes to present a research paper late next year. She also specializes in DOE (design of experiment) for the HRM function, specifically for HR development. Dr. Karling has many years of working experience in both the manufacturing and service industries with more years in the service industry as Head of Department. She has been involved in corporate training for more than 10 years and is a Certified Trainer from ACAP Australia. She also holds a unique Graduate Certificate in Adult Teaching and Learning from RMIT University, Australia. She is currently on a retainer with a listed local company as a HR consultant in all HR related matters from HR planning and recruitment to industrial relations. The consultancy work also extends to the subsidiaries of the listed company. Dr. Karling specializes in HRM related training as well as specific interpersonal skills and workplace behavior training aimed at improving workplace efficiency, effectiveness and relationships. She is committed to assisting organizations in their human resource development endeavors and specializes in assisting organizations design, execute, and feedback on training evaluation system for continuous development in the organization's human resource development efforts. Her current passion is in cross-generation management focusing on assisting organizations in tapping into the potentials of the millennial workforce and providing guidance to senior management in maximizing the talent of the new generation (Gen Y). She is also able to provide training workshops in specific supply chain management areas, specifically inventory management, warehouse system design, and purchasing management for effective cost down.

Dr. Mary Jo Bulbrook

Dr. Mary Jo Bulbrook, CEMP/S/I, is a practitioner and specialist in Energy Medicine, Dean of Continuing Education, Dean of the Institute of CAM Studies, Director of Complementary & Alternative Medicine, Akamai University, Distance Education, and President of Energy Medicine Partnerships. Mary Jo is a medical spiritual intuitive with over 40 years practicing, teaching, and researching energy-based therapies in multiple countries. She has brought energy therapies to Australia, New Zealand, South Africa, Peru, and Chile as well as throughout Canada and USA and is an advocate for empowerment of the individual to learn effective ways to manage their health and healing. She learned Touch For Health from Dr. John Thie and worked to bring TFH into the nursing and mental health fields. This has been presented at the American Holistic Nurses Association as an all-day preconference workshop and was well received in June 2014 and is based on the holistic nursing theory first introduced at the International Nursing Diagnosis Conference held in Calgary, Alberta in 1985. Since that time the theory has been advanced to this new level synthesized from the extensive application of the work worldwide within multiple cultural settings, different illness conditions and health challenges for all ages.

Dr. Seamus Phan

Dr. Phan has been an Asian pioneer in several fields, including computer-based training (CBT), service quality, digital prepress, and knowledge management. He was the first in-house developer of network-based learning with multimedia in 1987 for a major computer parts manufacturer, where at that time, all such programs were typically out-sourced to external development houses. In that capacity, Dr. Phan developed a total of 8 training programs, all with multimedia and interactivity, and online testing across an intranet, a first in Singapore in that era that predated the Internet. Dr. Phan has also been an external corporate educator and facilitator to many multinational corporations and government agencies, teaching about the adoption of vendor-neutral e-business, Internet connectivity, Internet security, wireless networks, business transformation and leadership. He is also a knowledge management pioneer, and his intranet solutions have been adopted by leading companies in law, manufacturing and retail. Dr. Phan has been credited as a credible and incisive journalist and editor and has served as contributing editor for Network Computing Asia (CMP), Asia correspondent for ETHIX, correspondent for TechTV, and has been a frequent on-air analyst for leading broadcast channels such as CNBC, Bloomberg, Channel NewsAsia and NewsRadio 93.8 and Capital Radio 95.8. He has consulted and helped many technology startups from USA, Israel and Europe achieve media presence in Asia Pacific. Dr. Phan received his doctoral degree in Business from Greenwich University, where he conducted a major dissertation concerning the use of the Internet as a self-analysis tool to improve small businesses in Singapore.

Dr. Kemal Yildirim

Dr Kemal Yildirm specialized in comparative politics and middle east specialization with other subsidiary subjects in Political history and social and economic history and has submitted my Thesisin Diplomacy- Main title is diplomatic practices in the foreign policies of early Islamic political realms. Dr Kemal Yildirm specialized in comparative politics and middle east specialization with other subsidiary subjects in Political history and social and economic history and has submitted my Thesisin Diplomacy- Main title is diplomatic practices in the foreign policies of early Islamic political realms. Dr. Yildirim has rcently completed the postdoctorate award in Democracy and Human Rights from Coimbra University, Portugal.

Dr. Mirjana Radovic-Markovic

Dr. Mirjana Radovic-Markovic is a full professor of Entrepreneurship. She holds B. Sc, M. Sc. and PhD Degrees in Economics, as well as Post-Doctoral Studies in Multidisciplinary Studies. After her dissertation completing, she continued her advanced studies in the Netherlands, United States and Russia. She visited famous universities in the US (Stanford University, Columbia University, University of Pittsburgh), and gave lectures at Lomonosow (Russia) and recently at Oxford University (UK), Franklin College, Lugano (Switzerland), OECD Experts' Meeting on the Black Sea and Central Asia Initiative held in Istanbul, Turkey and Faculty of Economics University in Hungary). She has served as professor at a number of international universities, foundations and institutes. In addition, she is a Member of Scientific Committee, National Ministry of Science, Serbia (2010-), head of the Scientific Centre for Economic Researches, Institute of Economic Sciences, Belgrade, Serbia (2008-), Member of Management Board of Institute of Institute of Economic Sciences (2008-)member of ERENET- Entrepreneurship Research and Education Network of Central European Universities, Corvinus University, Small business development Centre, Budapest, Hungary (2008-), fellow of ICAS ?International Convention of Asia Scholars (2007-), professor of the American School of Genealogy, Heraldry and Documentary Studies, a branch of the School of Genealogy, Heraldry and Documentary Sciences of Bologna, Italy and so forth. Recently she was a head of projects "Survey of Serbia", OECD, Paris, France (2009-2010) and "The Integration of Serbian economy into the European Union: Planning and financing of regional and rural development and enterprise development policy, financed by Ministry of Science of the Republic of Serbia (2008-2012). Professor is a founder and editor in chief of Peer international Journal of Women's Entrepreneurship and Education (JWE. She has written twenty-seven books and more than a hundred peer reviewed journal articles.

Dušan Marković

Mr. Markovic is a class instructor at Akamai University and an experienced instructor with Belgrade Business School and Vinca School of Computers with specialization in the fields of operational systems, database development and MS Project. His students include employed adults from many government agencies in Serbia, including the Ministry of Science. He has also been involved with projects in Yugoslav Prestige Institute for Nuclear Researching in Vinca for over 17 years. From June 2007 he has served as IT manager in Belgrade Business School. Mr. Markovic holds the Master of Technical Science degree from University of Belgrade. He is co-author of Management and the MS Project. He is pursuing his PhD thesis "Integration IT and Education Technology in Sineria of Virtual Factory and Virtual University"

Dr. Medani P. Bhandari

Dr. Bhandari is interested in teaching and mentoring in the field Community and Economic Development; Environmental Studies; Sustainability Studies; Peace, Diplomacy and International relations. His main interest as a teacher and researcher centers on the intersection of local and global interests (trans-society/trans-border) and capacities in addressing global political economy; green economy, natural resource management challenges, environmental sustainability, and the effects of climate change. He is also interested in risk analysis, public policies, and behaviors that contribute to the goal of catalyzing action across the global community, increase public awareness and change public attitudes on global climate change; natural resource governance issues, human rights abuse, sustainable development and environmental degradation. His goal is to utilize scientific and cultural knowledge, research skills, and extensive experiences to help address the challenges of global environmental change, the green economy, and sustainability. He is also interested as well in assessing the economic, social and environmental impacts on natural resources/ environmental sustainability. His ultimate objective is to cultivate and engage multidisciplinary knowledge-based networks to minimize the impact of climate change on marginalized societies and to reduce societal conflict over natural resources.

ENDNOTES

1. Sunday's Zaman January 31, 2014, Friday/ 18:41:00
2. September 21, 2014, Sunday/ 19:00:18/ MESUT DEMİR / ISTANBUL Sunday's zaman
3. The study of the Turkish Economic and Social Studies Foundation (tr: *Türkiye Ekonomik ve Sosyal Etüdler Vakfı* called İmam Hatip Liseleri: Efsaneler ve Gerçekler (Imam Hatip Schools: Legend and Reality) was published in October 2004. The 268-page document has an English summary (pages 39-53) and can be downloaded as PDF-file; accessed on 7 November 2012
4. Background written by the Ministry of National Education at the beginning of 2002 OVERVIEW OF THE HISTORICAL DEVELOPMENT OF THE MINISTRY OF NATIONAL EDUCATION; accessed on 3 November 2012
5. See an article in English Sabah of 31 March 2012 Modern Turkey's new liberal education system; accessed on 4 November 2012
6. See an article in English Sabah of 31 March 2012 Modern Turkey's new liberal education system; accessed on 4 November 2012
7. See an article by Andrew Finkel in International Herald Tribune of 23 March 2012 What's 4 + 4 + 4?; accessed on 4 November 2012
8. Songün, Sevim (27 February 2009). "Turkey evolves as creationist center". Hurriyet Daily News. Retrieved 17 March 200
9. "Turkish government rules out demands of Islamic sect Alevis". *Hurriyet*. 10 November 2008. Retrieved 22 December 2008
10. See an article in Voice of America of 25 September 2012 In Turkey, Religious Schools Gain a Foothold; accessed on 7 November 2012
11. See an article in Today's Zaman of 2 September 2012 Turkey to launch new Imam Hatip school for international students; accessed on 7 November 2012
12. See an article in Today's Zaman of 2 September 2012 Turkey to launch new Imam Hatip school for international students; accessed on 7 November 2012
13. See an article by Andrew Finkel in the International Herald Tribune of 23 March 2012 What's 4 + 4 + 4?; accessed on 7 November 2012

References

1. The study of the Turkish Economic and Social Studies Foundation (tr: *Türkiye Ekonomik ve Sosyal Etüdler Vakfı* called İmam Hatip Liseleri: Efsaneler ve Gerçekler (Imam Hatip Schools: Legend and Reality) was published in October 2004. The 268-page document has an English summary (pages 39-53) and can be downloaded as PDF-file; accessed on 7 November 2012

2. The TESEV reports cites studies of Suat Cebeci (1993), Türkmen (1998), Ünlü (1998)and Altunsaray (2000)

3. See an article by Andrew Finkel in the International Herald Tribune of 23 March 2012 What's 4 + 4 + 4?; accessed on 7 November 2012

4. See an article in Voice of America of 25 September 2012 In Turkey, Religious Schools Gain a Foothold; accessed on 7 November 2012

5. See an article in Today's Zaman of 2 September 2012 Turkey to launch new Imam Hatip school for international students; accessed on 7 November 2012

6. Songün, Sevim (27 February 2009). "Turkey evolves as creationist center". Hurriyet Daily News. Retrieved 17 March 200

7. "Turkish government rules out demands of Islamic sect Alevis". *Hurriyet*. 10 November 2008. Retrieved 22 December 2008

8. See an article in English Sabah of 31 March 2012 Modern Turkey's new liberal education system; accessed on 4 November 2012

9. See an article by Andrew Finkel in International Herald Tribune of 23 March 2012 What's 4 + 4 + 4?; accessed on 4 November 2012

10. Dogan, Yonca Poyraz (8 September 2008). "Prof. Soysal: Most Turkish universities are still autocratic". *Today's Zaman*. Retrieved

7 September 2008. "Before law No. 2547, rectors were appointed only by the president. Then upon the initiative of some of the universities, including Boğaziçi University, the system was changed. Now there is a middle ground: Both voting by the faculty and YÖK are involved in the process. As a result, YÖK and the president are involved in appointing rectors."

11. Blackmore, J. (2000). "Hanging onto the Edge: An Australian Case Study of Women, Universities, and Globalization." Globalization and Education. (Editör: Nelly P. Stromquist ve Karen Monkman), New York.

12. Buenfil, R. N. (2000). "Globalization and Educational Policies in Mexico, 1988-1994:A Meeting of the Universal and the Particular." Globalization and Education.(Editör: Nelly P. Stromquist and Karen Monkman), New York

www.ingramcontent.com/pod-product-compliance
Lightning Source LLC
Chambersburg PA
CBHW021350210526
45463CB00001B/54